Hunting the
American Terrorist

The FBI's War on Homegrown Terror

Terry D. Turchie

Kathleen M. Puckett, Ph.D.

With a Foreword by Louis J. Freeh,
former Director of the FBI

Published in the United States by
History Publishing Company, LLC
Palisades, New York

Library of Congress Cataloging-in-Publication Data
Turchie, Terry D.
    Hunting the American terrorist: the FBI's war on homegrown
    terror / Terry D. Turchie, Kathleen M. Puckett. – 1st ed.
    p.cm.
    Includes index.
    LCCN 2006938440
    ISBN-13: 978-1-933909-34-9
    ISBN-10: 1-933909-34-X

    1. Domestic terrorism–United States. 2. United
States. Federal Bureau of Investigation. I. Puckett,
Kathleen M. II. Title.

HV6432.T87 2007   363.325
                                  QBI07-600088

Printed in the United States on acid-free paper
9 8 7 6 5 4 3 2 1

First Edition

∞ ∞ ∞

To the victims and their families whose lives were suddenly changed forever by the crimes of Theodore Kaczynski, Timothy McVeigh, Eric Rudolph, and the Anthrax killer, still at large as of this writing, we dedicate this work.

Our deep respect goes, as well, to those men and women of federal, state, and local law enforcement who worked tirelessly for many years to bring these Lone Wolves to justice. Their selfless pursuit truly inspired us to tell this story.

∞ ∞ ∞

CONTENTS

FOREWORD

Hunting the American Terrorist is a gripping and fascinating inside account of the investigation that led to the capture of one of America's most dangerous lone wolf terrorists. Ted Kaczynski spent nearly 18 years killing, maiming, and terrorizing the country in a fanatical crusade to halt technology and punish those who didn't fit his twisted model of the world.

A brilliant scientist and mathematician, Kaczynski took extraordinary steps to avoid detection and to leave no trail that led back to him from his horrific bombing crimes. Operating out of a hand-built cabin in the Montana wilderness, without electricity or a telephone, the UNABOMBER, as he was dubbed by the FBI, arrogantly reveled in his belief that he was just too bright and canny to ever be found and brought to justice by the lesser mortals in the FBI who toiled for many fruitless years to find him. He was convinced that by breaking the most essential rules of civilized society, respect for human life and ideas, he could achieve his goal of remaking the world in his own self-aggrandized image.

What his superior intellect fatally miscalculated was the incredible competence of FBI agents like Terry Turchie and Kathy Puckett, and scores of their able colleagues on the UNABOM Task Force (UTF) and at FBIHQ. He also severely underestimated their intelligence, resourcefulness, and dogged persistence. Perhaps most of all, he grossly underestimated and misunderstood the relentless force of the Rule of Law and institutional nature of FBI culture, one of the Bureau's unique strengths.

I have the utmost respect for and a long history with many of the world's foremost law enforcement and security agencies. As a young FBI Agent working organized crime cases with the New York City Police Department, and later as a prosecutor who was part of a team of Italian National Police officers and investigating Magistrates, I had the privilege to learn and benefit from some of the best investigators in our business. Later, as a judge and FBI official, I was able to appreciate a much wider, global community of terrific law enforcement superstars and heroes.

However, in no single institution but the FBI have I found consistently, over the long term, such an integrated level of competence in investigative ability, intelligence, and sustained dedication to the mission. The unique strength of the FBI is its reliability and track record in resolving exceedingly complex, multi-jurisdictional matters—criminal, civil, counterintelligence, and counterterrorism. This reality and its history are not always understood.

For example, for those who naively suggest that the FBI's counterterrorism and counterintelligence responsibilities should be taken away, after over 60 years of solid experience, and given to a start-up, domestic "intelligence agency," some history is important. First of all, this misguided notion would in effect create a "secret national police," which Americans going back to the Founding Fathers have always rejected. In addition, the FBI's history in confronting successfully the most complex and dangerous challenges has been, with few exceptions, truly impressive.

Starting in the late 1930s and continuing until the Soviet Union's collapse in 1991, the FBI's lawyers, accountants, social studies' teachers, scientists, police veterans, soldiers, and sailors forged the most formidable counterintelligence force in the history of the world and bested the legions of Nazis and KGB professionals at their own game from one end of the planet to the other. More remarkably, the men and women of the FBI who won this fight pretty much played by the rule of law and kept their honor and integrity while doing it.

And when the FBI ultimately began to enforce the Nation's civil rights laws and the Constitution to protect Black Americans from generations of state-sponsored violence and hatred, all those who would deny any American his or her precious rights were on the way to being brought to justice. We regret that it took the FBI so long to enter that struggle.

After the tragedies of Ruby Ridge and Waco, the FBI learned that it was essential to fully integrate its operational and negotiation/behavioral sciences expertise. The Critical Incident Response Group (CIRG) was established, and SWAT leaders and social scientists were given equal seats at the crisis table. While it had been longstanding FBI and U.S. Government policy "never to negotiate with terrorists," the FBI used, for the first time, third-party negotiators to resolve peacefully the 1996 armed stand-off with the so-called Freemen in Montana. Interestingly, unlike Waco and Ruby Ridge, our 24 by 7 national media barely gave one full news cycle of attention to that successful and bloodless outcome. Only one life, that of dedicated FBI Agent Kevin Kramer, was lost in that long ordeal due to a tragic car accident.

Today, the FBI is the main agency that enforces our criminal, civil rights statutes. Similarly, the FBI is the primary agency that protects our citizens and residents from public corruption. When the FBI was given drug enforcement authority in the 1960s, it quickly distinguished itself by bringing some of the most complex drug investigations of international cartels to the country's 93 United States Attorneys' offices. The same can be said about anti-trust matters, complex fraud and securities cases, environmental investigations, and crimes against children.

The main point is that, once focused on a particular area of complex criminal or intelligence activity, the FBI has the proven ability to adapt itself to any challenge and deploy its best and brightest—for as long as it takes—to achieve a successful outcome. This, of course, assumes that it has the requisite legal authorities and the support and cooperation of its colleagues in the Justice Department. The second point is that from each new area of experience, the FBI has the institutional facility to learn new tradecraft as well as from its own mistakes. The last and most important point here is that the FBI performs this ongoing and evolving mission by adhering, with rare exceptions, to the letter and the spirit of the Rule of Law. All of this is made possible not by its immense power and international reputation, but by the honesty and integrity of the men and women who devote themselves to this calling despite great sacrifices and real dangers. For this special service, the Nation has a lot to thank them and their families for.

For all of these reasons, we are grateful to Agents Turchie and Puckett for giving us *Hunting the American Terrorist*. Together with their terrific UTF team and supporters at the FBI Lab and HQ, they devoted themselves to the task of unraveling one of the most complex and dangerous crime sprees in our history. Despite years of frustrating work and incredible effort without success, they never lost their focus, energy, imagination, and persistence. Just as importantly, they maintained their enthusiasm, sense of humor, and humanity. This last quality was exemplified in how they and their team cared for and interacted with the Unabomber's brother and mother. This is the high standard all FBI agents are taught to follow and is an integral part of the FBI's Core Values.

The UTF's painstaking years of detailed work, analysis, and innovative action enabled them to exploit fully the opportunity that Kaczynski carelessly provided when he mailed his looney manifesto. At that critical time, all of the prior forensic, investigative, and analytical work-product fell on the Unabomber like a legal anvil. Only the persistence, skill, and institutional, as well as personal, commitment of an agency as unique as the FBI could have performed such a Herculean task.

Finally, with the institutional capacity and fortitude to learn from both its successes and mistakes, the FBI commissioned the UTF in the able hands of Agent Puckett to prepare a study of the behavioral tools best used to work these excruciatingly difficult cases. Both for lessons learned and as a proactive treatise to deal more effectively with these matters in the future, Agent Puckett has produced a masterful work, which will long serve the FBI and other investigators in hunting down Lone Wolf terrorists.

As the Nation and countries around the world grapple with the destruction and threat of modern terrorism, perhaps the most important contribution *Hunting the American Terrorist* can make to the law enforcement and security communities at home and abroad is a reminder of one fundamental American truth: Our liberties and the Rule of Law should never become a casualty in the so-called war against terror. Ultimately, America wins by upholding its respect for freedom and the law, even when fighting terrorists who break every rule of human decency and commit the most brutal of crimes against innocent people. In the end, the state sponsors and purveyors of hatred and violent terrorism will fail, just as Kaczynski, Rudolph, McVeigh, and a host of single-actor terrorists have failed within our own country. Their judicially taken or slowly ebbing lives in the Super Max prison in Colorado are the results of their failed "causes."

America's legacy is being written on a much larger tablet, and the final and enduring strength of its success is directly dependent on real adherance to the Rule of Law—even under the most trying circumstances. We should look appreciatively to Agents Turchie and Puckett, along with their colleagues on the UTF and throughout the FBI, for providing the model for conducting complex investigations against ruthless enemies of the Rule of Law.

Louis J. Freeh
Director of the FBI
September 1993–June 2001

PREFACE

This book sets out the lessons learned after seven years of hunting for lone American terrorists, from the nature of their lairs to clues revealing the mystery of what makes them do the things they do.

We found that a physical search for a lone American terrorist is futile unless it includes an extensive psychological effort to understand him. His efforts to exhaust his hunters and throw them off the scent are formidable. By bringing together the scant physical evidence he leaves behind with elements of the psychological world he lives in, the possibility increases that we can track him down before he kills again.

We also found that considerable effort is necessary to keep an effective but outside-the-box approach from being undermined by even well-meaning traditionalists in an established bureaucracy.

We intend this book as a guide for the future we almost certainly face: where painstaking effort will be required to sort out the lone American terrorist from the international terrorist, to be able to capture him before he retreats for years into his solitary lair in between his terrorist acts against society.

And there's another ominous possibility that may be in our future. By demonstrating what we've learned about the lone American terrorist, we hope to spark discussion about the possibility that the same factors that give rise to lone domestic terrorists could lead to a lone international terrorist.

In that case, we'd be dealing with someone who, independent of the terrorist group whose ideology he shares, engages in a private campaign of terrorism against Americans at home and abroad, unreachable by invading armies, communications intercepts, informants, intelligence, and hostage rescue teams.

Every society harbors outliers and outcasts. Before any one of them becomes a lone terrorist, we need to know what motivates them to move against American society. And when a new terrorist emerges, we hope that the experiences we outline in this book will provide a blueprint for how—and how not—to deal effectively with the threat.

ACKNOWLEDGMENTS

We were continually encouraged and energized by our families. To Casey and Helen Puckett, thank you for the support you always gave and the confidence you always expressed in us. To Joy, Lindsey, and Kevin Turchie, thank you for your unselfish perseverance and daily phone calls.

This book would never have been written but for the dauntless efforts of the team of FBI, ATF, U.S. Postal Inspection Service, and U.S. Department of Justice members of the UNABOM Task Force. Their commitment to the rule of law took this case from investigation through capture and finally to conviction:

Dan Atchison, Karin Bagdon, Shirley Bridges, Leesa Brown, Sandi Callahan, Mary Cardenas, Dave Carr, Miriam Champion, Bob Cleary, Bob Conforti, Jack Culclasure, Don Davis, Rob Dugay, Tim Dumas, Rick Ethridge, Marilou Felder, Sandy Figoni, Jim Fitzgerald, Jim Freeman, Steve Freccero, Molly Flynn, Mike Grady, Bill Hagle, Penny Harper, Lee Hayden, Bernie Hubley, Jim Huggins, Alex Jacobson, Gordon Jenkins, Ken Kirk, Lenore Lamey, Steve Lapham, John Larson, Mark Logan, Phil Lowell, Tom McDaniel, Gordon McDonald, Mike Maggipinto, Sheila Martinez, Steve Merrill, Tom Mohnal, Kelly Moore, Joel Moss, Tony Muljat, Max Noel, Tom Nunnemaker, Chuck Pardee, Tom Ravenelle, Brad Reeves, Rob Rolfsen, Don Sachtleben, Shelagh Sayers, Lisa Seagraves, Joyce Seymour, Lee Stark, Maggie Stringer, Hector Tapia, Betty Throne, Pat Webb, Dave Weber, Paul Wilhelmus, Barbara Williams, Doug Wilson, Vicki Woosley, and Terry Wren.

For the same reason, although we can't mention them all, we would like to acknowledge the tireless work of the dedicated group of law enforcement officers and citizens in North Carolina that led to the eventual capture and conviction of Eric Robert Rudolph. We would like to especially thank Don Bell, Jim Eckel, Steve Gillis, Tom Golden, C.J. Hyman, Bill Lewis, George Lynch, Joel Moss, Tracy North, Danny Sindall, Charles Stone, Tony Suter, and Warren Thompson.

We were privileged to serve in the FBI and to work side by side with so many dedicated and compassionate colleagues. We admire their loyalty to the rule of law, their country, and each other. We have always been inspired by their integrity and tenacity in the search for truth and the ongoing quest for justice. It's our hope and belief that, despite the serious challenges they face in the new century and into the new Millennium, current and future generations of FBI agents and support employees will take the FBI to new heights of achievement while preserving the FBI's Core Values.

Our highest regard goes to former FBI Special Agent John Behnke, who proved to be a source of constant inspiration and encouragement in both the UNABOM and Eric Rudolph investigations, as well as in the realization of this book. Thank you, John, for everything.

Finally, we are admiring of and grateful for the youthful optimism of our publisher, Donagh Bracken, as well as the skill and professionalism of our editor, Thomas A. Cameron. For his early interest and faith in our project, we thank Rob Preskill.

Terry D. Turchie
Kathleen M. Puckett, Ph.D.

INTRODUCTION

A section of the "Supermax" prison in Florence, Colorado, called "Bomber's Row," is home to a number of notorious American terrorists. Among its most noteworthy, past and present, are Theodore Kaczynski, Timothy McVeigh, and Eric Rudolph.

In 1998, Theodore Kaczynski—the "Unabomber"—moved onto the Row. Oklahoma City bomber, Timothy McVeigh, until his execution on June 11, 2001, called one of these solitary cells home. And in August 2005, Eric Robert Rudolph, who placed deadly bombs at the 1996 Atlanta Olympics and at abortion clinics in Georgia and Alabama, joined the clique on Bomber's Row.

There's some irony in the fact of this little community of home-grown terrorists residing in an underground prison in Colorado. Now separated by thick walls, each terrorist already had been virtually as isolated before they were incarcerated. Being a member of a group was never in the cards for any of them.

In 1994, nearly a year after Kaczynski sent his most recent bombs, I took over the hunt for the Unabomber. Over the previous 16 years, twelve bombs exploded at **UN**iversities and **A**irlines (UN–A–BOM) all over the United States. Adding computer stores to his target list in 1985 resulted in the death of Hugh Scrutton in Sacramento. In the summer of 1993, UNABOM attacks nearly killed a geneticist in California and a computer scientist at Yale University.

We knew we were dealing with a wily and elusive bomber. Although he'd been in business since 1978, the only portrait we had of him was a shadowy composite drawing from a witness who'd seen him placing a bomb in Salt Lake City in 1987.

What we didn't know is that we were dealing with a kind of home-grown terrorist very different from the radical right- and left-wing groups law enforcement had dealt with for years. Kaczynski, like McVeigh and Rudolph after him, was not a member of any group. He never fit in enough to belong anywhere.

1

The lives of all three of these men were marked by the same social and psychological dynamics that eventually turned each into the most elusive of homegrown terrorists: a true Lone Wolf.

Loners by preference, they adopted radical ideologies as their companions rather than people. Even while scorning society, they longed desperately to be a part of something bigger, something important. Their anger grew, and their isolation kept them hidden from others as they planned a solitary campaign to capture the attention of the public as well as the government.

Lacking social connections, careful to leave no traceable evidence of bomb construction, Kaczynski and Rudolph retreated into their separate, isolated forests to evade capture. McVeigh? He probably would have gone underground as well had an alert state trooper not stopped him for a minor traffic violation. Why was he intent on such destruction of lives and property? In his angry mental state, he was intent on sparking a new American Revolution by targeting the federal government. He would watch the ensuing chaos from cover. Careful. They were all very careful, these Lone Wolves. Careful and very, very smart.

In 1994, we didn't know much about this kind of Lone Wolf. But the term "Lone Wolf" itself was known to law enforcement at the time. Militia and radical right-wing groups loved to talk about launching a stealthy lone wolf against their targets: a hero warrior who wouldn't endanger the group because he had no traceable connection to it. Someone who had no visible ties, who lived away from the group but did its bidding, who mysteriously emerged to strike at enemies of the group, and then disappeared from society until the next attack.

We in law enforcement worried about lone wolves, and, in the 1990s, monitored a growing number of radical Web Sites to try to prepare to deal with potential attacks. The language on the Web Sites was alarming, at the very least. Militia groups called for violent insurrection against the government. Any number of radical racist groups called for murder in the streets.

But over the years, it became clear that the lone wolf was more of an ideal than a reality, when it came to homegrown terrorist groups. The reason? Human nature. Most people are simply too social to spend their lives alone in the woods, or toiling in obscurity in a low-paying job while waiting for an opportunity to strike on behalf of the "cause."

This should have been good news. It was certainly a good thing that the lone wolf appeared to be more rhetoric than reality: wishful thinking on the part of extremist groups waving their flags and slogans at the public and then going home for dinner.

But lethal Lone Wolves do exist. What is the difference between these real Lone Wolves and the radical ideal?

Because of their own peculiar natures, real Lone Wolves either reject radical groups or are rejected by them. They operate by their own set of rules, unaccountable to group leaders, picking their own targets, and waging their own private wars with society. And because they're alone, smart, and careful, they're devilishly hard to catch by traditional law enforcement methods.

By April 1994, 16 years of investigation by University Police Departments, Sheriff's Departments, Municipal and state police agencies, the U.S. Postal Inspection Service, the Bureau of Alcohol, Tobacco and Firearms (ATF) and the FBI had come up empty. All worked intensively at different periods, sometimes even together, to identify the Unabomber. They never came close. Law enforcement officers came and went, but the Unabomber remained.

The team I assembled that April was in place and working when the Unabomber struck again in December. That attack cruelly took a father from his young family just before the Christmas holiday. Our investigation went into overdrive. And I learned a critical lesson.

The hunt for the Unabomber—who ended up being our first real "Lone Wolf"—demanded that we abandon tradition in favor of a new organizational and management approach. This meant that we stepped on toes in jurisdictions all over the United States, because we weren't operating in the traditional FBI way.

When I took over the UNABOM Task Force (UTF) in San Francisco, however, it didn't take me long to realize that the traditional FBI investigative structure was not going to help us solve the case. It hadn't done so for 16 years. This new type of offender would require us to both think and operate outside the box.

But as a result, I had two consistent opponents throughout the two years that I drove the UTF down new investigative highways.

One was the Unabomber. The other was an entrenched and often oppositional FBI bureaucracy that did not appreciate my outside-the-box approach, and was determined to forget we'd ever done anything differently than usual to catch the Unabomber. Opposition to our approach was so widespread that today, even within the home of the UTF, no exhibit on the UNABOM case has joined the ranks of historic cases in the executive hallways of the San Francisco Division. The UNABOM case files themselves now lie in a dusty heap on the floor of the FBI garage in San Francisco.

Our new strategy in UNABOM integrated analysis with investigation and behavioral analysis. Using this technique, we were to able to identify the Unabomber in 24 months. I used the same strategy to assemble a fugitive task force that drove Eric Rudolph so deep into the Nantahala Forest in North Carolina that he was prevented from unleashing another "Army of God" attack for five years before his arrest.

In 2000, as the first Deputy Assistant Director for the new FBI Counterterrorism Division in Washington, D.C., I asked Kathleen Puckett to conduct a behavioral study of Theodore Kaczynski and Eric Rudolph. Now a doctor in psychology, Kathy—a key member of the UTF—had worked on the fugitive search for Eric Rudolph. Through her extensive document review, interviews of case agents, and consultations with forensic psychiatrists and psychologists, Kathy linked Timothy McVeigh with Theodore Kaczynski and Eric Rudolph as prime examples of "Lone Wolves."

The object of Kathy's study was to learn what made real Lone Wolves tick, and to see if we could figure out a way to see them coming before they launched their attacks on society. The results showed startling behavioral similarities between Kaczynski, McVeigh, and Rudolph as a peculiar breed of Lone Wolf.

Then, right on the heels of 9/11, another wave of attacks paralyzed the east coast of the United States. During the week of September 18, 2001, five letters containing micronized anthrax were mailed to addresses between New York and Florida. They targeted journalists, U.S. Senators, and news magazines. As in the Kaczynski and Rudolph cases, the envelopes had fictional return addresses. Notes accompanying the mailings were supposedly from Islamic fundamentalists, and almost everyone in government and the media quickly cast blame in that direction.

For those of us who were involved in the domestic terror campaigns of the 1990s, however, the anthrax mailings had all the ear marks of a Lone Wolf.

We'd seen it before. Almost immediately after the Oklahoma City bombing in 1995, media outlets proclaimed the event the work of international terrorists—perhaps some new group of Muslim fanatics. Within days, however, the country was stunned to see all-American-looking Timothy McVeigh in handcuffs on the way to his arraignment for the bombing.

Unlike cases involving a homegrown Lone Wolf, miscalculation in a terrorism case where another country might be blamed for the attack had horrible consequences far beyond affecting diplomatic relations. We could actually unleash a retaliatory attack thinking we were on the right trail.

It's easy to criticize and chastise government agents and agencies for failures to connect the dots and both predict and prevent an act like the 9/11 attacks. In hindsight, anyone can overcome any obstacle, sort out good information from bad, and say: "See, why didn't you figure that out?"

Politicians engaged in 20/20 hindsight from the minutes after the first plane hit the first tower at the World Trade Center. It may have provided opportunities for juicy sound bites on the evening news, but it did not help or encourage those on the ground who were doing the work.

This book was written to give the public an intimate, inside look at two different aspects of doing the work on the ground. Part I is my discussion of how I departed from tradition and ran the UNABOM Task Force that captured Theodore Kaczynski and directed the fugitive search for Eric Robert Rudolph after his murder of a police officer in Birmingham in 1998. Part II is Dr. Kathleen Puckett's account of how she conducted the critical behavioral analysis in both cases, and the first public discussion of the study she produced for the Counterterrorism Division of the FBI on what makes lone terrorists like Kaczynski, Rudolph, Timothy McVeigh, and others tick.

As an FBI executive, one of the most important things I learned is that teamwork is everything. The more complex the case, the more important the quality of the team. In the long run, it's all about the people.

Hundreds—maybe thousands—of people took part in the hunt for the Unabomber during the 16 years before I took over the UTF. As I write this, however, I think of a handful of people—including the core of Team UNABOM—who brought us over the finish line to his capture.

THE TEAM ON THE HUNT

John Conway: Long-time FBI San Francisco UNABOM case agent. Using data based on crime-scene forensics, his mock-up of the first bomb provided evidence of the Unabomber's origins when it didn't fit into a nearby mailbox in a Chicago parking lot.

Jim Fitzgerald: FBI profiler from Quantico, who worked extensively on an analysis of the themes and phrasings in the UNABOM Manifesto that became the foundation for the behavioral analysis in the search warrant affidavit for Theodore Kaczynski's cabin.

Molly Flynn: FBI agent in Washington, DC, who—after picking up a document from the attorney for a cautious and anonymous witness—thought it was reminiscent of the UNABOM Manifesto. Her call to Joel Moss in San Francisco led within days to her becoming a de facto UTF member in February 1996.

Steve Freccero: San Francisco Assistant U.S. Attorney. Whip-smart and savvy, Steve knew the case inside and out, and gave us solid legal opinions while he kept a steady hand in the face of great pressures. He always reminded us that we couldn't afford to serve search warrants on the wrong person, because it would damage our credibility when the right person came along. With hundreds of suspects at any one time, his firm insistence on this point might have been Steve's greatest contribution to UNABOM.

Louis Freeh: FBI Director who became an honorary UTF team member. Part cheerleader and part seasoned mentor, Freeh made it possible for us to navigate through an entrenched FBI bureaucracy. He convinced Attorney General Reno that the search warrant on Theodore Kaczynski was solid and that the affidavit was trailblazing in its approach.

Jim Freeman: Special Agent in Charge of the FBI in San Francisco. Jim was a key player, who relished the unique challenges of UNABOM. We became a formidable management team, and Jim contributed his considerable experience and intellectual prowess to the case.

Penny Harper: An old friend and San Francisco FBI Supervisor, Penny ran the Administrative Squad, which spent countless hours sorting through the thousands of phone calls to the UNABOM hotline. She evaluated, as well, thousands of letters from all over the world from people who claimed to know the Unabomber.

Bernie Hubley: Assistant U.S. Attorney in Montana. A former FBI agent, Bernie was a straight shooter in every sense of the word. Bernie's experience was invaluable in the final, critical months of the case when we turned all our efforts to investigating the mysterious "hermit of Baldy Mountain" in Montana.

John Larson: The Chicago FBI equivalent of John Conway, Larson worked tirelessly and alone for many years exploring every lead in the frustrating and never-ending puzzle that was UNA-BOM.

Joel Moss: A close friend and San Francisco FBI Supervisor who became my "Executive Officer" on the UNABOM ship. A veteran of counterintelligence work, Joel was a tireless investigator who worked countless hours without complaint in both the UNABOM and Eric Rudolph investigations. He was the first to recognize conclusively that we had at last found the Unabomber.

Tony Muljat: Senior U.S. Postal Inspector. A veteran of the UNABOM case, Tony was the spitting image of Karl Malden in the 1970s crime drama *Streets of San Francisco*. Tony's focus was on the Unabomber's communications. His dedication to the case led Jim Freeman and me to ask for Louis Freeh's help in extending Tony's career past the mandatory retirement date.

Max Noel: FBI supervisor—a legend in the San Francisco office—worked Weather Underground fugitives in the 1960s, led assaults on airplane hijackers in the 1970s, and was a firearms and police instructor. By the late 1980s, Max was the office "go to" guy for organized crime investigations on the West Coast. He gave his all to UNABOM, fueling his prodigious energy by beginning and ending each day with shots of espresso.

Tom Nunnemaker: FBI Headquarters Supervisor, who dedicated himself exclusively to the UNABOM case and became indispensable in dealing effectively with other FBI and Department of Justice officials.

Kathleen Puckett: San Francisco FBI agent. One of the first female agents to join the Bureau, Kathy blithely told some of us that she had protested against the Vietnam War before she joined the Air Force and eventually the FBI. Kathy's background was primarily in counterintelligence rather than criminal work. She completed doctoral coursework in clinical psychology by the 1990s. Her behavioral analysis of Theodore Kaczynski became the basis for identifying the "Lone Wolf" mindset.

Janet Reno: U.S. Attorney General. Janet Reno understood the strategy we'd put in place in the hunt for the Unabomber. She put her own reputation on the line when she agreed to support our controversial recommendation to publish the UNABOM Manifesto in the summer of 1995.

Lee Stark: San Francisco FBI agent. Lee took on the challenging role, with Kathy Puckett, of dealing with the critical witness, David Kaczynski. Lee's solid background in criminal investigative procedure and the rules of evidence provided an anchor in the choppy seas navigated by the UNABOM ship in the final months of the hunt.

Maggie Stringer: San Francisco counterintelligence analyst, long-time FBI support employee, and daughter of an FBI agent. Maggie's keen intellect and relentless work ethic set the bar of performance for UNABOM analysts at a high level. We relied on her constantly throughout the investigation as well as the pretrial phase of the UNABOM case.

Terry Turchie: San Francisco FBI supervisor, promoted to Inspector and later Deputy Assistant Director. Pulled from the Counterintelligence "side of the house" by Director Freeh to take over the hunt for the Unabomber. Assembled a multi-talented and multi-agency crew and developed a new paradigm for the investigation of terrorism that is the focus of this book.

Paul Wilhelmus: San Francisco U.S. Postal Inspector, partnered with John Conway in determining that the first UNABOM device didn't fit into its intended mailbox. Paul's work was proof of the value of hours of meetings, debates, and analysis being invested in the case, and of his own dedication to the hunt for the Unabomber.

MONTANA, 1993

The bombs were perfect. The metal he'd so painstakingly cast glimmered in the dim light of the cabin. The hickory wood on the flipper switch was smooth and well shaped. The chemical compound had been perfected, and the targets selected. All that remained was to wrap them in heavy paper and add the addresses and the stamps. After a hiatus of over six years from his deadly mission, he was ready to remind them—all of them, all the unconscious drones in the technological nightmare the country had become—that he was still here, still dangerous, still watching them.

Here, in these woods, where he'd long hidden from the society he despised. People living tawdry, greedy little lives. All together, going to movies and dances and picnics, making friends, taking wives, acting as if it was no effort at all to fit in, to belong, to be part of the group. Something that always had been denied him; he, whose intelligence dwarfed theirs, who could read and write in languages he taught himself from textbooks, who thought deeply about the great mysteries of the world, and dealt fearlessly with the rigors of a wilderness life. He could never belong. No matter how hard he tried. No matter how much he read about societies, and philosophy; no matter how pure and dedicated his thought process, he always ended up the same way: on the outside. He'd made it his kingdom once, the Outside; he'd retreated to the wilderness to escape the pain and anger he felt in society. He'd exulted in those first years in the woods, where every day was a discovery, a triumph of his persistence, his ingenuity; there was so much to learn, to prove to himself that he could surmount any obstacle. He'd been proud of his accomplishments.

Then the intrusions started: the planes flying over his pristine forests, the motorcyclists roaring through the woods. He knew he was better than all of them, those drones—acting so happy, living piggish lives—how did they do it? What made it possible for them to so easily accept each other? No matter how much he studied and thought, he couldn't understand how that worked. Why no woman had ever wanted to be with him, no matter how he tried. He could howl with anger and humiliation at the thought that he'd actually joined a singles group during one work period in Oakland, and another time had put ads in the paper for a companion to join him. Just one woman, to share his physical as well as his intellectual life. It had never worked. Being brilliant didn't keep him from being a social cripple.

But it made it possible for him to be a towering presence in another way, a lasting, meaningful way, a way that would make his name known for generations, and go down in history. If he couldn't be part of a group, he was his own group. He'd stamped "FC" on these new devices as he had since he'd tried to take a plane down in 1979 and someone had called the papers claiming responsibility for his work. The group "FC." And he was the center of it. He was the one they all recognized but would never know, would stand in awe of but never find, because he was all alone, and no trails led to him in these woods. No one knew he was the Unabomber, but he knew it. And he was a towering figure in the midst of all those powerless to reach him. He would remind them, again and again, that he was in charge. And when he had their attention, he would send his words out into the world, where they would ring in the ears of all the dullards living their materialistic lives in a world increasingly polluted by their noise and their waste and their excess. He would bring them to their knees, in fear and in awe. Because when it all came down to it, his ideas—the purity and truth of his words—would live forever.

PART I

UNLEASHING THE HUNT

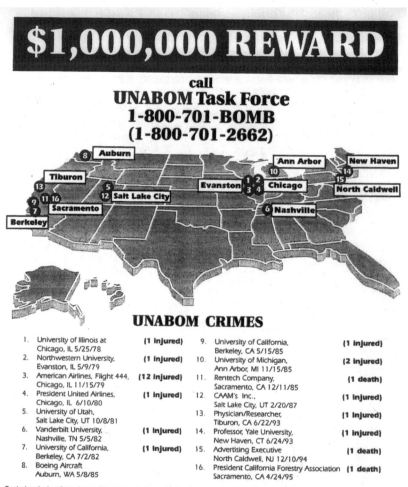

$1,000,000 REWARD

call
UNABOM Task Force
1-800-701-BOMB
(1-800-701-2662)

UNABOM CRIMES

1. University of Illinois at **(1 injured)**
   Chicago, IL 5/25/78
2. Northwestern University, **(1 injured)**
   Evanston, IL 5/9/79
3. American Airlines, Flight 444, **(12 injured)**
   Chicago, IL 11/15/79
4. President United Airlines, **(1 injured)**
   Chicago, IL 6/10/80
5. University of Utah,
   Salt Lake City, UT 10/8/81
6. Vanderbilt University, **(1 injured)**
   Nashville, TN 5/5/82
7. University of California, **(1 injured)**
   Berkeley, CA 7/2/82
8. Boeing Aircraft
   Auburn, WA 5/8/85

9. University of California, **(1 injured)**
   Berkeley, CA 5/15/85
10. University of Michigan, **(2 injured)**
    Ann Arbor, MI 11/15/85
11. Rentech Company, **(1 death)**
    Sacramento, CA 12/11/85
12. CAAM's Inc., **(1 injured)**
    Salt Lake City, UT 2/20/87
13. Physician/Researcher, **(1 injured)**
    Tiburon, CA 6/22/93
14. Professor, Yale University, **(1 injured)**
    New Haven, CT 6/24/93
15. Advertising Executive **(1 death)**
    North Caldwell, NJ 12/10/94
16. President California Forestry Association **(1 death)**
    Sacramento, CA 4/24/95

Explosive devices have been either placed at or mailed to the above locations. This activity began in 1978, and has resulted in three deaths and 23 injuries. The last device was mailed in April of 1995 from Oakland, California.

The **UNABOM** Task force will pay a reward of up to $1,000,000 for information leading to the identification, arrest and conviction of the person(s) responsible for placing or mailing explosive devices at the above locations.

Do you know the UNABOMBER?
Please contact the UNABOM Task Force at 1-800-701-BOMB / 1-800-701-2662.

UNABOM reward poster, 1995.

1

PICKING UP THE SCENT

The bomb that exploded on the morning of December 10, 1994, shattered the young family of Thomas Mosser forever.

Mosser, an advertising executive with Burson Marstellar in New York, opened the 15th UNABOM device in the kitchen of his home in North Caldwell, New Jersey. Mailed from San Francisco on December third, it was enclosed in a homemade wooden box placed inside a white cardboard outer box.

Each end of the 6- to 9-inch piece of aluminum pipe had been secured with metal plugs held in place by metal locking pins and a steel collar. Razor blades and green paneling nails, manufactured in the 1960s, served as shrapnel. Designed to detonate on opening, the "Mosser Device" proved lethally effective.

Barry Mawn, head of the FBI office in Newark, called me with the preliminary details. I called Jim Freeman—on a golf course in Half Moon Bay—and then Tom Mohnal, our point of contact at the FBI Lab. Mohnal, an explosives expert, left his northern Virginia home immediately and arrived in Newark several hours later. He called me that evening.

"It's UNABOM," he said a little shakily. He had instantly recognized the Unabomber's unique bomb-making signature in the blood-stained debris.

Within hours of the attack, Freeman, Max, and I stood around a speakerphone in a conference call with Headquarters. I began explaining our immediate strategy for the Mosser Event.

"We've already sent the UNABOM case agent to New Jersey. Neil Oltman knows the case well. He also knows Tom Mohnal from the Explosives Unit, and will be able to coordinate our interests at the scene. Neil is well versed in the science and forensics aspects of the case. We've already scheduled a conference call with him after he has had a chance to assess the situation. Meanwhile, we're already responding to some leads out here."

"What leads?" The Bureau supervisors said at once.

"Well, it seems that a call was placed to the Mosser residence some time before the bombing. The call was from an area code in California, so we're sending Joe Marinko and Tony Palumbo to check it out. They know everyone down that way and how to talk to them. Don't worry, we'll find out fast if the number's important, so that we can move on to the other leads that are pouring in," I said.

Joe and Tony eventually traced the call to the Calloway Golf Club Company. Thomas Mosser had been an avid golfer, and they were returning a call he'd made about buying golf clubs. Nothing in the call connected it to UNABOM.

"What about forensics?" said a voice from the Bureau. "At this point what do we have still up in the air? Are forensics gonna help get us anywhere?"

"The only forensics we've gotten recently that we're still working on concern the 'Nathan R' indented writing," Max said.

"Now, what are you talking about? Who's Nathan R?"

Max exploded while Freeman backed away from looking over our shoulders and spat an expletive. I tried to control my annoyance and speak in an even tone.

"'Nathan R' was indented writing found by the Lab on the letter the Unabomber sent to the two victims in 1993."

The Boss had heard enough.

"Hey, this is Freeman. We have some calls coming in we need to address. We've got to go now."

There was a final flurry of combined voices from the other end. "Don't forget to document all of this in tomorrow's 'Daily Report.' Maybe you should send something to us tonight in a teletype. We'll have another conference call tomorrow morning, and twice a day until the case is solved. . . ."

We hung up.

∞ ∞ ∞

In January 1995, FBI Director Louis Freeh came to San Francisco for one specific reason: to speak privately with all of the street agents and personnel of the UNABOM Task Force.

After initially meeting with high-level agency officials from the U.S. Postal Inspection Service, Alcohol, Tobacco and Firearms (ATF) and the FBI, I walked him into the UTF bullpen on a lower floor where the assembled throng was waiting.

Freeh was naturally at ease with FBI field agents. He had been one. He was a down-to-earth sort, and the agents clearly identified with him.

"I've discussed the UTF strategy with Jim Freeman and Terry Turchie here, and it's a good one," he told us. "Cases like UNABOM are solved through strategies and perseverance. You have my full support."

Freeh humbly reminded us of his work as an Assistant U.S. Attorney on another recent mail bomb case, called VANPAC, that involved the mail bomb murder of federal Judge Robert Vance. As he spoke, I realized we were lucky to have an FBI Director who had stood where we were standing now.

When Freeh finished his remarks, he looked around the room, in no hurry to leave. The attentive energy that had characterized the meeting suddenly froze in anticipation that somebody might say something crazy to the Director. A second or two went by, and then we all felt our hearts skip a beat when "Mad Max" Noel inhaled deeply and began to speak in a deceptively quiet initial tone.

"Director Freeh," he began, "I came to the task force in 1993, and I'm one of the original members still here working on the UNABOM case. There's not a person in this room who wouldn't work day and night to bring this case to an end. But we have three big issues that we just can't get resolved.

"First, we asked the profilers at Quantico for an updated profile of the Unabomber and for more timely and urgent analysis of the type of person we may be after. We're getting nothing. We need more interest in this case from Profiling and more answers to some of the specific questions we have asked of them."

"Certainly," said Freeh, "What else?"

The Director glanced at John Behnke, his trusted FBI head-quarters detail agent, who had worked with Freeh in Atlanta on the VANPAC case. Behnke was taking careful notes.

"The Explosives Unit at the Lab. We've been waiting too long to get back forensic exams we've asked for, and when we complain we get labeled as malcontents. It's not fair when we need those results urgently if we're ever going to piece all of this together."

Now Max's volume started to rise.

"And this gets to the problem that I see as the most serious throughout the Field.

"You say this is a priority, but the SACs in other Field Offices are not treating it as a priority at all. In some places, UNABOM isn't even getting major case status. We wait for weeks or months to get back the results of leads, when they should be coming back in days. What are we supposed to do? It slows down the investi-gation and it affects our morale."

Freeh eyed Behnke and Howard Shapiro, Legal Counsel at FBI headquarters, who had stood quietly while Max hammered through his points. He told us he would look into the issues that had been raised. Then he looked at me.

"I expect that any other issues that develop you'll take up with Terry and they'll be addressed," he said. All of us nodded in agree-ment, and Director Freeh left the room.

After several seconds of silence, Tony Muljat spoke up.

"Well, Max. . . thanks for holding back," he grinned, and everyone laughed.

The tone was set for future conversations with the Director. And the stage was set for resolving conflicts between the UTF and other major FBI players in the hunt for the Unabomber.

The next afternoon, Behnke and Shapiro walked unannounced into my office.

Their message was clear: the Director wanted the case solved. He would depend upon me to deal with the issues Max had raised and any others that developed along the way. He would be ready to support all of our efforts as we cut through layers of bureaucracy to bring the UNABOM attacks to an end. John Behnke would be my point of contact with the Director.

Although it wasn't printed on anyone's organizational chart, John Behnke, Howard Shapiro, and Director Freeh himself had become part of Team UNABOM. And Freeh would be counting on me to gun the engine and make it work.

The Director's visit to San Francisco, so soon after the attack that killed Thomas Mosser, reminded all of us that we were engaged in a race against time. The Unabomber would continue his terrorist attacks until we stopped him. And although we were energized by the attention devoted to us by Louis Freeh, I would continue to wear the double yoke of hunting the Unabomber and keeping a number of Bureau executives in Washington and in the Field out of our way while we did it.

A month later, Freeman and I traveled to Washington, D.C., to brief the Director and his staff on the progress being made in the case. Before we left, Jim asked me to meet him in his office after one of our morning task force management meetings.

"Louis is going to want to talk more about strategy," he said. "Where do you think we are at this point? I don't want to go back there and blow smoke. I want to solve this case. That's what we're about. Solving the case."

When I'd first met Jim, he had just arrived as the new SAC in San Francisco. I was supervising the Palo Alto Office and was a little nervous during our first encounter. He was tall and wide-chested in his dark suit, and he had a deep voice with a kind of languid growl to it. The UNABOM case had stirred Jim's intellectual as well as professional determination, and he was lightening fast in absorbing detail. Had it not been for UNABOM, I would never have been able to work this closely with him. We had become a team in managing and leading the UTF.

I pulled a memo out from among the papers under my arm. It set out a number of investigative projects that were simultaneously under way—all related to the growing intensity of the re-investigation of the 14 UNABOM attacks before the Mosser Event and the ongoing activities surrounding it.

Included were Tony Muljat's work on the History of Science project and the written letters that the Unabomber had mailed to two of his victims, as well as the indented writing impression of "Nathan R" on a letter to *The New York Times*. Thirty-two aspects of physical evidence from all 16 crime scenes strongly suggested that the Unabomber might be affiliated with the airline industry. Also on the list was the analytical opinion of the FBI, ATF, and Postal crime labs that the Unabomber most likely had access to a foundry, where he melted aluminum, and to a machine shop, given the precision with which he crafted his bombs.

"We could do a hand-out that looks something like this," I said to Freeman.

I started sketching some notes on a large white napkin that had been left on his conference room table. Across the top I wrote, "12/10/94 New Jersey Event."

Jim grabbed another napkin and started adding notes of his own. After 30 minutes, we had an updated strategic plan to guide the UNABOM ship into the stormy seas of 1995.

Our plan called for releasing a revised composite drawing of the Unabomber from the witness of the 1987 Caams Event in Salt Lake and using the opportunity to unveil a new and aggressive media strategy. Freeman would conduct more frequent news conferences. They would be designed to focus the public on known facts about the Unabomber, using information that would not impede the investigation or eventual prosecution.

To follow up on the additional leads we anticipated would come as a result of the media effort, we would add additional telephone lines and more agents to the UNABOM 1-800 Hot Line. In trying to uncover every grain of evidence, we would update the UNABOM behavioral profile and re-investigate all UNABOM events. Re-investigations would involve the core members of the UTF, those who knew the case best. We would launch around-the-clock computer-aided analysis to identify potential UNABOM suspects. And we would establish strict protocols and criteria to guide every step of the investigation, insuring that the case remained under our strict control.

A new document I'd developed, "Known UNABOM Facts, Fiction, and Theory," would serve as a guide for the investigation. By keeping it current, we could clearly focus our efforts and thereby develop a foundation for collecting and analyzing the thousands of pieces of information being developed across the country. It would also be a training aid for current and future UTF members.

Freeman and I compared napkins as the discussion ended. We exchanged glances of approval.

"Okay. Looks good," said the Boss. "Let's make it work."

He seemed relieved as we walked out of his office, adjusting his tie as if already preparing for the on-camera interviews to come. Handing over his napkin notes, he said:

"You may want to put this on regular paper before we go back to see Louis."

Theodore Kaczynski's Montana cabin, April 1996.

We are an anarchist group calling ourselves FC. Notice that the postmark on this envelope precedes a newsworthy event that will happen about the time you receive this letter, if nothing goes wrong. This will prove that we knew about the event in advance, so our claim of responsibility is truthful. Ask the FBI about FC. They have heard of us. We will give information about our goals at some future time. Right now we only want to establish our identity and provide an identifying number that will ensure the authenticity of any future communications from us. Keep this number secret so that no one else can pretend to speak in our name.

553-25-4394

Letter from the Unabomber to *The New York Times*, 1993.

2

MINDHUNTING AND FORENSICS

In 1991, a chilling film called *Silence of the Lambs* riveted audiences with its depiction of a series of gruesome crimes as well as the mysterious world of criminal profiling in the FBI. I saw the movie with a number of other agents, and I remember that we grinned at each other when we saw the agent Clarice Starling working out on tank trails at the Quantico Marine Base in Virginia, where the FBI Academy was built in 1972. There were other images of life at the Academy, including the sub-basement where the original Behavioral Profiling Unit was located, that were familiar to us.

A number of years later, we were in the middle of the UNABOM case when John Douglas—one of the more famous alumni of the Profiling Unit—published a wildly popular book called *Mindhunter*. FBI criminal profilers gained even more luster in the public imagination, and were soon expected to perform at superhuman levels of knowledge combined with intuition, like a cadre of latter day Sherlock Holmes.

I've known and worked with a considerable number of FBI profilers, who now work under the Critical Incident Response Group at a new location near Quantico. Their most recent title is the Behavioral Analysis Unit.

In 1994, as in other FBIHQ positions, profilers were agents from the Field who got to Quantico on a promotional career path. All of them had college degrees, all of them had worked investigations in the Field, and all of them were interested in the complex field of predicting future human behavior based upon past human behavior.

Few of the profilers at Quantico were psychologists or psychiatrists. Their training consisted of courses taken at various colleges and universities, usually in Virginia, on-the-job training, and mentoring by the profilers who had established the Unit. They also attended various in-service seminars and had exposure to some of the real experts in the field, like renowned forensic psychiatrist Dr. Park Dietz. All FBI profilers were assigned to Quantico, but they trained agents in the Field at a number of the larger offices to effectively funnel work that came from inside the Bureau as well as from other law enforcement agencies in the United States and abroad who sought their help.

Two of these profiling representatives were assigned to the UTF. They were primarily involved in the "Victimology" project, conducting interviews of UNABOM victims from over the years to see if there were any common threads or contacts that might point us to the Unabomber.

In view of the 1993 attacks, I wanted the UNABOM profile updated, and was eager to get more direct assistance from Quantico. Specifically, I wanted more assessment of the Unabomber's known writings; the thinking behind his mailing of some bombs and placement of others, and his comfort level with university environments and possible reasons for the pauses that had occurred in UNABOM attacks between 1982–1985 and 1987–1993. I was particularly interested in the renewed frequency of the attacks and what this indicated about future expectations.

I asked our two Field reps to facilitate an updated profile, to provide a more current status of where we might be and who we might be looking for based on the most recent UNABOM attacks. They said there was no need for any further profiling of the UNABOM subject.

"The profile is the profile," they said.

They also said they already knew who the Unabomber was. He was the return addressee on the first bomb in Chicago, in 1978.

Essentially, they thought the professor at Northwestern University—by 1994 he was in his 50s—had built a fake bomb and put it in the parking lot. When the package made its way back to him, he replaced the fake with a real device that exploded when a University police officer opened it, and the professor stood away from the blast.

Why? Because the professor and the officer had been involved in a disagreement over a parking ticket, and the professor wanted to get even.

They also suspected the professor because the man agreed to attend a Victimology Conference in San Francisco even though his wife was ill at the time. In their view, his attendance at the conference proved he was more concerned with what the UTF was developing about him than he was about his wife. And that type of personality was consistent with how they saw the Unabomber.

I was dumbfounded.

"Okay, you think you have a viable subject. Prepare a timeline. Let's see where he was during UNABOM events."

Several weeks later, I received an updated profile of the UNABOM subject. It bore an amazing resemblance to the professor at Northwestern. A timeline referencing UNABOM events was included. Although there were numerous conflicts ruling him out completely, there were also numerous attempts made to rule him back in.

Some UTF members were puzzled by this, but assumed that the experts were the experts. The rest of us were restless and worried that we would have a real problem if our Quantico reps were unwilling to consider any new suspects we surfaced. I decided abruptly one day to take action.

I bolted out of my office and into the hallway, running into agent Rick Smith, the Media Representative.

"Have you seen Kathy Puckett?" I asked. Rick nodded towards the adjoining hallway.

"I just passed her. She's on her way to lunch, I think."

I intercepted Kathy as she swept out of the Golden Gate Avenue side of the Federal Building in her long black raincoat.

"I'm going to lunch at this great new place on the corner," she said. "Want to come along?"

I should have known that she was headed for a vegetarian restaurant, and—true to form for Kathy—an expensive vegetarian restaurant. Once I found something on the menu I could live with, I told Kathy I wanted her on the UTF. I needed her skills and talents to be applied to UNABOM-related psychological profiling. I also needed someone who could work with other members of the task force, who would be a true team player.

During her days on Squad 12 Counterintelligence, Kathy had returned to graduate school to pursue her true passion: Clinical Psychology. She moved within a year or two from the Masters to the Doctoral level. She had mastered the art of studying and assessing human behavior even before she finished her degree, and was one of the original six agents selected for the Behavioral Analysis Unit of the National Security Division, whose "profiles" were of spies rather than serial killers. She would become an insider in the UTF operational structure who would capture the attention of the Director for her insight and competence, and she would play a major role in the ultimate solution to UNABOM.

Within weeks of her arrival, Kathy completed and disseminated to us her analysis of the book *Ice Brothers*. The bomb sent to Percy Wood in 1980 was concealed in a hollowed-out copy of the book, and it was preceded by a letter urging the victim to open the book because it was a "work of great social significance." The letter marked the first time the Unabomber had corresponded in any form with one of his victims. Sheltered through the anonymity of the mail and hiding behind a fictitious name, maybe he identified with *Ice Brothers* because of a personal event in his own life. At the time, Percy Wood was president of United Airlines. Maybe the Unabomber was employed by the airline and maybe, just maybe, he had lost his job and attributed the loss to Wood. It would be a question the UTF had to answer if the UNABOM investigation was to have any credibility at all.

Knowing another attack could come at any moment, Kathy also concentrated on the previous profiles provided to UNABOM investigators by Quantico. Eleven years after the Wood Device, Quantico's profile of the Unabomber read:

A white male who spent his early years in the Chicago area, had a high school education with some college or trade school attendance, experienced early encounters with the law for nuisance offenses, lacked social skills, had low self-esteem, may have had problems dealing with women, had real or imagined flaws, had an employment history of menial jobs that required little social contact, was obsessive compulsive, and was probably a quiet and ideal neighbor.

Kathy pressed Quantico for an update, to include information gleaned from the Epstein, Gelernter, and Mosser Devices in 1993 and 1994.

In March 1995, two Quantico profilers traveled to San Francisco. We spent two hours discussing our differences of opinion. Reiterating that "the profile is the profile," one profiler said that recent events had no bearing on the initial observations of the Unit, which dated from 1980. The Unabomber was who he was when the first UNABOM device exploded, and he was the same person now.

"The profiles," I said, "did little to address potential motivations for the UNABOM attacks—could any more be done?"

There had been several serial bombing cases over the past 50 years. Could Quantico produce a study of the lone serial bombers identified and arrested in those cases? Wouldn't a study of past bombers and those investigations enhance our ability to conduct the UNABOM case? Couldn't Quantico evaluate the profile in light of each new event to determine whether it was validated or impacted in some way by new information?

No, the profile was the profile. There were no resources at Quantico to deal with further UTF requests, and they certainly couldn't waste profiling manpower by sending someone from Quantico to work on the UTF.

I thought we were dead in the water. But several weeks later, Quantico Unit Chief Steve Mardigian traveled to San Francisco with a brand new profiler in tow. Supervisory agent James "Fitz" Fitzgerald, who had just transferred to Quantico from the FBI in New York, would be assigned in San Francisco as the full-time Quantico representative to the UTF. With Fitz and Kathy working together, we had a functional behavioral team.

∞ ∞ ∞

The Explosives Unit at the FBI Laboratory was legendary in its own right. Over the years, the Unit had developed significant authority over the direction and management of FBI cases that involved bombings. Their centralized operation and the specialized knowledge of their bomb examiners was of critical importance in "making" many cases. As a result, like the profilers at Quantico, their forensic successes allowed them to play a large and influential role in forging directions in complex cases.

This was problematical for me in setting the UNABOM ship in a new direction. By 1994, the Explosives Unit had thoroughly analyzed the evidence from the new bombings in 1993. With no new forensics, in much the same way that the Profiling Unit said the profile was the profile, the Lab considered their UNABOM work done—at least until the next bombing.

It is certainly true that, at the end of the day, the FBI Lab and the other crime labs (ATF and Postal) that played a part in the UNABOM investigation made substantial contributions to sealing the fate of the Unabomber at trial. But they had little to do with the identification of Theodore Kaczynski.

In fact, the Unabomber would never have been identified through forensics. And this was a hard pill to swallow for many traditionalists in the FBI, let alone the legendary Explosives Unit.

The Lab had concluded in 1980 that a serial bomber was at work. As with the first bomb in 1978, a second device, discovered on May 9, 1979, also had a connection with Northwestern University. It was placed on a table in a room at the Technical Building— a gathering area for graduate students, faculty, visiting scholars, and teaching assistants.

A member of the Civil Engineering Department opened the colorfully wrapped package and suffered burns and lacerations as it detonated. ATF took the lead in the investigation, and the debris was sent to their lab.

The device was built from scratch, almost completely improvised by the maker without the need to purchase components at any store. Only the "Phillies" cigar box, the wrapping paper, the batteries, the glue, and the tape used in constructing the device could be traced backwards to try to identify the maker, and they never led anywhere.

On November 15, 1979, the pilots of American Airlines Flight 444 felt a "thump" when the plane was at 34,500 feet. The passenger cabin of the Boeing 727 started to fill with smoke. En route from Chicago to Washington National, the plane was diverted to Dulles Airport for an emergency landing. A bomb had exploded in the baggage compartment. Because this was a crime aboard an aircraft, the FBI had jurisdiction.

The pilot and copilot later said that if they hadn't been able to land when they did, all 75 passengers and crew would most likely have perished. The fire caused by the explosion was burning its way towards the main hydraulic support. Had they lost hydraulics, the plane would have crashed before making it to the airport.

The bomb, improvised from a large juice can, was designed to fit inside a homemade wooden box. It had smokeless powders and chemicals used in fireworks. Four C-cell batteries were wired to a modified barometer switch, and a loop switch to two improvised wooden dowel initiators. As the airplane gained altitude, the barometer initiated the explosion.

Unit Chief Chris Ronay at the FBI Lab examined the bomb fragments and concluded the bomb was uniquely made and different from any he had seen before. Chris had done forensic exams on thousands of bomb fragments and components. He photographed his findings, prepared a report, and circulated the results to the FBI's 56 Field Offices, requesting that contacts be made throughout the forensic community to determine whether any similar bombs had been discovered.

The Chicago FBI located the ATF reports on the May 1978 and May 1979 devices. Ronay concluded those devices were made by the same individual who attempted to destroy AA Flight 444. There was only one inescapable and troubling conclusion: a serial bomber was on the loose.

While Ronay and the FBI lab are credited with connecting the first three bombs to the same maker, the Lab's work during the duration of the UNABOM investigation illustrates clearly that sometimes forensic science simply cannot lead investigators to an offender's door. And in some instances, relying on forensics can blind the experts to the real solution in a difficult case.

When the Lab drives the train and offers the only hope of resolving a case, other avenues are discounted. Forensic reports to investigators are delayed because of other priorities, and inaccurate theories may persist for years when the Lab isn't accountable to people working the case in the Field.

In 1994, we wanted the Lab to re-examine previous UNABOM device components. We also wanted Lab reps to attend UNABOM conferences where the overall case and each individual bombing were constantly dissected and re-examined.

A new Explosives Unit Chief didn't see it that way. In his view, given all of the FBI's other responsibilities and large workload, there was little time to devote to going over something repeatedly. Lab technicians did not have the luxury of repeated analysis to find something they may have missed earlier, and they were not about to do it merely to please us.

After Director Freeh's visit to San Francisco, the Explosives Unit called for a gathering at FBIHQ to discuss the UNABOM case. The agenda listed me as one among a number of proposed speakers. I called and asked that Max and Neil Oltman, the UNABOM case agent, be added to the speakers list.

Neil, a young agent, was uniquely suited to talk about the scientific aspects of UNABOM. He had come to the FBI from McDonnell Douglas in Los Angeles, and his background and education were in engineering.

By the time I arrived to take over the task force, Neil had developed a theory that the Unabomber might be a former or current employee somewhere in the aviation field. This theory interested the Explosives Unit, and Mohnal and the other examiners thought highly of Neil. I was also intrigued, as the forensics dovetailed with other indicators in some of the UNABOM events to suggest that a disgruntled airline employee might be responsible for the bombings.

Following the death of Thomas Mosser in New Jersey, I had sent Neil to secure the interests of the UTF and to become familiar with the principals of that particular event: the victim's wife; the Assistant U.S. Attorney for New Jersey, Robert Cleary; and Barry Mawn, head of the FBI in Newark. He worked around the clock to piece together the facts. By the time he returned to San Francisco, he was exhausted, but he was the ideal person to accompany Max Noel and me to Washington, D.C., for the Lab meeting.

When we arrived at the J. Edgar Hoover FBI Building, we found well over a hundred people waiting in the auditorium, most of whom we didn't recognize. Neil stood to my side at the door.

"Who in the world are all these people?" he said, aghast. Max frowned at me, and we took our seats.

The meeting began with an introduction by the Assistant Director of the Lab, who began by praising the FBI's efforts in the

UNABOM case. He took particular care to thank all of the people who were there, including government prosecutors from the Department of Justice; a variety of Laboratory examiners who had conducted UNABOM forensic analysis; desk supervisors from the Criminal Division; Lab supervisors, Unit chiefs, and countless others. Then one speaker after another listed his or her contribution to the case and praised all of the teamwork and help that everyone had given one another.

During all of the discussion, Max, Neil, and I sat in the very last row of the auditorium, with no one behind us and a clear path to the massive exit doors. With each speaker, Max became more restless. Eventually he was alternately moaning or groaning in disgust. Neil heard him, and seemed increasingly nervous at the prospect of talking to this large group of luminaries.

When my turn came to speak, I played the diplomat. Realistically, I didn't expect to learn anything useful from meetings at this level. Our mission was simply to listen, establish stronger relationships where we could, and identify potential team recruits at the Headquarters level.

I discussed our strategy, staked a claim to the management of the investigation by San Francisco, and introduced the group to the UTF view of the "UNABOM Facts, Fiction, Myth" approach that summarized over 16 years of investigation across the United States. Then I carefully introduced Neil, explaining the special role he played in the case and the unique aspect of assigning responsibility for such a massive and complex investigation to an agent who'd only been in the FBI for a year.

Neil's talk was short and to the point. As he returned to his seat, he passed Max, who was already up and headed for the stage.

True to form, Max began in a relatively calm manner. He said he was glad that all of the FBI Headquarters people in the room who had spoken before him were so proud of their work and their effort in UNABOM.

He himself couldn't claim to be so proud, he said, because we hadn't solved the case. In fact, while everyone here appeared content to pat themselves on the back, the Unabomber had killed another victim, and was just as elusive today as he had been for the last 16 years.

I caught a glimpse of Jim Tobin, who was the lead Lab metallurgist in the UNABOM investigation and a bit of a maverick in his own right. It was clear from the grin on his face that he was thoroughly enjoying an agent from the Field—an old-timer like himself—lambasting the brass.

On my right, Neil wasn't so amused. The longer Max talked, the farther into his seat Oltman sank, rolling his eyes and taking deep breaths. Finally, he pulled himself up in the seat, pulled out a piece of notepaper, and wrote on it in large letters, "Can't you stop him?"

I scribbled, "No," and tried to smile at him as he cringed at Max's every word. When Max finally returned to sit next to me, the auditorium was momentarily hushed until the next speaker took the stage, cracked a few one-liners, and the meeting moved along again. But not before I saw several prominent supervisors and Unit chiefs stalking toward the exits.

A few minutes later, an arm poked through one of the doors, beckoning me to follow. I was met in the hallway by a group of Bureau supervisors. We all walked quietly to their office. Once inside, with the doors closed, their boss turned around, pointed at me, and said, with a chilly smile: "A bridge builder, Mr. Noel is not."

The others shook their heads. I smiled big.

He handed me a handwritten note.

"The Explosives Unit Chief wants to have dinner with you tonight in Old Town Alexandria. Here are the directions."

I met the Unit Chief in front of one of the picturesque restaurants in the quaint suburb of Old Town. He was on his very best behavior. He smiled broadly and shook my hand, then led me into the restaurant. We ordered drinks as we looked at the menu. I was starved and tired from the tension of the day, but my companion didn't mention the conference.

I ordered a huge prime rib end cut with all the trimmings. During dinner, we eventually discussed some of the Lab's efforts in UNABOM in greater detail, and he appeared to sympathize with our needs for more attention from his Unit. While I had nothing but positive things to say about his chief UNABOM examiner, Tom Mohnal, I wanted his boss to know that Mohnal was overloaded and overworked, and was having a hard time keeping up with the needs of the UTF. We were finishing our cheesecake and coffee when he peered across the table at me, and his tone changed dramatically.

"Terry, you're doing a great job with the UTF. But Max Noel has to go!"

He waited a beat, then continued.

"His presence today embarrassed people. His comments were totally unprofessional, and I want you to know I will not tolerate it."

I put my coffee cup down and looked back across the table.

"Max is no diplomat, it's true. But he's dedicated to finding the Unabomber, and I need him."

Dinner was over.

When I got back to the hotel room, I had two messages: one from Neil and one from Max. I returned Neil's call first.

"Terry, today was awful," he said. "I don't see how I can stay on the UTF."

I assured Neil he'd done fine and told him the UNABOM case would likely grow stronger because of the meeting. Then I called Max. He was clear. He wanted off the UTF.

"Well, Max," I said, "I was told by the Explosives Unit Chief over dinner tonight that I need to get rid of you anyway."

He paused, surprised.

"That just makes it easier, then."

"No, Max, it really doesn't," I said. "I'll tell you what I told him. You aren't going anywhere until we solve the UNABOM case. Good night."

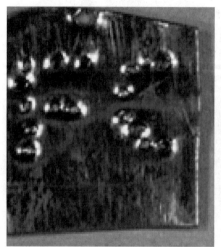

Metal found in the debris from a UNA-BOM device, stamped with the initials "FC."

Remnants of a note found in the debris from the first Cory Hall bombing at U.C. Berkeley in 1982

3

FOLLOWING THE TRAIL

Every week, investigators on television shows like *CSI*, *Without a Trace*, and *Law and Order* effortlessly—or at least attractively—sweep up crucial and unambiguous evidence, outwit suspects, and solve the case in an hour.

In real life, things are never that simple, or attractive, for that matter. But in my view, they're even more interesting.

It's tedious and frustrating to comb through thousands of pieces of debris from a crime scene that seem to shed light on absolutely nothing. But when evidence hard-won over long years leads to a suspect's doorstop, there's little in law enforcement that compares to the deep and heady thrill of it.

No one solves a crime alone, and every investigator needs the help and advice of his or her colleagues. There are DNA, fingerprints, and bloodstains to analyze; witnesses, victims, and family members to engage; and trained professionals to consult on the mysteries of the human mind. But in a case that lasts years, long strings of "fact" are often woven into a confusing web of fiction, folklore, and favorite theories that poses a serious obstacle to its solution.

For 16 years before our new UTF, hundreds of investigators had worked to find the Unabomber.

Each time a bomb exploded, active investigation would last only as long as the attention span of the bureaucracies involved would allow. To confuse matters further, there were constant personnel changes in every location where a UNABOM crime occurred. As the years stretched out with no solution in sight, UNABOM became a frustration of such magnitude that it was practically radioactive. Getting involved with the case could put the brakes on a career. How could you measure success when the Unabomber was still out there?

After I was assigned as the UTF supervisor, I spent weeks reviewing hundreds of FBI files, evidentiary reports, and psychological profiles from the FBI Profiling Unit, ATF, and even the public at large. Many agencies had kept no reliable records of their investigations, or had been absorbed by other agencies. Witnesses had died or were otherwise unavailable. The biggest speed bumps were often a long series of investigators from agencies all over the country who had pet theories and pet suspects, and who defended their positions well past reason.

I concluded that analysis had to become our foundation. We needed to link all that had been done in the past with all we knew in the present, and with all we would develop in the future.

This may sound elementary, but it's a tedious process in any complicated investigation. In UNABOM, it was exquisitely tedious. Criminal investigators are generally action-oriented, and wading through acres of ancient data isn't something they long to do.

But I had an advantage. The investigators at the core of Team UNABOM came primarily from the counterintelligence side of the house in the FBI.

Long and twisted puzzles weren't something new to me. I'd chased wily Soviet spies at the United Nations in New York for the better part of a decade. I had also supervised aspects of the national FBI effort against Soviet intelligence in Washington, D.C.

Joel had moved into counterintelligence work from his early White Collar Crime roots (he had an accounting degree), when he became fascinated by the intricate and arcane world of spy and counterspy. In the 1980s, the Bureau had sent Kathy to Washington for a year to learn Russian, and she later specialized in long and detailed research interviews of Americans convicted of espionage.

Even Freeman had spent a good part of his FBI career in counterintelligence, which was rare for an SAC in the Field.

Espionage, counterintelligence, and organized crime cases can—and often do—last for years, with maddeningly small infusions of information or luck. As a result, agents who work these kinds of cases are used to taking a longer and wider view. The pure intellectual challenge of UNABOM was not repellent to us; it actually added to our fascination with it. And after long years in other hunts, we were used to keeping the faith that expertise coupled with persistence would eventually lead us to the Unabomber.

That faith didn't extend to how we felt about the technology that existed at the time to help us. I wasn't as anti-technology as our Lone Wolf bomber turned out to be, but I noticed early on that the long printouts from the Massively Parallel Processor left behind by my predecessors hadn't led us anywhere significant. Lists of all Illinois driver's licenses issued over 25 years had not spit out the name of the Unabomber. (Interestingly, it turned out that Theodore Kaczynski's name was in one of those vast lists of data. Eventually, with the right variables loaded into it, the computer just might have spat out his name—by 2050 or so.)

In mid 1994, I called a UTF conference to update the team. I announced that we would immediately begin separating fact and fiction in the case. Myth and folklore had been woven into fact for years, and it was essential to finally pull them apart. Instead of relying on long printouts of data, we went low tech. We kept a chart, organized by categories and incidents over time, that summarized our "UNABOM Fact, Fiction, and Theory" guide. We updated it constantly, often daily. As we moved into 1995 and approached the 17th anniversary of the first UNABOM event, there was a new attitude in the hallway on the 12th floor of the John Burton Federal Building, home of the San Francisco UTF.

Our motivation quickened with the brutal killing of Thomas Mosser in New Jersey, and our morale was lifted by Louis Freeh's visit and pledge of support. There was a new momentum in the work we were all doing, a feeling that what we were doing meant something, and that eventually we were going to track the Unabomber down.

Freeman and I went to Washington early in the year, where Jim schmoozed with FBI Headquarters executives, and I spent some time with the Director's assistant, John Behnke.

Tall and reedy looking with a lock of brown hair over one eye, John was young, confident, and aggressive. The Director, particularly bothered by the inconsistencies in the investigation, had instructed Behnke to address the issue with the FBI's Interstate Property Crimes Unit in the Violent Crimes Section.

Even though the challenge in the UNABOM investigation was to track a terrorist, in May 1978 there were no clear statutes determining jurisdiction. The FBI had worked the case from a unit that handled crimes involving interstate property in the Criminal Division.

Behnke smiled as he told me that a new supervisor had been transferred into the unit that managed the UNABOM case from Washington. This new guy had agreed that he would stay in the unit assigned exclusively to UNABOM for an extended period of time.

It was welcome news. I only hoped that his personality would be a fit with us, and that we could secretly co-opt him as a headquarters UTF member, or as Jim Freeman always said, "put the team jersey on him."

We were all prepared to pound our new Headquarters supervisor into the type of point person we thought we needed. But the first words out of Tom Nunnemaker's mouth when I picked him up at the airport convinced me he'd already bought the team jersey.

"I hope we're not going to spend a lot of time in the office talking about UNABOM. I mean, I want to get to know and understand all the known facts about the case. But what I really want to do is go to the sites of the crimes that happened here in the Bay Area and see the terrain for myself. I want to feel that I'm standing where the Unabomber stood."

He sounded sincere. There was little that could slow us down if we had a reliable and trusted anchor in Washington. I smiled approvingly.

"Whatever you need. We'll spend just enough time in the office to get you grounded so things will make sense, and then we'll do a road trip for the next couple of days."

I held expanded UTF conferences at least once a month to update or adjust our Known UNABOM Fact, Fiction and Theory list, and they were starting to bond everyone. One of our analysts, Sheila Martinez, a baker before joining the FBI, made dozens of cookies the night before these conferences to keep the sugar rush high. I often suspected that munching on her cookies had a lot to do with our full attendance.

Bringing their work to the table in front of their peers did wonders for people's work ethic. It also let all of us see who was cutting it and who wasn't. People were rotated off the task force after some of these meetings, because they simply were not doing the job.

Before the creation of the new UTF, no one who had any sense had wanted to be involved in the case. Many ace criminal investigators felt imprisoned and stymied enough in the grind that was UNABOM that they would do anything to get off.

Now things were changing quickly, and the rotations gave us opportunities to further unify the team as we replaced people who didn't want to be there with people who were up to the challenge of identifying the Unabomber. It was all part of our strategy to galvanize the investigation by empowering each investigator and analyst to pursue long, twisted paths they might not have been able to walk down before.

We had used the UNABOM conference experience to brief high- level government officials and prosecutors from around the country on the status of the case. Now we arranged a conference to brief Tom Nunnemaker, our new Headquarters supervisor.

"Think of it this way," I said as I introduced case agent Neil Oltman. "We're running a big mutual fund here, and everyone around the table is a mutual fund manager. Some of our investment choices are going to fail, but others are going to pay off, big time. We're looking for a balance: risk versus growth, and, at the end of the day, we'll put together the combination that gives us a 100% return. Then we'll have the Unabomber."

Neil began his briefing.

"The FBI Lab and crash investigators from the National Transportation Safety Board have looked at the physical evidence from UNABOM crime scenes, and we have a report on similarities between the way some of the bombs were crafted and standard practices used in the airline maintenance industry.

"There were scribe marks on pieces of sheet metal that housed the batteries in the first bomb that was placed at U.C. Berkeley in

July 1982. Scribe marks are formed when sheet metal is formed and cut in patterns. This is a prominent technique in the aircraft sheet metal fabrication.

"In the bombs placed outside of Rentech in Sacramento in December 1985 and Caams in February 1987, there was shimming. Shimming is the practice of filling in gaps when mating structures. It can involve hard shimming, like thin sheet metal, or liquid shimming with epoxy.

"Overhead lights in the passenger compartments of airplanes are operated by battery packs where the batteries are soldered in a series. It looks similar to the way the Unabomber carefully solders batteries in his devices."

Neil detailed another dozen or so similarities between UNABOM craftsmanship and aircraft industry practices while Nunnemaker took copious notes. I found the aviation theory enticing, and I interrupted.

"The fascinating thing about all of this is that when we interviewed Percy Wood, who was president of United Airlines in June 1980 when he got his bomb, we asked him about his enemies. He told us he couldn't think of anyone. But when we interviewed other airline officials, we learned that United laid off 5,200 employees during Percy Wood's time as president.

"Some of the lay-offs were actually furloughs, and those employees returned to United in Chicago in the 1984 and 1985 time frame. But some of the employees left for good and migrated west to Salt Lake City, where they went to work for Western Airlines, which was ultimately bought out by Delta. One of the more time-intensive projects we have under way is to identify and interview those 5,200 employees, find out where they are now, and whether they have any connection to UNABOM.

"But it's just one project of many," I sighed.

Nunnemaker grinned.

"You're telling me you need another 100 agents, right?"

For the next hour or more, we provided Tom with a map of the many roads the UTF was traveling in an attempt to identify the Unabomber. Since his first attack in May 1978, he had mailed or placed 15 bombs to targets associated with universities, airlines, computer stores, and—at the end of 1994—an advertising executive. In the early years, he was called the "Junkyard Bomber," because his devices were almost entirely handmade from materials picked up at random locations and were impossible to trace back.

The Victimology project had found no commonalities in victims of the attacks that would link them, even after bringing many of them together to discuss the matter. But the re-investigations of each of the UNABOM events and new analysis of information and evidence were starting to produce some promising results. In the process, old theories, fiction, and folklore about the case were being scrubbed away.

John Conway educated Nunnemaker about the Dungeons and Dragons project. The first two UNABOM events involved an abandoned package with $10 in uncanceled stamps left beside a parked car at University of Chicago Circle Campus in 1978, and a bomb left in a graduate student room at Northwestern University in Chicago in 1979. ATF and the FBI had identified a group of college students who used a room on the same floor to play the game Dungeons and Dragons, or "D&D." One of the students was enrolled at Northwestern and then transferred to Rensselaer Polytechnic Institute. His professor at Rensselaer was the addressee on the first UNABOM device in 1978.

As a result, the FBI in Chicago had made nearly everyone who ever knew the student and played the D&D game with him at Northwestern a UNABOM suspect, and many had never been fully resolved.

One former Chicago agent, newly assigned to our UTF, was convinced of a massive conspiracy involving more than one of the D&D players. She was certain that one or another of them was the Unabomber. One day, she made an impassioned and angry plea to Steve Freccero for a federal search warrant to arrest them. The FBI in Chicago knew who the Unabomber was, she said firmly, and San Francisco was wasting time.

Steve was familiar enough with the case that, after he listened politely, he smiled and told the agent to stay focused on the facts, and to methodically eliminate one D&D player at a time.

That job had actually fallen to the team of John Conway and Paul Wilhelmus, who now happily advised Nunnemaker that the

UTF had identified over 900 D&D players nationwide and over 20 players at Northwestern in Chicago. None appeared to be connected to the investigation, and most had been positively eliminated as suspects. Paul and John had made a good connection with several of the original Chicago D & D players, some of whom had begun to seriously consider that one of their own might be the Unabomber. (They'd even been writing a book about who it might be. After we arrested the real Unabomber, one of them contacted us and said plaintively, "Are you sure?")

"Tom," Tony Muljat interjected, "I agree that we need to eliminate suspects and theories and possibilities as best we can to keep the investigation moving forward. Some things we're only going to develop so far, and then we'll just stop and go on to the next project." Tony turned to me.

"I know it isn't my turn at bat, but I want to comment on the Eugene O'Neill stamps, since we're talking about loose ends."

I nodded.

Tony settled himself in his chair and readied himself for a long exposition on his work in the case.

"There were three mailed UNABOM devices with Eugene O'Neill stamps on them. In 1982, one bomb was mailed from Provo, Utah, to State College, Pennsylvania. It had three Eugene O'Neill stamps. The bomb on American Airlines in 1979 had two of the stamps, and the first device—the one that was found in the parking lot at Circle Campus—had ten Eugene O'Neill stamps on it."

"What does that tell us?" Tom interrupted.

"Well, we think the bomber has a Bay Area connection. The Eugene O'Neill house is just a few miles from here across the Bay, in Danville. I don't know, maybe there's a link there we need to look at, that's all I'm saying. A possibility, you know?"

Hearing a little defensiveness in Tony's voice, Paul Wilhelmus jumped in.

"There's one other aspect of the stamp project you need to understand. Stamps are issued in coils and sheets. All three devices had the sheet version of the stamps, so we'll work on determining where they could have been purchased."

"And," Tony waved his hand, "We'll probably visit the O'Neill house some fine day as well." He looked intensely at Nunnemaker.

"We're being thorough, Tom. You know what I mean."

Nunnemaker smiled. He was aware that, as a young FBI supervisor, he might be treading on sensitive ground in second-guessing a senior Postal Inspector.

"Paul, could you talk about the Boeing Device?" I said. I was particularly intrigued by new information we were developing about this bomb.

"Yeah, the Boeing bomb was mailed from a return address on Hegenberger Court in Oakland, an industrial area about a mile from Oakland International Airport. All mail for Boeing was generally sent to its main address in Seattle. But this bomb was addressed to a facility used only when immediate delivery was required, and was used mostly by machine shops and other fabrication facilities."

Tom was listening carefully.

"You're saying that might be further indication of someone in the aviation industry—or someone in a blue collar capacity in a machine shop that supports the industry?"

"We can't rule it out," Paul said.

"Max, this is a great time for you to talk about your visit to Chicago," I said.

Max's booming, energetic voice picked up the pace.

"A pattern is developing in some of these areas where the Unabomber has operated. We didn't see it before, because no investigators ever traveled to all of the areas and saw all of the pieces together.

"The return address on the bomb mailed in 1980 was in the North Ravenswood neighborhood in Chicago. The Ravenswood area is very similar to the Hegenberger Court area in Oakland. Lots of machine and tool and die shops. There's a community college that specializes in industrial manufacturing and machine tool technology in Elgin, Illinois, about 20 miles from Ravenswood. That could be important, because we think the bomb on American Airlines Flight 444 was mailed from a Postal Substation in Gromer's Market, which is in Elgin and not far from the college."

Tom was intrigued and impressed.

"We're learning so much," he said.

I had promised Nunnemaker he would not spend his entire time in San Francisco listening to briefings in the office. After we adjourned the conference, we left San Francisco and crossed the Bay Bridge. We pulled into a parking space near Cory Hall at U.C. Berkeley.

"I used to come over here to the movies on Telegraph Avenue in the 60s," I told Tom. "It was nothing but hippies everywhere you looked. Today, it seems as if everyone's hair is shorter than mine."

Students and professors hurried by on bicycles and on foot in the busy, colorful atmosphere that was Berkeley. From his East Coast perspective, I think everybody still looked like hippies to Tom. We walked into the building that had been the scene of two UNABOM attacks in the 1980s.

Cory Hall housed the College of Engineering, which included the Department of Electrical Engineering and Computer Science. On the street-level entrance, we passed photographs of professors lining the wall. We came to a set of wide double doors leading to a second floor mezzanine. After climbing 18 steps, I pointed Tom to our left, and we entered a narrow hallway where two people couldn't walk past each another at the same time without touching. I stopped in front of door 264.

"This is where the Unabomber placed the May 1985 bomb that almost killed John Hauser, a graduate student. It was disguised as a three-ring loose leaf binder. When Hauser picked it up, the blast blew his Air Force Academy class ring off his finger with such force that it dented the wall on the other side of the room. You could see the impression of the insignia. He almost bled to death, and he never got a chance for the astronaut career he'd planned."

We walked up 58 stairs inside a fire exit stairwell to a small break room in a dead end corner. During summer break in 1982, Professor Diogenes Angelakos was seriously injured when he found a bomb here. In the debris after the bombing, the investigators discovered a piece of paper with the typed notation, "Wu, it works. I told you it would. R.V."

The typewriting didn't match any previous typewriting connected with the Unabomber.

"This doesn't seem like a place you would feel comfortable coming to if you weren't familiar with the building," Tom said.

"Absolutely!" I agreed. "I've brought over 30 people here. It's become the main stop on my training of new UTF people, and they all say the same thing. You've got to feel comfortable to walk down these hallways while you're carrying a bomb. In fact, this room is very similar to the room at Northwestern in Chicago where the second UNABOM attack occurred in 1979. The bomber feels comfortable in these tight environments. At the very least, he must blend easily into a college setting."

"Do we know who Wu is?"

"We've identified hundreds of people across the country with the last name Wu. At selected college campuses, we've pursued more limited investigation on everyone with a first name that begins with R and last name that begins with V. So far, nothing. In fact, if you noticed the nameplate at the top of the second floor mezzanine, it has the name of the department chair. His name is Wu."

Tom shook his head as we walked back to the second floor of Cory Hall.

"You probably noticed the construction across the street when we came in here," I continued. "Construction has been going on here for years, and we've identified at least a hundred contractors and several hundred subcontractors who were working around Cory Hall in the July 1982 time frame and then again in May 1985."

Tom was thoughtful as we left Cory Hall and walked out onto the street.

"When I walk around here, it's like you can feel the Unabomber. Somebody would have to be mighty at ease in this neighborhood to risk carrying not one, but two bombs into the same building." He stopped and looked at me.

"So, what's the plan? How in the world will you eliminate all the hundreds of possibilities?" He sounded sympathetic and tired at the same time.

"Interesting you should ask," I said. "Jim Freeman and I have to anchor this effort somewhere, and we're comfortable in saying that the Unabomber originated in the Chicago area. We're going to start making that a major part of our media blitz in the next few months. The analysts are building their common denominator searches around the notion of people with an Illinois Social Security number showing up at multiple places where the Unabomber also showed up. Hopefully, we'll get lucky."

"Any potential suspects shown up using that strategy yet?"

"Well, we're moving forward. We've been running name searches now for a couple of weeks on an experimental basis."

Here was where I needed to make my first pitch to our new UNABOM ally.

"One of the favors I need from you is to convince Headquarters that we need more analysts so we can start doing computer searches and comparisons 24 hours a day, during three eight-hour shifts."

"How many analysts do you need?"

"About 50, I guess, for about six months."

Tom blanched.

"We don't have that many counterterrorism analysts in the entire FBI. We'd have to take every one from every other Field division." I could tell he was thinking of how many irate FBI executives he'd have to face off with.

"I don't want to appear greedy," I said promptly. "How about 48?"

He smiled wryly.

"About your experimental run. Any suspects?"

"We started with millions of names," I said. "We've narrowed it down to thousands, so we're making progress. They all have Illinois Social Security numbers, were in Chicago in the late 70s, and have a connection to one or more other locations of UNABOM events."

As we got back to the car, Tom looked one last time at Cory Hall and the U.C. Berkeley campus.

"It really feels like he was here," he said.

We didn't know it then, but in less than a year we would knock on the cabin door of one Theodore John Kaczynski, whose name appeared only once in the vast UNABOM computer databases: as an Assistant Professor of Mathematics at U.C. Berkeley in the late 1960s, whose classroom in the Mathematics Building was only yards from Cory Hall.

Selected Statements of Defendant
Concerning the Northwestern University Bomb

"The bomb mentioned just above used match-heads as an explosive. Earlier this month I left it . . . at the Technological Institute at Northwestern University. The bomb was in a cigar box and was arranged to go off when the box was opened. I did it this way instead of mailing the bomb to someone because an unexpected package in the mail might arouse suspicion, especially

GX 18-2003B, p. 2

since a short while before there had been an incident in the news where cops in Alabama had been killed and maimed by a bomb sent them in the mail. According to the newspaper, a 'graduate researcher' at Northwestern was 'hospitalized with cuts on the arms and burns around the eyes' . . . Unfortunately, I didn't notice anything in the article indicating that he would suffer any permanent disability. I figured the bomb was probably not powerful enough to kill (unless one of the lead pellets I put in it happened to penetrate a vital organ). But I had hoped that the victim would be blinded or have his hands blown off or be otherwise maimed. . . . maybe he would have had burns <u>in</u> the eyes if his glasses hadn't momentarily retarded the flow of hot gasses. Well, at least I put him in the hospital, which is better than nothing. But not enough to satisfy me . . . . I wish I knew how to get hold of some dynamite."

Kaczynski's admission to the second UNABOM device placed at Northwestern University, Evanston, Illinois, in 1979.

The ruins of the Murrah Federal Building in Oklahoma City.

4

A TERRORIST IN CAPTIVITY

Early on April 19, 1995, another day on the UNABOM Task Force began the way hundreds had before. Max Noel and I left our quiet and manicured neighborhoods east of San Francisco and hit the Starbucks in Castro Valley before we joined the traffic over the Bay Bridge to the city.

When we got to the office, we immediately plowed into files and reports, returned phone calls, prepared for meetings, and pondered the resources we would need to maintain momentum in the Bureau's priority investigation.

I was in the same Federal Building on October 17, 1989, and I remember exactly where I was standing and who I was looking at when the Loma Prieta earthquake struck San Francisco, setting the Marina District ablaze and collapsing a section of the Bay Bridge that we crossed every day.

And I remember exactly where I was standing in the same office space six years later when news came from Oklahoma City that the Murrah Federal Building had been hit by a massive truck bomb.

The phones started ringing immediately. Bob Conforti, the Section Chief who oversaw the unit handling the UNABOM case, was one of the first to call. Bob didn't rattle easily, and although he was new, he seemed to know and understand more about the UNA-BOM case every time I talked with him.

"I guess you're following the news out of Oklahoma. The Seventh Floor 'execs' are asking me if there's any possibility this is the Unabomber."

"We're going into a meeting with Freeman and the staff here, but I've already talked to Kathy Puckett. She does not think it's connected. The Unabomber is a killer, but he's selective. The size of the bomb, the way it was delivered in the Ryder truck, none of that seems like UNABOM."

"Keep us posted on what's going on out there," Bob said. "We're going to be tied up for who knows how long with this tragedy, but we can't lose sight of the UNABOM case while we're working the Oklahoma bombing."

I empathized with those who were now engaged in the search to identify and catch whoever was responsible for the horrific destruction and loss of life at the Murrah Federal Building, and with the thousands of relatives and friends who had lost loved ones. I knew that all over the country—all over the world, in fact—hundreds of FBI and ATF agents would be fanning out to conduct interviews, trace explosive residues, and follow any possible lead to find the bomber(s). The pieces of the Ryder truck would be reassembled and traced to its origin, and thousands of data points would be painstakingly put together before those responsible could be conclusively identified.

But it didn't take the media any time at all to find the bombers. News commentators from CNN to Fox and all the regular networks trumpeted their conclusion: Muslim fanatics had struck the U.S. again. Harkening back to the truck bomb that exploded underneath the World Trade Center in 1993, a swirl of accusations against Middle East terrorist groups hit the press.

I earnestly hoped that the Oklahoma City investigators wouldn't be handicapped by the furor in the media. I knew some of them, and thought it unlikely they'd allow their best instincts to be second-guessed by wild speculation.

Stay on track and follow the facts, I thought to myself. We were moving forward in UNABOM using that strategy, and the unbridled raging in the media and by government executives, who should have known better, only reinforced my determination to keep us on course.

Thanks to an alert Oklahoma State Trooper, we didn't have to wait long to find out who was responsible for the deaths of nearly 200 men, women, and children, and the injury of hundreds more.

When the trooper stopped a car because it had no rear license plate, he apprehended Lone Wolf Timothy McVeigh as he attempted to flee the carnage he'd created.

All of us on Team UNABOM were excited and depressed at the same time. The swift success in Oklahoma was inspiring, and we were immensely proud of our law enforcement colleagues. But UNABOM was still unsolved. We needed to get back to work. We desperately wanted to find the Unabomber before he could kill again.

But our Lone Wolf had already made his move to take another life.

When McVeigh drove the Ryder truck to the Oklahoma City Federal Building, the Unabomber was already in the San Francisco Bay Area, preparing to mail his 16th bomb on April 20, 1995.

While he was there, he mailed four letters, including one to Warren Hogue, the Assistant Managing Editor of *The New York Times*, and one to a Yale professor the Unabomber had previously targeted with a bomb when he re-emerged after six years off the radar in June 1993. All of the letters were postmarked Oakland, California, two with return addresses and two without.

One of the letters had a return address of Ninth Street and Pennsylvania Avenue, NW, Washington, D.C.—FBI Headquarters. By now, the Unabomber was so confident that he was taunting us.

∞ ∞ ∞

On April 24, 1995, the overhead page sounded in the office: "Mr. Turchie, please call the switchboard immediately."

I instinctively realized that the news would not be good. I was away from my office, so I went to the closest desk and dialed the operator.

"Please hold for SAC Ross in Sacramento."

My stomach churned as I waited for Dick Ross to come on the line. He confirmed my worst fears the minute he started to speak.

"Terry, I'm out here at the office of the California Forestry Association in Sacramento. A bomb just went off inside the office of the association president. Everything is sketchy right now, but it seems to have all the hallmarks of a UNABOM attack."

"Was anyone hurt?"

"Yes, the president was killed instantly. We've frozen the crime scene. Most of what we know is from witnesses who reported picking up the mail and then giving the victim a package that had a San Francisco return address. But we haven't been able to get inside yet to begin a crime scene. We've closed off the area, and the police agree with us that it should be treated as UNABOM until we think otherwise."

We'd had problems earlier with the Sacramento Division of the FBI, just as we had with Salt Lake. Although the Unabomber had killed his first victim in the December 1985 attack on the Rentech Computer Store in Sacramento, the Division was slow to accept UNABOM as a priority after the bomber resurfaced in June 1993. Just months before the attack that killed California Forestry Association president Gilbert Murray, a Sacramento FBI squad supervisor argued that he had many other priorities, and was working on a major bank robbery that to him was just as significant as UNABOM.

Ultimately, Freeman and I met with Ross, the Sacramento SAC, and he'd agreed that attitudes and priorities about the case in Sacramento had to change. He was now an important ally.

"Dick," I said, "I'll send Pat Webb and some of the San Francisco Evidence Response Team technicians to Sacramento to help you with the scene. They should be there within the hour."

I reached Pat, who swiftly got the address of the Forestry Association and said he would talk to me after he got to the scene. Webb, the FBI Supervisor of the San Francisco Terrorism Squad for many years, was an accomplished explosives expert. His influence in the office extended far beyond that of a regular squad supervisor, and I relied on him in crisis situations.

Pat worked hard, was constantly in motion to solve problems, and served as a mentor to younger supervisors, including me when I first arrived in San Francisco. He had a rakish sense of humor and loved clowning around at the office Christmas party, where he played Santa. But when a bomb went off, Webb was all business.

While Webb and an evidence team were en route to Sacramento, the management arm of the UTF consulted briefly before meeting with the entire task force. When we broke the news that the Unabomber had killed again, the mood of the group darkened, and I could feel the tension in the room as everyone looked at each other and shook their heads.

We had a plan ready to deal with new UNABOM attacks. Chief Postal Inspector, Don Davis, dispatched postal inspectors to mail distribution centers throughout the San Francisco Bay Area. As additional information came in from the crime scene, Postal learned that the envelopes containing the letters were most likely processed through the main post office in Oakland, California, between 7:00 a.m. and 4:30 p.m. on April 20, one day after the destruction in Oklahoma City.

In a gruesome coincidence, the Unabomber had already been on the road, set to deliver another deadly bomb and taunt his pursuers, when McVeigh pulled his Ryder truck to a stop in front of the Murrah Building over a thousand miles away. At the time, however, we didn't know this, and initially thought he had tried to step back into the limelight after being trumped by the bombing in Oklahoma.

Soon after he arrived at the bombsite, Pat called me. He was breathing heavily and coughed as he talked.

"I'm here with Dick Ross. I just came out of the building. This is definitely a UNABOM attack. There's still a lot of smoke inside, so we're waiting for it to clear before we go back in. But there's no question. It's UNABOM. I found an end plug about ½ inch in diameter, with a locking pin through it, and a Eugene O'Neill stamp."

"You all right?"

"Yeah. We're out here in the street sitting on the curb. Someone just brought us some food. I don't even know who it was but yeah, we're okay." Pat coughed again. "Maybe this will be the one time where he made a mistake, and we can end up at his door."

I smiled at his stubborn optimism. I had thought optimism was a symptom of youth, but he was proving me wrong.

"Give me the phone," I heard Ross say on the other end.

"Thanks for sending Pat and the evidence teams. I talked to Jim Freeman a few minutes ago. I'll plan on meeting you all in San Francisco tomorrow so we can go over all that we've learned by then."

"Okay, Dick, see you then," I paused. "Wait. Please let Pat know that I talked with Tom Mohnal. He should be in Sacramento today to help you finish up."

"Mohnal from the Lab?" Ross said. "How is he going to be here today from 3,000 miles away?"

"He's in Oklahoma City—flew in on a Bureau plane. They've collected evidence at the scene there for the past two days. It's being sent back to Washington, and Tom will fly on to Sacramento before he goes back east. He'll take the UNABOM evidence with him, as well. I don't think he's had any sleep for days."

"I don't think any of us will be sleeping much for days," Dick said.

That evening, I called a UTF meeting to get status reports on all aspects of the investigation that were ongoing while we dealt with the Sacramento bombing. Freeman was absent, but we all agreed that the UNABOM ship was coming up on its next dramatic turn. There was so much activity, and the need for rapid operational as well as administrative decisions was so great, that the core of Team UNABOM decided that Freeman should work with us exclusively until the case was solved.

I approached him the next morning before the Division management meeting.

"Jim, we've decided that we need you to work with us on UNA-BOM full time. I think we can do a better job that way of making more rapid decisions, of avoiding conflicts with other squads in the office, and in dealing with Headquarters. We'll just have more juice if we do things this way."

"Get outta here," he scoffed, but he smiled broadly. "No agent wants the SAC micromanaging a case."

I could tell he was intrigued. Jim was fascinated with the case, and his intellectual curiosity had been engaged along with his determination that UNABOM would be solved under his watch. But it was a very unorthodox thing to do.

"You're a great help," I continued. "We've been through the Mosser crisis and in the last few days the Murray bomb, and you add a lot to this. We think you should be involved full time."

"So, you're like the case agent and I'm the squad supervisor?" His eyebrows wiggled with interest.

"Exactly!"

Shortly thereafter, Freeman turned over the day-to-day management of the San Francisco Office of the FBI to his Associate SAC, and the UTF took another dramatic turn from Bureau tradition. Although it served us well, traditionalists in the Bureau were so unhappy with the unusual management structure of the UTF that Jim's and my active roles in the investigation became a bone of contention during the next San Francisco Inspection at the end of 1996. Luckily, we'd caught the Unabomber that April.

In early summer, while Gilbert Murray's grieving family was still coming to terms with his loss, FBI Deputy Director Bill Esposito came with Supervisor Tom Nunnemaker and Section Chief Bob Conforti to San Francisco for an update on the investigation of the Murray bombing. Esposito listened patiently as I provided a summary, then cut to the chase.

"What do you need to bring this case to an end?" he said.

He looked first at me, then at Freeman. Jim nodded back in my direction.

"Well," I said, "right now we have one UNABOM squad, about 20 FBI agents, five Postal inspectors, and three agents from ATF." I cocked my head slightly, wondering if it could be this easy.

"We need three squads: one to work suspects, one to do the re-investigations of each UNABOM crime, and one administrative squad to coordinate input from the 1-800 number. We also need about 50 analysts, so we can compare and analyze data seven days a week, 24 hours a day."

Esposito stood up and asked Freeman for a phone line to FBIHQ. The two of them disappeared into Freeman's office for about 20 minutes and then returned.

"I spoke with the Director." Esposito said, glancing at Freeman. "We're transferring 50 agents into San Francisco Division to staff three UNABOM squads. Ten each will come from the next three new agents training classes at Quantico and 20 from the Office of Preference list. We're transferring in as many analysts as we can move, hopefully somewhere between 25 and 50 on a rotating basis, 30 days at a time. We're also giving you more money to staff a 24-hour 1-800 number with multiple lines." Esposito looked pleased.

"Anything else you need?" he smiled.

"No," was all I could muster.

"One more thing," said Esposito. He looked pointedly at me. "We're making UNABOM a Division within San Francisco. You'll be Assistant SAC, Terry."

I was astounded and a little numb. A battlefield promotion.

"Thank you," I managed.

"Now, solve this damn case, would you," Esposito growled, and he and a grinning Freeman vanished again, leaving Nunnemaker, Conforti, and me to work out the details.

Several days after my battlefield promotion, I decided to take a rare, short break from UNABOM and spend the morning with my ten-year-old son, Kevin.

At his urging, we went to Diablo Vista Park on the border between Danville and San Ramon and began unloading two canvas bags of Little League equipment on the Minors baseball field. Kevin suddenly stopped, looking intently towards the Majors field about 200 yards away.

"Dad," he said, pointing excitedly at a figure slowly jogging around the outfield fence of the adjacent ball field. "Dad, that's Dennis Eckersley!"

Kevin loved sports, and he was thrilled to spot a top Oakland Athletics relief pitcher within meeting distance.

"We need to go back home so I can get my baseball and have him sign it!"

I peered across the field. "Kevin, he looks like he's working out. I don't think he would want you to bother him."

Kevin heard nothing I said as he stuffed helmets and bats along with an extra layer of dust into the canvas equipment bags. We hurried back to the car, and as we drove back home I kept telling him that by the time we got back, Eckersley would be gone. He paid no attention and hurriedly ran into the house, retrieved bats, balls, an Athletics baseball cap, and a Topps card with Eckersley's photograph. We set off again, back to the park.

"Dad, hurry! Drive faster," he urged me as we returned to Diablo Vista.

As we drove up, I could see Kevin searching the Majors field for his hero, but Eckersley was nowhere to be seen. Just as my son's face began to fall, however, Eckersley reappeared, running the same pattern as before, 200 yards from the car. In an instant, Kevin's legs were a blur.

"Dad, come on, let's go!" Kevin shouted back to me.

"I don't think you should bother him, Kevin. . . ."

I was thinking of how to handle the crushing disappointment he would feel when Eckersley ignored him. I saw Kevin come to a stop at the center field opening in the fence, while Eckersley slowed to a stop just inside the center field grass.

For a second, neither moved. Then Kevin walked tentatively to within ten feet of Eckersley. I watched as the Major League pitcher motioned for Kevin to walk towards him. He then dropped to one knee, patted my son on the head, and proceeded to sign the cap, the ball, the bat, the card, and everything else Kevin had brought. There was no press, no cameras, no one else watching as Eckersley's small and private act of kindness painted a smile on Kevin's face that lasted for days.

My young son's persistence and faith was an inspiration to me. And the whole event was a fresh reminder that, despite all the evil we had been chasing, there was good in the world. My batteries recharged, I went back to work.

∞ ∞ ∞

Much later, Kathy's behavioral study "The Lone Terrorist" would include Timothy McVeigh in company with fellow Lone Wolves Theodore Kaczynski, the Unabomber, and Eric Robert Rudolph, the Olympic Park bomber driven into the forests of North Carolina by another relentless task force I had the privilege of directing.

Had it not been for the Oklahoma State Trooper who'd stopped McVeigh as he fled the devastating destruction he'd wrought at the Murrah Federal Building, he might have gone to ground and joined the ranks of the most elusive homegrown terrorists known as Lone Wolves. He was already one of the most deadly. As it happened, however, McVeigh, unrepentant, was executed for his crime before Kathy's study was even finished.

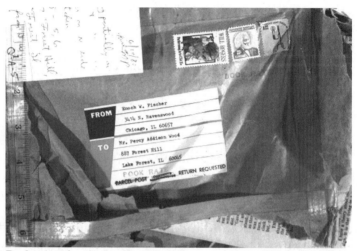

Packaging for the bomb sent to the president of United Airlines in 1980 in the book *Ice Brothers*.

Remnants of the bomb sent in 1980 to the president of United Airlines, concealed in the book *Ice Brothers*.

5

TAUNTING THE HUNTERS

"The *San Francisco Chronicle* just got a letter from the Unabomber." Freeman reached me on the phone in the Bureau car. "I need you to get to the office now. I'm arranging for us to interview the editor."

We'd been working at a feverish pace since the murder of Gilbert Murray in Sacramento, trying to anticipate how the Unabomber would follow his April letter to *The New York Times*. In it, he'd said "the terrorist group FC" would "desist from terrorism" if the *Times* published a 30,000 word article.

A hundred thoughts raced through my mind. Was this letter to the *Chronicle* the prelude to another bomb? Was there a manuscript, or was the Unabomber just enjoying the freedom he'd had to taunt his hunters for so long? With the Murray device, he'd demonstrated that he could operate freely right under our noses, since law enforcement had been unable to identify him for almost two decades.

The letter to the *Chronicle* warned:

"The terrorist Group FC is planning to blow up an airliner out of Los Angeles International Airport sometime during the next six days." He'd put a bomb aboard an aircraft before, and his devices had become much more sophisticated since then. This time he might succeed in blowing one out of the sky.

But this time, things were different.

He'd changed the equation with his threat against the general public by threatening LAX, and also by extorting the press to publish his manuscript. He'd crossed the threshold from law enforcement to public policy. Now, his threats as well as his actions would bring government and the media together to hunt him down before he could kill again.

FBIHQ activated the Strategic Information Operations Center (SIOC). After the first World Trade Center bombing in 1993, Congress gave the Bureau funding for a crisis command center that would be capable of handling several terrorist or other law enforcement incidents at the same time.

Now, FBI supervisors, ATF personnel, and FAA officials convened in SIOC to coordinate a nationwide response to the Unabomber's latest threat. Dozens of agents kept a sharp eye out for any evidence or breaking news stories that might be a sign of his next move. Agents also communicated constantly with FBI Field Offices all over the country to ready them for any type of UNABOM emergency.

The FBI in Los Angeles set up an emergency command post inside their headquarters office and a forward command post at LAX. San Francisco mobilized agents throughout the office, re-assigning them to chase down UNABOM leads and answer switchboard calls with tips from the public. The Evidence Response Teams waited for deployment to a crime scene. ATF and the Postal Inspection Service had people in each command center, forming a tight communications circle that was a force multiplier where skills and capabilities were critical.

The FBI nationwide went to a 24-hour-a-day emergency mode. And then we waited. We waited for the Unabomber to com-municate again, not knowing whether he would use words or bombs.

The FAA slowed airline traffic to a halt, adding a layer of security unseen before the threat. For the first time, passengers throughout the country were asked two questions before they could board their flights: Did you pack your own bag? Has it been in your sight continuously?

Early the next morning, Freeman and I shuttled between his conference room, the UNABOM squad areas, and the San Fran-cisco command post to assess the latest developments and to get ready for a conference call with FBIHQ.

"San Francisco, this is Bob Conforti. We have Attorney General Reno, Director Freeh, Deputy Director Esposito, and, on the line from Quantico, Jim Wright at the Investigative Support Unit."

"Good morning, Ms. Reno, Louis. This is Jim Freeman." Jim nodded and grinned approvingly in my direction. The Attorney General had never spoken with us directly, until now.

"Terry is here with me, and also Steve Freccero and Kathleen Puckett, our resident psychologist. We have Don Davis, the Chief Postal Inspector on the UTF and Tony Muljat. I believe, Louis, you're familiar with Tony."

"Yes, good morning Tony. How are you?"

The Director's letter to the chief of the Postal Inspection Service requesting that Tony's mandatory retirement be postponed had sent a clear message. The FBI cared about solving the case, and the Bureau would go to bat for people from other agencies who were critical to its solution.

"Director Freeh, I'm very grateful for your letter, and I thank you for keeping me around." Tony said.

The UNABOM case was Muljat's life. We all appreciated his passion and persistence, and I smiled as he proudly nodded his approval.

The Director got down to business.

"I want to discuss our response to the letters and copies of the UNABOM manuscripts that have been received by the *Times*, the *Post,* and others," he said.

There was no bomb aboard an aircraft out of LAX—at least, not this time. The Unabomber had used the threat to seize the attention of the public as well as the media.

Then, the manuscripts started arriving in the mail.

"I think you've all received copies by now," Tom Nunnemaker began. "The originals are with Mohnal in the FBI Lab being processed for prints and any other forensic evidence we can use."

"Tom," I interjected, "we have the letter that went to the *Times*, dated June 24 and mailed from San Francisco. Then we have the letter received by the *Post* on June 27—also dated June 24th; a letter to Bob Guccione at *Penthouse*, also mailed from San Francisco; a letter received by *Scientific American*; and a letter addressed to a professor of Social Psychology at U.C. Berkeley. All the letters included copies of the manuscript except the one to *Scientific American*."

"Right, that's what we have here."

Director Freeh spoke again.

"What's your assessment of the threats outlined in the letters he sent this week—Quantico? Kathy?"

Louis' acknowledgement of Puckett's behavioral role immediately placed her on a level playing field with the Quantico profilers.

"This is Jim Wright at Quantico. Director Freeh, we have cause to be concerned about the safety of law enforcement personnel. The recent letters were all mailed from San Francisco, so the bomber is not afraid to operate right under the nose of the Federal task force trying to hunt him down.

"All four letters mailed on April 20 from Oakland give the same message. The April 24 letter mailed to Dr. Gelernter at Yale had FBIHQ as the return address. The June 24 letter to the *San Francisco Chronicle* had Frederick Benjamin Isaac Wood as the return addressee. So it doesn't take too much imagination to see that he wants to rub our noses in it, while, at the same time, playing with everyone who's been making comments about his supposed fascination with wood."

We never thought much of the Unabomber's use of terms and phrases related to wood. The idea that references to wood were crucial clues in the case came from amateur investigators and the press. I constantly reminded everyone on the UTF to stick with the facts rather than spin off into speculation of this sort. If I'd thought it had merit, I would have made the wood theory the subject of an investigative project. But it appealed to the imagination, and even some of our most experienced investigators picked up on the opinions of people like crime writer Robert Graysmith, who later wrote in *Unabomber, A Desire to Kill* that "the investigators were fully aware of the bomber's pathological obsession with wood, both physically and with name-related connections."

Theodore Kaczynski himself seems to have been somewhat exasperated by this theory, and in a letter to *The New York Times* in June 1995 wrote: "The FBI's theory that we have some kind of a fascination with wood is about as silly as it can get. . .the FBI must really be getting desperate if they resort to theories as desperate as this one."

Director Freeh continued.

"We'll prepare something here to get out to all Field Offices, and talk to Postal and ATF to make sure they do the same. Any assessments on the documents themselves, the words? Anything about their relevance to the case?"

Freeh had been an FBI agent, as well as a prosecutor and a judge, and talking with him was like talking with a colleague. Many SACs didn't appreciate his hands-on approach. But to have high-level policy makers directly involved in the case worked brilliantly for us. Major decisions could be made in a matter of minutes rather than the hours, days, or months that the normal, lumbering bureaucracy could take.

Wright spoke from Quantico.

"We need time to look at the manuscript and see what it says. Generally, however, we've discussed the Unabomber's offer to desist from committing terrorist acts. We believe his primary goal is to broadcast his words to the public, and we don't think he'd risk his credibility by continuing his attacks after his manuscript is published."

Kathy broke in, looking a little pained.

"I don't think we can take his word for anything. He's been bombing for almost 20 years, and it's possible he can't stop now, even if he wants to. He gives himself an out by reserving the right to commit sabotage, a distinction he makes from committing terrorist acts. But acts of sabotage kill people, too. He'll rationalize whatever he wants to fit whatever position he wants to take."

There was murmuring all around on these differing opinions. Wright spoke again.

"The key question will be: Do we break a long-standing U.S. government position of refusing to negotiate with terrorist demands?"

"This is Freeman. We negotiate every time there's a kidnapping for ransom. We advise the family to do what they feel is best, and if they choose to meet a ransom demand, we use it in a tactical way, to our advantage. Would this be any different?"

Jim viewed the Unabomber's written words just as Kathy, Joel, Tony, and I did, as the potential key to track this Lone Wolf to his lair.

The Director sounded a closing note.

"Jim and Terry, prepare a formal recommendation and send it back to us by the end of the week. We'll meet here at Headquarters and decide what our next steps should be."

Suddenly, there was a new voice on the line, calm and deliberate.

"I want to tell all of you that I know how hard you've been working, and I know of your dedication to UNABOM," she said.

We had almost forgotten that the Attorney General had been listening in.

"But let me ask you, there are so many pieces of this case. How will you know if the Unabomber comes across your screen? What is in place to make sure that if we have an opportunity, we'll recognize it in the first place?"

There was silence from the FBIHQ conferees and in our San Francisco conference room. I looked across the table at Steve Freccero, who rolled his eyes upward as if to say: Who wants to chase that answer for the A.G.? I motioned that he should answer, since he worked for her directly, while I reported to her only through the FBI. But I was just joking. Steve was an attorney, so he frequently took two minutes worth of issues and talked about them for three hours. We didn't have time for him to answer.

"Ms. Reno," I said. I couldn't believe I was talking with the Attorney General of the United States.

"The UTF knows this case inside and out, and we get a clearer picture every day. We'll know the Unabomber when we see him."

I could see everyone catch a breath. What kind of answer was that for the Attorney General?

"Excellent!" she said immediately. "I'll look forward to a longer briefing on the case when you come back here next week."

The Attorney General was wearing the team jersey.

```
            ""              WARNING
The terrorist group FC, called unabomber by the FBI, is planning to
blow up an airliner out of Los Angeles International Airport some
time during the next six days. To prove that the writer of this
letter knows something about FC, the first two digits of their iden-
tifying number are 55.
```

The Unabomber's 1995 warning to The *San Francisco Chronicle* that he planned to blow up an airplane out of Los Angeles International Airport.

6

NEGOTIATING WITH A TERRORIST

Jim, Kathy, and I paced inside the Director's reception room on the 7th floor of the J. Edgar Hoover FBI Building. Every agent who waits in this room faces decades of FBI history. On the wall opposite dark blue leather couches are portraits of every FBI agent lost in the line of duty. Serious young faces wear hairstyles and suits cut in the 1920s and 30s during the gang wars. The wide lapels of the 1940s recall the days of chasing Nazi spies. Some wear the pencil thin ties of the 1960s, when the Bureau went after civil rights violators, and some sport the long sideburns of the 1970s popular in the Watergate era. Female faces appear in the 1970s and forward, along with a widening variety of ethnic groups from all over America.

Everyone in law enforcement has a similar tribute wall, and every officer and agent who looks at those faces weighs his own worth against theirs. Now it was our turn.

I had expected only a handful of people to be at the meeting with Director Freeh. As usual, when we walked through the conference room doors, we maneuvered through about 30 dark-suited Bureau executives who thought they might have a dog in this hunt.

All the way across the country, I had silently practiced what I would say to the Director. I anticipated a flood of protest against our plan. After days of vigorous debate, the core of Team UNABOM had hammered out a strategy to use the publication of his "Manifesto", the nickname given to the manuscript, as the key to identifying the Unabomber.

It was long-standing U.S. policy to refuse to negotiate with terrorists. When the Unabomber made his offer to "desist from terrorism" if the *Times* or the *Post* published his essay, a furious national debate began. Should the press submit to extortion from a killer? What encouragement would this be for future terrorists? Publishers of both papers pushed for a guarantee from the FBI that printing the Unabomber's words would save lives.

In San Francisco, we had huddled for long hours trying to work out a solution. There were only a few of us who strongly believed the Manifesto was the key to identifying and eventually capturing the Unabomber.

Jim Fitzgerald looked sober as he described his and his fellow Quantico profilers' position on the Manifesto.

"The Unit believes it's important to the Unabomber that he isn't viewed as a terrorist," he said. "In the June 24th letter to the *Times*, he puts distance between himself and terrorism when he says he deplores the indiscriminate slaughter that resulted from the Oklahoma bombing. We think the publication of his words is most important to him."

Kathy frowned and shook her head.

"You're saying we can give the *Times* the guarantee they want," she said. "But we can't. I don't believe that he'll keep his word. However important his word is to him, he's not a man of words—he's a man of bombs."

Although they often disagreed, Kathy and Jim Fitzgerald ("Fitz") were a good behavioral team. Fitz was calmer in his delivery, but no less passionate in his beliefs than Kathy. Unlike his colleagues at Quantico, however, he willingly conferred with her, and the UTF reaped the benefits of their often spirited collaboration.

For months, Fitz had shuttled between the East and West coasts as a kind of profiler diplomat. He walked a difficult line both personally and professionally in his work with us, but we had developed great trust in him. Before the FBI, he'd spent years as a Pennsylvania state trooper. His grounding in law enforcement the East-Coast way was a great counterpoint to Kathy's West-Coast maverick nature.

Max stepped in.

"Well, Jim, what's the Bureau expecting? Did Louis give you any indication of what he's thinking about all of this?'"

"Not really," said Freeman. "He's looking to us." He looked resolutely at me.

"And we're going to give him something solid. I don't want those guys at the Bureau dictating what we should do here. We're the ones that know the case, and we're the ones who know best how to proceed."

"Kathy," I said, "Go on with what you were saying."

Kathy looked at Fitz.

"Basically, the decision we make should depend less on believing what the Unabomber says, and more on our feeling about how publication may help us identify him."

"I agree," said Tony Muljat. "He's communicating with us now. We never had that before. We've been doing a lot of work on his previous letters, you know, the ones to McConnell and Percy Wood, and we know a lot we never knew before. I think we could learn even more if we kept him talking."

"What if we push to publish the manuscript and he sends another bomb and kills someone else?" Max said, agitated. "Our credibility will be gone, someone else will pay with his life, and we'll lose control of the investigation."

"I've gotten calls from other SACs," said Freeman. "They say we'd be crazy to publish. They say it's a no-win situation."

"So, Jim, what do you think?" Don Davis from Postal was always direct and diplomatic at the same time.

"I go back and forth. We negotiate with kidnappers for ransom all the time. We negotiate with hostage takers so they'll release people. They're all tactical moves to seek an advantage. How is this different?" He shook his head. "On the other hand, we haven't done this before, and this case has gone on for 17 years. Another bombing after we've stood behind publishing the manuscript would probably mean we'd all be looking for jobs. So would Louis."

"Can they do that to us?"

Penny Harper grinned as we laughed at her quip, and some of the tension in the room dispersed. Her timing was perfect, but it was her drawling Georgia accent that always made us laugh.

Penny and I had been friends for many years. We met when we were working Soviet counterintelligence in New York. She was transferred to San Francisco a couple of years after I got there, and it was fun dealing together with the challenge of being squad supervisors in a large office. When the UTF expanded, I asked Penny to supervise the Administrative Squad, which handled the 1-800 line, among a hundred other things.

Jim picked up his pen. He was one of the few Bureau executives I had ever known who took his own notes at a meeting. He looked up at us.

"Let's look at the policy and operational aspects of any decision we make."

Joel spoke first, calm and steady. He spoke in clear paragraphs, having quietly thought everything out beforehand.

"The major policy issue we face is the public's perception that we have acceded to a terrorist demand.

"But at the end of the day, all the public will remember is whether our decision to publish or not to publish the manuscript led to the Unabomber's arrest.

"If we refuse to publish the manuscript, or the Unabomber doesn't get an answer about publication before the September 24th deadline he's imposed, we risk another bombing attack.

"But if the manuscript is representative of his lifelong views, then it's entirely possible that publication will result in someone seeing it who will recognize him and call us."

Max gestured animatedly from his chair.

"Well, he could be published, but it doesn't mean he's going to stop mailing bombs and killing people," he said forcefully. "We're in the same place we've always been in UNABOM. We've got no meaningful evidence. We need forensics and witnesses and information that will lead to the Unabomber. I've said it before and I'll say it again: this is all just words, and not evidence of anything."

There was a growing division in the UTF, and Max was reflecting the majority view. Many saw the UNABOM manuscript as a red herring, part of our crafty adversary's strategy to toy with his pursuers and throw us off the track. Max and his cohorts worried that the preoccupation Kathy, Joel, Fitz, Freeman, and I had with the Manifesto was becoming a major distraction in the case.

"Sirs, if I might," Tony said as he shot a pointed look towards Freeman and me.

"The Unabomber's words can help us find him. This is our break. I think we should take it."

He settled down and chose his words carefully.

"In the manuscript, the Unabomber refers to a book, *Ancient Engineers.* There were two editions. The Ballentine version was limited in its distribution. The other was published by Doubleday. The UNABOM manuscript quotes from page 17 of the Ballentine edition of the book."

This discovery was proof that encouraging individual initiative and creativity in the UTF was paying off. Tony and his partner Robin Shipman excelled at tackling the facts surrounding the Unabomber's own words.

"Chicago has located a professor who taught at Northwestern University during the 1978 to 1980 timeframe. He used *Ancient Engineers* in a class called 'The History of Engineering and Technology.'"

"At Northwestern—the site of the second UNABOM device!" I exclaimed.

"Yes, now that's just it," Tony nodded. "We have the names of the students who were in that 1978 class. The analysts did some checking and identified two students who ended up at U.C. Berkeley in the 1982 through 1985 timeframe."

"Where two devices were placed at Cory Hall," Joel contributed evenly.

"What's the status of those two students as suspects? Where are they now? What about the professor? Have we interviewed him?" The Boss could have rattled out ten more questions, but Tony wanted to respond to the first.

"We've located them, and we're coordinating leads with Joel's suspect squad. As for the professor, if we want to interview him, we need to get back to him fast. He's 88 years old."

Tony's point was the operational high note of the discussion. It contributed analysis of fact to the behavioral view that there was a positive argument for publication of the UNABOM manuscript.

We eventually identified and eliminated as suspects all of the students who took a History of Engineering and Technology class at Northwestern from 1978 to 1980, including the two students who had ended up at U.C. Berkeley in 1982.

But at the meeting, Tony's point also led us to an initially dispiriting conclusion. If we could proceed by analysis of the Manifesto and other UNABOM writings alone, why did we need to give in to a terrorist demand? Grimly, we adjourned to my office to draft our recommendation against publishing the UNABOM manuscript.

When we got there, I looked at the long faces around my own conference table. Kathy and Joel looked at each other and shook their heads. Fitz sighed, and Tony threw up his hands. Mark Logan, a tall Assistant SAC from ATF I always think of whenever I see Sidney Poitier or Denzel Washington, looked at me with a level expression.

"We made the wrong decision in there," he said.

Logan was a class act. By 1998 he was ATF SAC in Charlotte, and put his stamp of approval on my use of strategies I'd learned in UNABOM on the fugitive hunt for Eric Rudolph in North Carolina.

"Yes," Kathy said firmly. "We need to argue for publication. We need to set out our options on how best to do it, and develop a strategy to take advantage of it. Somebody out there knows this guy, and they'll recognize his words."

"So now I go back to the Boss and tell him we've decided to recommend doing just the opposite of what we decided after hours of debate?" I said.

They all looked at me, then at each other. They nodded.

"Yeah," said Max, "We'll have some more coffee and wait here while you go deal with the Boss," he grinned. His eyes danced as the rest chuckled in agreement.

I went back to Jim's office. He was buried in paperwork, his glasses perched on the end of his nose. His well-thumbed copy of the UNABOM Manifesto sat in the middle of his desk.

"Already?" he looked up at me. I gestured as I sat down opposite him.

"When we got to my office, we decided we'd made the wrong decision. We all believe we should recommend publication of the manuscript. We think it may be the piece we're looking for to solve the case."

Jim looked at me, surprised. He took his position as part of Team UNABOM very seriously, and he seemed a little insulted that things had turned around without him. After he thought a minute, though, he nodded.

"Interesting the way it went full circle. I agree. Now get it down on paper, and we'll see how it sells in Washington."

∞ ∞ ∞

It was crunch time in the Director's conference room. Dozens of FBI luminaries milled around the massive conference table. Next to me stood Jim Kallstrom, the Assistant Director in Charge of New York. Kallstrom shot me a genial glance. He'd worked with the Director on the Pizza Connection organized crime case in the 1980s, and they were close friends. It was a hot summer day and the air conditioning was laboring. I started to sweat in my patterned brown suit, which suddenly seemed out of place in that sea of dark blue. I could feel my confidence flowing south, running through my soaking feet and onto the floor.

"You're going to do great. Our position is solid. We're recommending the right thing."

I looked back at Dr. Puckett, our UTF ship's doctor. She knew exactly what I was thinking, and smiled encouragingly as she took a seat down and across from me at the table, next to the profiling expert from Quantico. He gave her a cool nod.

To my right, I saw Freeman working the room. They were mostly SACs from other offices, and had been colleagues as they moved up through the FBI ranks together. Two of them approached Jim, and I heard them say they'd reviewed our position paper.

"We couldn't disagree more, Jim. We can't negotiate with a terrorist—it would set too dangerous a precedent. You need to go another way."

Before Jim had an opportunity to respond, Louis Freeh walked in, and a hush fell as they all took their seats at the table. Kallstrom sat next to me and Freeman, and the Director took his seat at the head. Towards the middle of the long table sat Kathy and the profiler from Quantico, chatting politely.

I had been a supervisor at the Bureau in the late 1980s, but I had never been in this kind of company before. My stomach was again in turmoil. In addition to the many SACs, there were FBI lab representatives, officials from the Violent Crime Section that ran the case, and other high ranking executives I had only heard of previously. I was going to have to sell this crowd. When I heard Director Freeh introduce Jim, I knew the countdown was on.

Freeman spoke briefly and then turned it over to me for the details. Before I began, my father's face flashed before me. I heard his voice telling me to sit up straight and speak slowly and clearly. My vision tunneled a bit, which was lucky, since an initial scan of the faces around the room showed mostly disapproving glares. I focused on the Director. He nodded occasionally as if to say, "I get it; continue." I caught occasional glimpses of Freeman nodding approvingly at me and raising his head in support against the growing level of silent opposition around the table.

After I gave our rationale for publication, I told them we preferred that *The Washington Post* be the vehicle, since we would be far more able to put surveillance on *Post* sales venues than those used by the more widely distributed *Times*. I said we thought the Unabomber would be highly motivated to actually see his work in print, and might try to purchase a copy himself. We had already identified and eliminated as suspects all regular *Post* subscribers in the Western United States. From the corner of my eye, I could see Kathy and the Quantico profiler nodding their behavioral agreement with this operational strategy.

At some point, I felt my confidence return. Our UTF had a substantial grasp of all the known facts about UNABOM, and had pieced them together in an intricate mosaic unlike any previous effort in the case in the nearly two decades before us. Instead of waiting for non-existent forensics and informants, we had painstakingly established connections between UNABOM events and the mind of the terrorist who was committing them. We had built such a solid foundation that we could be certain of one key thing, and I concluded my talk with it.

"We're not recommending publication because we believe the Unabomber will stop the bombings if he's published. We're recommending publication because we feel it represents the lifelong work and philosophy of the Unabomber. We think someone might recognize it and call the 1-800 Hot Line. If they do, we are confident we know enough about this case and the bomber we're pursuing to bring him to justice."

I was immeasurably relieved to arrive at the finish line. But no one was cheering.

The room was silent.

Jim turned to the Director.

"We don't view this as negotiating with a terrorist. We view it the same way we deal with kidnap for ransom, or with hostage takers. Our purpose is to gain the tactical advantage so that we can end the crisis at hand.

"We believe we can resolve this case if we accompany publication with a massive media campaign focusing the public's attention on the known facts of the UNABOM case."

From his seat next to Kathy, the Quantico representative spoke up in an authoritative tone.

"The Unit believes that the Unabomber cherishes his credibility and will refrain from mailing or placing another bomb if his manuscript is published. But therein lies the problem. Once he has our attention and we're walking down that path, how many other demands is he going to make? In addition, there are no assurances that someone will identify the manuscript, or any of his writings at all."

Around the table, the group responded with approving looks and nods. The Director looked down the table.

"Kathy, what do you think?" he said.

As often happened, she was the only woman in the room. I knew she was nervous, but she didn't show it. Her voice was clear and steady.

"The Unabomber said he would stop committing terrorist acts, but he reserved the right to commit sabotage. He defines sabotage as attacks against property, while he says killing people is terrorism.

"But he also says that people could be 'accidentally killed' if they happened to be at the wrong place at the wrong time."

She paused, glancing to her left, where the polite demeanor of her fellow behaviorist had now turned to icy disapproval.

"Here's where I disagree with my colleagues at Quantico. We aren't convinced he truly intends to stop bombing if he's published.

He may not be able to stop, even it he wants to. This is what he does, and it defines him.

"So, although the *Times* and the *Post* would like a guarantee that by publishing him they'll stop him from bombing, we can't give it to them. The reason to publish is exactly what Terry said. He's left us no other path that leads to him for almost 20 years. We believe that publishing his Manifesto will cause someone who knows him to come forward and identify him to us."

Kathy told me later that, from the corner of her eye, she saw Director Freeh nodding slowly and continually as she spoke. Now he looked up and asked for input from his Field and Headquarters executives.

"I've reviewed the UTF's written proposal. It was sent ahead of time to all of you. I assume you've reviewed it also. Terry, Jim, excellent presentation. I like the idea.

"Let's hear what others think."

The room remained silent. I could almost hear the gears spinning. The Director said he liked the idea. Did that mean they should like the idea, too? Or did he like the idea because the presentation was interesting? What other kind of ideas might he like to hear? The quiet became ridiculous. Finally, Jim Kallstrom's New York accent broke the silence.

"Lou, I agree with Jim and Terry. I agree that we should take a chance. If this will enable the public to help us identify the Unabomber, then that's justification enough."

Heads suddenly nodded all around the table. The Director looked at everyone.

"I'll meet with the AG tomorrow morning. I'll take Jim, Terry, and Kathy. Thanks for your time."

In the hallway near the elevators, I overheard someone sarcastically ask the profiler whether he was going along to brief the Attorney General.

"Guess I'm going back to Quantico," was the curt response.

∞ ∞ ∞

The following morning, we all walked in the early, sticky heat of a Washington summer across Pennsylvania Avenue to the Department of Justice Building. Balancing on her heels, Kathy carried an armful of files and her briefcase, as well as her pocketbook. Jim Kallstrom had come along and offered to carry the briefcase; Kathy shook her head in thanks, but declined. Then the Director offered his assistance.

"Like I'd ever live *that* down!" Kathy exclaimed to everyone's amusement.

Director Freeh walked up to the giant doors that stretched from the sidewalk 20 feet into the air, and knocked. No response. He grinned something about the doors of Justice being closed to us and then walked us around the building to another entry, where an armed guard waited. The guard looked at his watch. Freeh turned and rolled his eyes.

"I don't get over here enough. Maybe they don't recognize me," he said. Turning back to the guard, he said, "I know it's early, but we have an appointment with the Attorney General in a few minutes." He glanced down at his own watch.

As we walked off the elevator into a fifth floor corridor, we followed the long, historic hallway that houses America's top law enforcement officials. I knew it from my early days as a clerk at FBIHQ, when the Bureau was on the lower floors of the building.

When the J. Edgar Hoover Building was completed, the FBI moved out of the Justice Building forever. I smiled as I recalled an old-time agent telling me that the Director's office on the Seventh floor of the building now looked down upon the Justice Department across the street.

The Attorney General's office suite is contained by high walls with colorful murals from the WPA era of the 1930s. I had delivered mail from the FBI to this space in the 1970s. My hands were sweaty then, and they were sweaty now. This time, I would be giving an overall briefing on the case as well as our publication strategy for the manuscript. I didn't have long to worry about it, however, because almost as soon as we were seated, Attorney General Janet Reno entered the room. She wore a charming smile and greeted everyone warmly, telling the Director—whom she called Louie—she was looking forward to finally being briefed on the UNABOM case. Louis introduced us.

"General Reno, you know Assistant Director Bill Esposito and Jimmy Kallstrom, but I don't believe you've met Jim Freeman, the San Francisco SAC; Terry Turchie, the head of the UNABOM Task Force; and Kathleen Puckett, the UTF behavioral expert."

Director Freeh obviously held AG Reno in some regard, and seemed to make a special effort to make everyone feel at ease in front of her. She was personable, but tall and imposing. I believed she was taking in every word being spoken and every name being mentioned. As her eyes trailed from one introduction to the next, they focused intently on each of us, as if she were rapidly assessing our credibility.

Introductions over, I started my briefing. Ms. Reno crossed her arms in front of her, leaned into the conference table, and followed every syllable. I had one chance to make a strong case to her, and I knew it had to be flawless.

"As you know, no forensic evidence in 17 years has led us to the Unabomber. We have no fingerprints of any reliability, no DNA samples we can positively state belong to him, and no bomb debris from UNABOM crime scenes that we've been able to trace back to where they were purchased or otherwise acquired."

She nodded, eyebrows raised.

"Months ago, we began aggressive re-investigations of each UNABOM event by a core team of investigators assigned to that event. It was their responsibility, whether they were from the FBI, Postal, or ATF, to evaluate each crime, analyze what they collected, and then do it all over again."

Director Freeh interjected.

'This strategy has become so successful and produced so many new discoveries that I approved the UTF's growth from 25 agents and two analysts to well over 50 agents and 50 analysts working fulltime around the clock on a variety of investigative projects and leads."

"That doesn't include agents from other Field offices and the help we're getting from Postal and ATF, does it?" Ms. Reno asked.

The Director confirmed her statement and nodded for me to continue.

"The foundation of the UTF effort has been to develop known facts about UNABOM and to separate fact from theory and fiction as we move the case forward. By now, we've categorized 45 known facts about the Unabomber and his bombs. We've separated the known facts from 35 theories about the case, and we've listed 10 high-probability personality traits of the terrorist we are chasing."

I stopped and glanced at Kathy. "Our behavioral expert will outline for you some of those traits."

I opened my mouth to continue when the door swung open abruptly and a well-dressed and rather officious woman stalked into the room and flung herself into the seat next to Kathy. She motioned for her assistant to bring her coffee cup, and, as she took it, she shot a question at me about overall UTF strategy. The Attorney General cut her off.

"You're late, he's already discussed that," she said, directing a cool glance at the late arrival. Her calm voice registered as a distinct slap, and Deputy Attorney General Jamie Gorelick fell into a chastened silence.

For the rest of the hour, I gave the AG all we had learned about the Unabomber in painstaking detail. She absorbed it all effortlessly. She seemed to understand what we were feeling: that the Unabomber's face was becoming known to us, and that despite the care he'd given to his nearly two decades of bombs, he'd also made mistakes. He wasn't invulnerable to law enforcement; he was human. And we were finally closing in on him.

I told her we were still wrestling with contradictory pictures after thousands of hours of re-investigation of UNABOM events.

On one hand, we knew the Unabomber was comfortable in the blue collar islands of big city oceans. Return addresses on his bombs had referenced the Ravenswood neighborhood in Chicago, which included machine shops, foundries, community colleges that emphasized machining, and a large Polish émigré community. He'd also referenced a nearly identical type of neighborhood, Hegenberger Court, near the Oakland airport in the return address used on the mail bomb sent to the Boeing Fabrication Division in 1985.

Although the addresses were fictitious, the neighborhoods were real. UTF investigators had visited every one and determined that almost all of them included businesses that had contracted either to United Airlines or Boeing over the years.

So we were still aggressively pursuing the notion that the Unabomber was connected somehow to the airlines.

But he was just as familiar with the university environment. From his first attacks, he'd signaled his familiarity with Northwestern University, the University of Chicago, and Rennselaer Polytechnic Institute. We had no doubt that he had also walked the hallways of the University of Utah in Salt Lake and the narrow corridors of Cory Hall at U.C. Berkeley.

We'd also discovered that many of the colleges and universities involved in UNABOM had connections with the airline industry. When UTF analysts launched a comprehensive computer search for people who were common to these universities and the airline industry, thousands of names surfaced. To narrow the field, Joel's suspect squad was investigating these potential suspects.

AG Reno leaned forward.

"I'm beginning to understand why you told me that you would recognize the Unabomber when you saw him," she told me. "You're making sure to connect all the possible pieces in advance."

"Exactly," I responded looking first at the Attorney General and then at Kathy across the table, silently sending the discussion her way.

Kathy offered the latest behavioral assessment we had on the Unabomber. He valued academic success, might live in a rural environment, and probably used libraries for reference materials. His writings were likely autobiographical, and there were no indicators that he was ever in the military.

Kathy emphasized that, although the *Times* and the *Post* had wanted us to guarantee that publication of his Manifesto would stop the bombings, we were unable to provide one. Even if he wanted to stop, she said, he might not be able to at this point. But publication would launch his words into the public domain, and that's where we hoped someone who knew his words would recognize him and come to us.

Freeman, Kathy, and I joined the Director in recommending to the Attorney General that the Manifesto be published. It was our first real opportunity to jump ahead of the Unabomber and let him play into our game.

We realized there was a hailstorm of opposition to our plan, and that our recommendations were not politically correct. The U.S. government does not negotiate with terrorists. We knew that if another bombing occurred, we would be accused of complicity in it. But we also believed that his attacks would continue whether he was published or not. This might be our only opportunity to conclusively identify the Unabomber, before he faded back into hiding for another span of years.

Attorney General Reno looked at the Director.

"Louis, can I see you in my office?"

She stood to walk out of the conference room almost immediately as he reached her side, but not before smiling a warm thank you to all of us as we stood to wait for Louis to walk back with us to the Hoover building.

They were gone for only a few minutes, and they were both smiling as they walked back into the room. Handshakes all around, and we started walking towards the elevators in the outer hall. Louis turned to us before we left the room, still smiling.

"The A.G. said that was the best briefing she has ever had on a Bureau case. She'll join us this afternoon when we meet with the *Times* and the *Post* to recommend publication." We looked at each other with a clenched kind of relief. Then Freeh glanced back at the conference room and said, with a mischievous glint in his eye, "Didja see the A.G. slap the Deputy down?"

Theodore J. Kaczynski
Documented Efforts to Erase or Avoid Leaving Fingerprint Impression Evidence

GX 18-778B, p. 1

"two 10¢ stamps, purchased from vending machine in Kent St. Post Office, Missoula, March 1995. They do not bear the impression of this writing and are <u>clean</u> in that I have not handled them, but they may have been handled by postal employees who put them in the little envelopes that go in vending machine. They have been treated with salt-water and soybean oil."

Theodore J. Kaczynski
Documented Efforts to Erase or Avoid Leaving Fingerprint Impression Evidence

GX 18-20410, p. 4

"The tube should be worked over with fine emory paper to remove any fingerprints - wiping is not enough. Even if your own prints are not on the tube, store employees' prints may enable FBI to trace tube to store where it was bought."

The Unabomber was careful to remove his latent fingerprints from any potential evidence that could connect him to his bombs.

7

STRANGE BEDFELLOWS

"Thanks for coming," said Louis Freeh. He paused, and the silence was heavy.

"We don't see each other often enough," he added.

The tension in the room broke as everyone chuckled and exchanged glances.

We were strange bedfellows, indeed.

On opposite sides of the long table in the Director's conference room at the J. Edgar Hoover Building sat the owners and editors of *The New York Times* and *The Washington Post*. Their arms were tightly folded against the table edge, and they looked about as comfortable as cats in a dog's den.

Director Freeh and Attorney General Reno sat on the *Times* side, while Freeman and I sat with the *Post*. Although there were initial pleasantries as everyone filed into the room and sat down, years of distrust, suspicion, and anger marked the relationship between the FBI and the press. Neither the *Times* nor the *Post* considered it their business to help the federal government. Their business was more often to call government on the carpet in front of the American public. Today, things were different. Both papers had joined the long roster of UNABOM victims. The Unabomber had extorted both with a promise to "desist from terrorism" if they published his Manifesto. If they refused, he'd implied that more victims would die.

The American press is as averse to being extorted or blackmailed as is the U.S. government. No publisher or editor will willingly submit to outside control by anyone, whether it's the FBI or a notorious terrorist. But now they were in a major dilemma.

Should they publish the Unabomber in the belief that lives would be saved, as he promised? What if he didn't keep his word? Should they cooperate with the FBI in dealing with this terrorist? The prospect that the press should be under the control of federal law enforcement was anathema to them. And there was a deadline.

Everyone in the room felt the sting of urgency and the dread of failure. We were being forced to discuss how to handle this together.

"We recognize that we're making history with this meeting today," said Louis. "We intend to be forthright with the information we give you. That's the only way you're going to feel comfortable with the decision we ask you to make."

There was a rustling in the room, and then a chorus from our guests.

"You recommend we publish?"

"Absolutely," the Director said. "And there's only one reason to do it.

"We strongly believe that publication of the Manifesto will attract the attention of the whole country. Because of that, we believe someone who knows the Unabomber will recognize the words and content as his, and will be moved to turn him in."

Louis Freeh knew the idea of meeting a terrorist demand was against every precedent in recent history. He also knew his own reputation rode on whether this tactic worked to solve the case, or whether the Unabomber claimed new victims. He didn't hesitate to take the responsibility. His guests, however, weren't so comfortable with it.

"If we do publish, we need to be able to say that the FBI told us to, and the government accepted the responsibility for the consequences. We're not going to be responsible if he kills someone else after publication."

We'd anticipated this. No one wanted to be responsible for making the wrong decision in this intricate situation. The Attorney General spoke slowly and clearly into the agitated atmosphere of the room.

"You can state that the Attorney General of the United States and the Director of the FBI wanted the Manifesto published, asked that you publish it, and that I, Janet Reno, accept full and complete responsibility for whatever happens as a result of the publication."

There was a sudden hush as everyone held their breath. I remember thinking that true leadership was about stepping up to the plate when it was your turn and doing the right thing when you got there. This Attorney General and FBI Director intended to do the right thing. The confidence they both expressed in the work of the UTF would give us the final boost we needed to bring the Unabomber to justice.

There were short nods of acknowledgment from our guests, and then we all shifted in our seats as we began to discuss the nuts and bolts of publishing the UNABOM Manifesto.

"He said he wanted it published as an insert, all 29 chapters or 37,000 words at once," said the editor of the *Times*. "We don't really have the capacity to print an insert of that nature."

Eyebrows raised, the editor from the *Post* let the hint of a mischievous grin light his face at this admission as he spoke.

"We could probably do an insert," he began, "but it would be costly and. . ."

"We could split the cost of publication," the *Times* editor broke in. "If the *Post* does the insert, the *Times* could pay half the cost."

Splitting the cost also meant splitting the risk, and we all knew it. Despite assurances from the highest levels of American law enforcement, no one wanted to stand alone in making the decision to publish the Unabomber's screed. The results of this combined law enforcement and publishing dynasty strategy remained to be seen, and it was impossible to ensure success. At the same time, it was impossible to do nothing.

Director Freeh moved forward.

"We'd like to use another investigative strategy, along with publication," he said. "It might help us identify the Unabomber."

"Our behaviorists believe he'll want to buy at least one trophy copy of the paper when he's published. We intend to conduct surveillances of all *Post* distribution points in the Western United States on that day."

The delegation from the *Post* looked confused.

"We're not sure we can provide that information to you. We don't know for certain where all of our papers are sold throughout the United States, due to the nature of our distribution system."

The *Times* contingent sat up in their seats. Their body language said, "This is interesting. . . ."

Louis shot me a look. I cleared my throat and spoke for the first time.

"Actually, we know where the papers are distributed," I said.

They all turned to me. The *Post* delegates looked a little stricken, while the *Times* group looked like they were thoroughly enjoying the show. Eventually, the *Post* regained its voice.

"Well, even if the FBI knows where our papers are sold, there are so many copies and so many buyers that, even if you wanted to, you couldn't possibly cover them all at the same time."

I glanced at Louis and then at Freeman. Both looked comfortable with where I was going, so I continued.

"The *Post* has more limited distribution in the West than the *Times*, and there are far fewer venues selling the *Post* on the date of publication. That makes it easier for us to see if the Unabomber shows up to buy a trophy copy."

It seemed strange to disclose this sort of business detail in front of competitors, and I wouldn't have gone further except that the *Post* couldn't resist blurting out, "How many papers and places are we talking about?"

The *Times* group looked at me with undisguised delight.

"There are four retail outlets in San Francisco that sell twelve copies of the *Post* on weekdays," I said. There was a beat as they waited for more, but that was it.

Louis Freeh smiled sardonically.

"I guess that confirms what most of us know anyway," he joked. "No one else in the country cares much about what goes on here in Washington." There was laughter all around, but the chuckles from the *Times* group sounded a little louder, I thought. The editor from the *Post* decided self-deprecating humor was his best bet.

"Guess we'll need more copies on the day we do the insert," he said.

The remaining business of the meeting went quickly. The Unabomber's Manifesto would be printed in a *Washington Post* insert on September 19, 1995, jointly published by the *The Washington Post* and *The New York Times*.

Before it was published, SAC Freeman and I gave a series of interviews discussing specific known facts about the Unabomber. In addition, selected passages from the Manifesto itself were published as previews in publications all over the country. This strategy in itself might have led someone to contact us, and we might never have had to gratify the Unabomber's full demand at all, even if for tactical reasons.

A *New York Times* editorial before publication read:

> The rejection of violence in favor of reasoned discussion and debate is a choice which is cherished by all intelligent men. . . . FC may have a message important for all of us. The *Times* remains interested in exploring the opportunity presented by FC in its most recent letter.

No reference to the FBI was made in the editorial.

SAC Freeman conducted interviews with several major news magazines and media outlets. Jim had clearly mastered the art of working the media, and used his considerable skills to stress the known facts about UNABOM.

"When you think of the Unabomber, think of Chicago in the 70s, Salt Lake City in the 80s, and the San Francisco Bay area from the mid eighties to the present. Think about those locations in the context of the composite drawing from his 1987 bomb in Salt Lake, and then read the Unabomber's own words. If you can put them all together, call the UNABOM Task Force."

In a *Post* interview, I stressed phrases from the Manifesto. I highlighted our belief in the link between the *History of Science* reference in the 1985 McConnell letter and an academic connection with the Unabomber.

On September 20, 1995, *The Washington Post*, with the financial assistance and mutual support of *The New York Times,* published the entire UNABOM Manifesto.

We released a carefully worded statement from UTF Headquarters in San Francisco. We told the public that the decision to publish was "reached after much consultation between officials of both newspapers and law enforcement experts."

Howls of protest were immediate, from the media, academia, and law enforcement circles. "This was the wrong thing to do!"

thundered one of our former Quantico Field representatives—now retired from the FBI—on the nightly news.

Director Freeh had offered to temporarily send a thousand FBI agents to the Western United States if necessary, to conduct surveillances of newsstands that sold the *Post*. In San Francisco, however, we had already narrowed the task to two locations in the city: Nick and Mel's at Kearny near Market, and Harold's, on Geary Street. They both opened at 6:30 a.m., and each normally sold five daily copies of the *Post*. We'd already determined that no normal customers at the newsstands were of concern to us, and only two other locations sold one copy each of the *Post* on a daily basis. We decided to funnel any *Post* customers to Nick and Mel's and Harold's, so we had agents buy these other copies immediately.

Thirty agents, Postal inspectors, and Special Surveillance Group members were assigned to follow and identify every person who bought a copy of the *Post* on September 20. Based on past observations of business at the newsstands, we thought we'd more than covered our bases.

But an hour before Mel's and Harold's opened, the line stretched around the block. Fifty-five copies of the *Post* were available that day. Harold's sold all of its copies within ten minutes. Mel's sold its lot in an hour. Surveillance scrambled, and quirky circumstances abounded.

Somebody drove up to one of the newsstands in a car with Illinois plates. When he was told the *Post* was sold out, he flew into a noisy rage. We followed him to a transient hotel, where he stayed the rest of the day until he left to wander around the Castro district. We later determined he had no UNABOM connection.

In other parts of the city, other surveillance teams were watching UNABOM suspects who had already been identified. Some had taken a History of Engineering and Technology class at Northwestern University in the 1978-1979 timeframe, where one of their textbooks was *Ancient Engineers*, one of only four books referenced in the UNABOM Manifesto. None of them tried to purchase a *Washington Post* that day, and none of them turned out to have any connection to UNABOM.

One of the surveillances really got interesting. A man our people described as "acting very weird" purchased several copies of the *Post*. Surveillance took him around and around several city blocks, while he stopped periodically to look around as if someone were watching him. He then jumped onto a Bay Area Rapid Transit (BART) train with surveillance hot on his heels. After three stops he got off the train, walked around several more city blocks, and then got on another BART train. Two stops later, he was off the train again; he walked a few blocks and climbed onto a city bus, still looking around suspiciously. He got off in South San Francisco and went into a high-rise apartment building.

By this time, we were more than intrigued. We identified the apartment he'd entered, and an investigative team swooped in to knock on the door.

The door opened slightly, and the man peered out at them while they identified themselves to him and cajoled him enough to let them in.

The small, 9- x 10-foot room was even more claustrophobic, due to the yellowing newspapers and magazines stacked floor to ceiling. Since there was no place to sit, the agents stood to talk to him. As they tried to feel him out, he asked repeatedly why they were so interested in him. When they finally told him they'd seen him buy copies of *The Washington Post*, he nearly collapsed on the floor.

We later learned that he was a prolific letter writer, who corresponded regularly with his elected representatives and was also a frequent visitor to the FBI and other government agencies. His main complaint? He believed that the U.S. government was following him everywhere he went, and knew everything he read. For years, he'd received constant reassurances that he was not the subject of any investigation. He'd never believed it, and was sure he was being lied to. And here, on September 20th, 1995, he finally had proof that it was so.

Smiling as much reassurance as possible, the agents politely took their leave.

Selected Statements of Defendant
Concerning the McConnell Bomb

"Experiment 100. Raid 3. An iron water pipe, bought at Rock Hand, August 1985 . . . [It is] galvanized on the outside. . . The lids are made from a 3/4" diameter iron rod. . . . Each lid is held by 2 iron bolts . . . The first part of mixture #3 was placed under the igniter wire on the afternoon of October 8th. . . . The ends of the pipe are reinforced with collars made from an iron pipe . . . The device will be hidden inside a pile of Mead's brand typing paper, arranged as follows: The pieces of paper have been glued, one to the other, by placing Elmer's glue around the edge of each sheet, making a pile . . . After preparing the package, a strip of strapping tape will go around the package in such a way that it will fasten the door to the trigger. . . . As strapping tape is cut, the door and the piston will be released and the circuit will close, and boom . . . With plastic electrical tape, we fasten 1 package (62 little balls, 1.2. oz.) of Water Gremlin split shot (lead weights for fishing). . . . We decided to use 4, D batteries and 6, AAA batteries (all alkaline, Duracell, 1.5 volt). The metallic covers have been taken off. . . . A while back I obtained 2 human hairs from the bathroom in the Missoula bus depot. I broke one of these hairs into two pieces, and I placed one piece between the layers of the electrical tape I used to wrap the wire joints inside the package. . . . The reason for this is to deceive the policemen, who will think that the hair belongs to whoever made the device. . . . We placed enough postage on the package for zone 8 and for 7 lbs. We sent the package on Nov. 12, 1985."

GX 18-2033A, pgs. 238-245

Kaczynski's description of how he assembled the bomb he sent to Professor James McConnell at the University of Michigan in 1985.

del exp.100, La carta estaba en un sobre prendido con cinta al paquete. El sobre llevó la dirección, pero ningún sello. En el propio paquete había bastante sellos para el y la carta juntos

Department of History
University of Utah
Salt Lake City, Utah 84112
November 12, 1985
Dr. James V. McConnell
2900 E. Delhi Road
Ann Arbor, Michigan 48103

Dear Dr. McConnell:

I am a doctoral candidate in History at the University of Utah. My field of interest is the history of science, and I am writing my dissertation on the development of the behavioral sciences during the twentieth century.

This dissertation aspires to be more than a mere collection of facts. In it I am attempting to analyse the factors in society at large that tend to promote vigorous development in a given area of science, and especially I am attempting to shed light on the way in which progress in a particular field of research influences public attitudes toward that field in such a manner as to further accelerate its development, as through research grants, increased interest on the part of students, and so forth. I have selected the behavioral sciences for study because I believe that they illustrate particularly well my

Carbon copy of the letter sent to Professor McConnell, found in Kaczynski's cabin in 1996. The letter refers to a dissertation draft to follow. Hand written notes–in Spanish–describe how Kaczynski sent a bomb instead.

8

THOUSANDS OF UNABOMBERS

After the *Post* and the *Times* published the UNABOM Manifesto, we'd thought we'd be inundated by calls and letters from the public. That was the plan, after all. But we had no idea of what was actually to come.

Within days, thousands of calls came in over the 1-800 UNABOM hotline in San Francisco. Within weeks, the number of "tips" we received was well over 50,000. Thousands and thousands of people both inside and outside the United States were convinced they knew the Unabomber, and they sent and described millions of pieces of information and documentary "evidence" to prove it.

In law enforcement, work generated by a tip is called a "lead." If you have 50,000 leads, you need a lot of manpower to cover them, and organizing the flow of information in and out is a staggering task.

By October 1995, agents and analysts temporarily reassigned from other FBI Divisions streamed into San Francisco. Analysts worked around the clock on computer-aided assessments, identifying hundreds of potential UNABOM suspects. Agents ran down thousands of leads, interviewing people all over the country in connection with information they'd provided or to resolve emerging links that connected them somehow to the case.

Most were on 90-day temporary assignments, and their work involved set tasks that didn't require them to string long timelines or volumes of information together. Even so, many of those assignments were extended due to our ravenous appetite for manpower.

Millions of pieces of data, like blood in the veins of the UTF, flowed through Joel's suspect squad and Max's incident reinvestigation squad. Every day, the pulse quickened, and every day it seemed we were getting closer to identifying the legendary Unabomber.

At the same time, we continued to be plagued by bureaucratic nonsense. On one memorable occasion, our whole management team dealt for weeks with a delegation from Information Systems at FBIHQ. They wanted to put UNABOM on the Automated Case System (ACS), and we'd fought to be exempted from it. ACS was the first attempt to computerize FBI files. It wasn't designed to handle a major case like UNABOM, and its deficiencies were glaringly obvious several years later when the execution of Timothy McVeigh was delayed because of issues related to the OKBOM Task Force's reliance on ACS to document their case.

In UNABOM, we held our ground, and we winced later at the experience of our OKBOM colleagues, who were among those who suffered as a result of the notorious FBI computer inadequacies that have cost close to a billion dollars over the past decade. After nearly 20 years of frustration in UNABOM, we didn't need a dodgy computer system to slow us down when it came to finally prosecuting the Unabomber for his crimes.

While the UTF sifted through piles of mailings and phone calls in the fall of 1995, the Department of Justice suddenly decided they needed more direct control of UNABOM. Perhaps the Deputy Attorney General was still smarting from being slapped down in front of us a few months earlier, because she suddenly directed that a DOJ attorney would replace Steve Freccero as primary legal counsel for the UTF.

One afternoon, I was called to a meeting in the U.S. Attorney's Office in San Francisco, where Steve waited with his boss and a young Department of Justice attorney in a starched white shirt and designer necktie. A pleasant enough fellow, the young visitor noted that the new DOJ attorney would have "regular phone conferences" with all the other U.S. Attorneys around the country who had a piece of the UNABOM case. I forced myself to use my inside voice when I responded.

"As it stands now, we go to Steve's office—which is five minutes away—when we need a subpoena to get whatever information is required. He's completely familiar with UNABOM, so it doesn't take him long to decide whether to issue the subpoena. It takes two hours, tops. Are you saying you now want us to deal with someone new who's also 3,000 miles away every time we need a subpoena?"

The young man from Washington was diplomatic.

"I think what we could do is that all of your subpoena requests could be sent to the DOJ trial attorney for review, and after he approves them, Mr. Freccero could issue the subpoena from San Francisco," he smiled.

I saw Steve was only barely containing his temper. It was pretty insulting for an experienced senior trial attorney like him to be relegated to acting as the errand boy for a hotshot DOJ attorney in Washington. As for me, my hold on my own temper lessened as the knot in my stomach tightened. Having to ask daily permission from a lawyer in Washington to run our case would put us all in the hospital. Steve constantly handled agendas and interests that conflicted with ours. Without him, we'd be bogged down in political quagmires all day long instead of focusing on catching the Unabomber.

"With all due respect to you and the Deputy Attorney General," I said, "I have no interest in working this case by committee. We don't have the time to brief all new people at DOJ so that they can direct how we run it."

"I think you may be worried over nothing," our visitor said smoothly. "This arrangement is being used in the Oklahoma City bombing case, and it's working very well."

Still in my inside voice, I said we'd heard that before, and added that the task in a case lasting two decades had little in common with resolving prosecution in a case that was solved the day the bombing occurred. There was an awkward pause, and then our visitor said politely that he'd discuss our concerns with the Deputy Attorney General when he got back to Washington.

A DOJ attorney was eventually selected, and he traveled every four weeks to San Francisco to listen to updates on the case. We all politely ignored him. He usually flew in on a red-eye and back the next afternoon. For Washington bureaucrats, careers aren't made outside the Beltway, and it's not healthy to be away too long.

∞ ∞ ∞

Meanwhile, the intensity of the work on UNABOM increased as public response hit a crescendo. The number of suspects—in locations all over the country and even overseas—multiplied daily. For me, the leadership task in UNABOM was changing from my original role in galvanizing creativity and imagination in investigators and analysts. I was more of a trail boss now, controlling the pace and direction of the hunt while letting the UTF unleash its considerable energy in the drive to capture our Lone Wolf.

With hundreds more suspects, I had dozens of investigators with fire in their bellies about their favorite ones. When a dogged investigator is convinced he's on the right trail, all hell can break loose when you try to pull him off it. And, although fans of Clint Eastwood's *Dirty Harry* may disagree, bad things can happen if a maverick investigator charges after his suspect out of control.

By fall 1995, the number of potential UNABOM suspects had been carefully winnowed down to a couple thousand people who had serious potential to be the Unabomber. In general, they were all U.S. resident males between 30 to 60 years old, had never served in the military, and had no criminal record. Several hundred had college degrees, and some had a Masters or Ph.D. Despite the huge public response, almost all were developed as suspects through proactive investigation and data-base analysis. Only a handful were a result of calls to the hotline or mailings from the public.

A later analysis of all of the UNABOM suspects was conducted in preparation for the trial of Theodore Kaczynski. They came from just about every state in the union and represented numerous professions and trades. They ranged from accountants, airline employees, and attorneys to scientists, corporate executives, and government employees. Even a dog musher, a masseur, a pastor, and a psychic came under observation. They were all screened by Joel's suspect squad, and none made it past a final evaluation. None were the Unabomber.

Sometimes the media was so carried away with UNABOM that they saturated the public with information about famous fugitives still at large, trying to make them into the Unabomber. These made for entertaining stories, but they were always wrong, and the problem was that they interfered with our efforts to focus the public on the real facts related to the case. Sometimes, things really got out of hand in the media. Freeman had to issue an FBI Press Release categorically stating that longtime federal fugitive James William Kilgore—on the run since his days in the Weather Underground in the mid-1970s—was not a prime suspect in the UNABOM investigation.

The media also hyped another fugitive from the seventies as a UNABOM suspect: Leo Frederick Burt, who'd been missing since the bombing of a math building at the University of Wisconsin. Media interviews with one of Burt's professors led to the titillating revelation that Burt once wrote a term paper on anarchy. But we found nothing that tied Burt to UNABOM.

Crime writer Robert Graysmith advanced the idea in 1995 that the infamous San Francisco serial killer from the 1960s, the Zodiac, might be the Unabomber. The Zodiac killer was never identified, and Graysmith painstakingly outlined facts that he believed showed similarities in the two unsolved cases. We never worried too much about this after one morning meeting in Jim's office when Kathy pointed out that whereas the Zodiac had shot or stabbed his victims, the Unabomber never confronted any of his victims directly, and insured his own safety and security while mailing or covertly placing his bombs. They were two different animals, she said.

But the real challenges to my trail boss role came from our own law enforcement herd, not from the media. Steve Freccero walked into my office one day while I was on speakerphone with a veteran SAC from another FBI Field division and his legal counsel. They were passionate about someone they were sure was the Una-bomber, and they wanted to take immediate action.

"He meets the profile. He's from Illinois, earned his college degree in a scientific discipline there, worked at U.C. Berkeley for a number of years, has had some minor run-ins with authority, and has had trouble holding down a steady job for a number of years.

"He's very familiar with the San Francisco Bay Area and is getting ready to board a plane tomorrow to fly to Oakland. We think we have enough to stop him from boarding the plane, so we want to detain and search him. We think it's urgent. He could be carrying a bomb to Oakland."

I knew they were overreacting, because the UNABOM case agent in their Division was a friend who had already told me they were barking up the wrong tree. I told them I didn't see the urgency they saw, and I didn't believe their guy met the criteria. The SAC was adamant, and his voice started to boom over the line.

"Listen, he fits the profile, and we have to move fast before something happens. I'm not letting him get on that plane knowing what we know!"

Steve looked at me, raised his eyebrows, and spoke into the mike.

"Excuse me, this is Steve Freccero."

"Who are you?" the SAC shot back.

"I'm the Assistant U.S. Attorney, working with the UNABOM Task Force in San Francisco," Steve said. "Sorry, but nothing you've laid out constitutes probable cause to detain and search this guy."

"Well, we disagree," the SAC growled. "I've talked to our AUSA, and if you don't authorize a search warrant, he will!"

"That's not going to happen," Steve said. "I suggest you have your AUSA call me before you create a big problem for yourself." Steve wrote me a short note that asked me to keep him posted and then left for a hearing.

Within an hour, Bob Conforti contacted me from Headquarters. We had grown to trust each other's judgment and appreciated each other's candor during our UNABOM adventure, and he especially understood the emotions the experience evoked in everyone the case touched. The SAC had called him, shouting that I was arrogant and hadn't given his arguments the respect they (and he) deserved. We went over the facts together, and Conforti agreed that the FBI didn't have any probable cause to detain and search the suspect. I agreed to put surveillance on the suspect when his plane landed in Oakland.

The guy was picked up by a friend at the airport and the two drove to a local cafe. While agents listened from an adjacent booth, the suspect told his friend that the FBI had talked to some of his neighbors. "You're not gonna believe this," he said. "The FBI thinks I'm the Unabomber!"

They both had a hearty laugh, and another suspect was on the way to being eliminated.

∞ ∞ ∞

Sometimes it was FBI Headquarters that jumped the gun on a new, "hot" suspect. Freeman took a call one day from a high-level official at the Bureau who said Director Freeh wanted us to do a "sneak and peek" on a suspect.

A sneak and peek search warrant allows entry into a private residence without the owner's consent or knowledge. Max, Joel, and I were in Jim's office when he told us what the Bureau wanted. This suspect was reported to have an old-fashioned typewriter in his house, and if we could get a glimpse of it, we could see whether it might be consistent with one of the typewriters used to produce some of the UNABOM documents.

A sneak and peek is risky, but in exigent circumstances—like when human life is endangered—it may be warranted. Freeman told Max to do it the next morning.

Joel was in my office when I walked in later that afternoon.

"We can't do this," he said.

He'd gone to talk to Freccero, who told him a sneak and peek wasn't supported by law, and it would cause more trouble than it was worth. We exchanged grimaces. None of us thought the suspect was the Unabomber, and it didn't make sense to take the chance.

Max was unusually quiet on the drive home. It was obvious he didn't want to do the sneak and peek, but the SAC had given him an order. We all respected Freeman, and we knew that he, too, was following orders, but it didn't make us feel any better. As we pulled into Max's driveway, I looked over at him and asked him if he wanted to do it.

"No."

"Okay," I said. "I'll let Jim know that I cancelled it until we can discuss it further."

The next morning I left a note on Jim's desk. Max and I went down to the cafeteria for coffee, and I was just loading up on the cream and sugar when I got an urgent page to come to Freeman's office. He glared up at me over his glasses when I got there and pointed a long finger at the chair next to his desk. As I sat down, he leaned towards me.

"You countermanded my order."

I thought fast, but the words came out of my mouth before I could measure them.

"Boss, we're not trying to ruin your day."

"I know that!" he howled.

Since my loyalty was not at issue, his tone and demeanor changed dramatically. We agreed that we should assemble Team UNABOM and further discuss the sneak and peek. In the end, we decided not to do it, and no one from the Bureau ever asked about it again. We concluded that the idea had come from the active imagination of another Bureau executive, and not from Director Freeh.

∞ ∞ ∞

One day a young UTF agent approached me, led me into a vacant office, and closed the door. He was bursting with excitement.

"I think I've identified the Unabomber. I want to brief you on what I've developed, but you need to promise that you'll keep this a secret until we can be certain we have the guy." He paused for a reaction.

I kept my face impassive, although I know I raised my eyebrows.

"Who are we going to keep a secret from?"

"Everybody. I don't want the SAC to know, I don't want the Bureau to know. I don't want to open a suspect case. I just want to go out and work on this until I have something concrete, but I think this is the guy."

This sounded a little too Hollywood to me, and I suspected that dreams of solitary glory and a leading man role in the UNABOM movie were behind this more than dedication to the team. But the last thing I wanted to do was throw cold water on any kind of enthusiasm for solving this case.

"Why don't you tell me what you've found and let's go from there," I said gently.

"Okay." He drew a long breath. "We know the Unabomber originated in Chicago. This guy is from Chicago. The first UNA-BOM device was found in the parking lot at Circle Campus in Chicago. This guy went to Circle Campus. He's lived in the Bay Area since the 1980s. He has a science background, and got into some trouble early on in his life when he put a fake pipe bomb into someone's gym locker at school."

Another breath, and then the build to the finish.

"The Postal Inspectors believe that the bomb that killed Thomas Mosser was mailed from the Postal Annex near San Francisco International Airport. This guy works within a two mile radius of the Postal Annex, and close to the United Airlines Maintenance Operation Center. And he has reddish blonde hair, like the witness in Salt Lake described in 1987."

I was pleased at his intensity, and the fact that he'd built his case on the known facts surrounding UNABOM.

"You've easily crossed the threshold for initiating a suspect investigation," I said. "But we have to tell SAC Freeman, and we have to tell the Bureau. We're going to need to set up on the guy's residence, use the Special Operations Group for surveillances, and let the Lab know that we'll be sending potential evidence their way for comparison. We can't do all this in secret."

He looked stricken.

"Terry, you know what's gonna happen," he said, almost pleading. "This looks pretty interesting, and somebody at Headquarters is just going to take it over, and then we'll have a mess. Why can't we. . .?"

"No," I put my hand up to stop him. "You need to know something. If we don't do this right—regardless of the fact that what you're worried about probably will happen—we'll lose control in the end, anyway. We can't have secrets from each other and do things the wrong way. Good intentions aren't enough, trust me. I know what I'm talking about."

We opened a suspect case, advised the Bureau, initiated surveillance and a trash cover of the suspect. Almost immediately, the Lab found DNA on a single strand of hair from the trash that they couldn't positively eliminate as being a match to DNA found on a strand of hair at a UNABOM crime scene.

All of the agent's worst fears came to pass. Bureau officials jumped in with both feet and tried to micromanage every move in the suspect case. Jim Freeman and I were tied up in one conference call after another trying to keep their rush to judgment from impacting our strategy of just following the facts. Max even wrote an analysis of all we knew about the suspect, including the fact that he had walked with a noticeable limp for over ten years. The 1987 witness at the Caams bombing in Salt Lake had gotten a good look at the bomber in disguise, who walked quickly from the scene without a limp. The suspect wasn't the Unabomber. But the Bureau wanted science to make that conclusion, not our assessment.

We all eventually agreed that the Lab would conduct a highly sensitive DNA test on the hair found at the earlier UNABOM crime scene. The test would be conclusive—either the DNA came from one source or it did not—but it would use up the entire hair, and there could be no future tests.

We green-lit the test. If this was the Unabomber, we had to swiftly eliminate or hone in on the suspect sooner rather than later. The DNA test was the only way we would know for sure. The pressure grew nearly unbearable—especially for the young agent who'd started it all—but after several days, the Lab found the DNA didn't match, the hairs didn't match, and the suspect wasn't the Unabomber.

∞ ∞ ∞

We had constant, divisive disagreements over suspects on the UTF; it was part of the process. The amount of time and effort needed in a suspect investigation was considerable. The decisions on which suspects to pursue were so crucial and the margin of error so narrow that only Joel, Jim, and I made the ultimate determination on when a case should be pursued further or discontinued.

We knew that making the wrong decision might possibly result in obliterating the only trail leading to the real Unabomber. But running too long and far after the wrong guy could also forever tarnish someone's reputation if word leaked out he was under investigation. Balance was paramount, and the stakes were high. Suspect cases truly served to remind us that we had dual responsibilities as FBI agents to identify the bad guy while protecting his and everyone else's civil rights. One bad move would rob us of our credibility, and would devastate the morale of everyone on the hunt.

One particular suspect case demonstrated this more than any other.

A mix of several Assistant U.S. Attorneys, aggressive FBI and ATF agents, and police officers became convinced that they had identified the Unabomber. Their suspect had connections to Chicago earlier in his life, had been in Salt Lake City on numerous occasions in connection with his job, and was highly familiar with the San Francisco Bay Area. On the day the bomb that killed Thomas Mosser in New Jersey was mailed from a Postal Annex in San Francisco, the suspect was nearby.

There were other reasons the suspect appealed to this group, some of which had to do with professional associations they shared. The group of investigators and attorneys grew more and more convinced that he was the Unabomber, and they began to mix fiction in with fact to better support their conclusions.

While it became readily clear to Max, Joel, and me that their suspect was not the Unabomber, it wasn't easy to call a halt to their pursuit. An Assistant U.S. Attorney is highly independent and can pretty much pursue whatever he or she pleases. Stubbornly, the group discounted information that tended to alibi their suspect while their dark suspicions led them to erroneous confirmations that he was the Unabomber. For example, they developed information that their suspect was an avid Sherlock Holmes fan. They concluded that this was consistent with the Unabomber's desire to taunt his hunters, and also explained why he was so clever at avoiding detection. As a disciple of the great detective, he had learned how to stay beyond the reach of the investigators on his trail!

I finally got everyone to sit at the table and give Kathy a rundown on their suspect. They were convinced they were right, and they didn't want to hear why they were wrong. Their arguments got more and more forceful. Kathy listened to it all politely, and then conclusively dismantled their arguments based on aspects of the behavior and personality of their suspect relative to the Unabomber.

They refused to give up. I worried that they might do something to alert the suspect to their suspicions of him, and that their pursuit had the potential to ruin a person's life and career if it remained un-checked. I finally had to order the FBI agent in the group to cease any involvement in the suspect case or risk disciplinary action. We then worked to stop the others from pursuing the matter any further.

But it all became moot after we received a call one winter afternoon that eventually turned the UNABOM ship northeastward under full steam towards Lincoln, Montana.

Kaczynski's cabin near Lincoln, Montana, in early spring 1996.

9

When Words are Evidence

When the Unabomber sent his manuscript to the press, only a few of us recognized it as the turning point in the investigation. Freeman, Fitz, Joel, Kathy, and I couldn't get enough of it. On the afternoon it arrived, I spent the night in my office, lying on the couch and reading it until I fell asleep. We went over and over it during the day. We called each other to talk about it in the evening. We read it in cars, on planes, at airports, at home during the late night news. On more than one occasion, I woke up in the middle of the night with phrases from "Industrial Society and Its Future" (the actual title of the Manifesto) by FC ringing in my head. It's not an overstatement that a handful of us were obsessed with the document, and it was that obsession that fueled the creation of our final strategy to identify the Unabomber.

While we focused on the manuscript, the rest of the UTF stayed with their primary assignments. Agents painstakingly working suspect cases continued to test new suspects against what we knew about our quarry, and after resolving one they moved doggedly to the next logical suspect. Max's squad traveled to the site of past crimes, developed closer bonds with investigators in Sacramento, Salt Lake, and Chicago, and worked continually to tie aspects of the case together.

Where the UNABOM Manifesto was concerned, the UTF fell into three camps. There were we five "true believers." After that, the majority found it intriguing, but didn't think it was evidence; many of them never read more than a few sentences. Then there was a small and very vocal group who continually wondered—often loudly and with considerable irritation—what all the fuss was about.

I was so intent on exploiting the Manifesto to get us closer to the Unabomber that for some time I had no idea how divisive this issue had become. One day, a young agent who was one of our most dedicated workers came to me and said he wanted off the task force. He was in the camp with the vocal and volatile doubters, and he told me with great frustration that the Manifesto was simply "a red herring." I was astounded when he said he had never even read it. He represented the strong views of this small group that only physical evidence would lead us to the Unabomber, and scoffed in disgust at the idea that careful analysis of the document could provide information about the Unabomber as well as lead to his identification.

It wasn't normal law enforcement practice in 1995 to focus on linguistic analysis as evidence. But UNABOM investigators had been unable for nearly two decades to follow any other trail of evidence to the Unabomber. We needed to throw the net wider, and to include new kinds of analysis and information vectors to point us in the right direction.

We had several early samples of Unabomber writings. They'd been analyzed in great detail for years. He'd sent letters under assumed names with fictional return addresses to two of his victims, United Airlines president Percy Wood in 1980 and Dr. James McConnell at the University of Michigan in 1985. Those letters were designed to ensure his victims looked for and opened the packages—one a "book of great social significance" and the other a "dissertation draft" on the History of Science—that concealed the bombs he sent to them.

When he'd resurfaced with a more compact and powerful bomb design that gravely wounded Drs Gelernter and Epstein in 1993, the Unabomber had also sent his first letter to *The New York Times* as "the anarchist group FC." He included an identifying number "so no one else can pretend to speak in our name."

In April 1995, at the same time he mailed the bomb that killed Gilbert Murray in Sacramento, he'd sent a longer letter to the *Times* claiming responsibility for the bomb that had killed Thomas Mosser in New Jersey the previous December. He wrote of Mosser's "misdeeds" as an advertising executive, claiming that Burson Marstellar had helped Exxon clean up its public image after the Exxon Valdez environmental disaster.

In that *Times* letter, he wrote that his bombs were intended for "specialists in technical fields which included certain areas of applied psychology, such as behavior modification." He also described "FC" as a group of anarchists dedicated to the destruction of the world industrialized system. It was in that letter to the *Times* that he proposed "a bargain:" he made an offer to "desist from terrorism" if they published his essay.

A biologist at MIT and a geneticist at New England Biolabs also received letters from "FC" on April 24th, in which they were warned, "it would be beneficial to your health to stop your research in genetics."

And on the same date, the Unabomber cruelly taunted one of his 1993 victims, Dr. David Gelernter at Yale University, who'd nearly bled to death from his injuries before he received medical treatment. The return address on the letter to Gelernter was 9th and Pennsylvania Avenue in Washington, D.C., FBI Headquarters. Wily as ever, "FC" wrote to Dr. Gelernter, ". . . people with advanced degrees aren't as smart as they think they are. . . apparently people without a college degree don't count." (During the search of Theodore Kaczynski's cabin, we found a carbon copy of the letter with a handwritten note that "this will make them think I don't have an advanced degree.")

Intrigued by the publicity value, another publisher wanted to get into the act. Bob Guccione released a statement urging the Unabomber to send him the manuscript, which he would then publish in his raunchy magazine, *Penthouse*. Meanwhile, a public debate about the perils of caving in to a terrorist demand continued to rage in the press and within the government.

At the end of June, the Unabomber himself squelched all the arguments when he sent a letter to the *San Francisco Chronicle* stating "The terrorist group FC is planning to blow up an airliner out of Los Angeles. . . during the next six days." At the same time, a final flurry of letters arrived at *Scientific American*, *The New York Times*, *The Washington Post*, *Penthouse*, and the office of social psychologist Dr. Tom Tyler at U.C. Berkeley. All but the letter to *Scientific American* were accompanied by carbon copies of a 65-page screed that soon became known as the UNABOM Manifesto.

In these last letters, the Unabomber referred to the threat against an airplane out of LAX as "one last prank." He had simply wanted some fanfare before his Manifesto arrived. He wrote that he'd agree that *Penthouse* could publish his work only if the *Times* and *Post* did not. In a bizarrely prudish way, he wrote Bob Guccione that if *Penthouse* did turn out to be the publisher, FC "reserves the right to plant one (and only one) bomb, intended to kill, after our manuscript has been published."

We had never wanted to gratify the Unabomber by ensuring that he was published. But after the painful decision was made and the Manifesto arrived, we had to ensure that it was of immediate use in tracking him down.

We "true believers" knew that the Unabomber's words would lead us to him. But how to follow those words was a problem we had never faced before. There were no rules or guidelines, and no useful precedents, so we were on our own in learning how to do it. We were also free to develop new techniques in doing so, and we proceeded to do just that.

One day, Fitz reported that his colleagues at Quantico had come up with some preliminary behavioral analysis on the Manifesto.

"Whoever wrote the manuscript has taken years to develop his belief system," he said. "The manuscript represents how he feels, and he's probably felt this way for some time. We think the paper is well written, and that he sounds like a social scientist. He may have shared his themes with others, and publication might help someone recognize his words and come forward."

Fitz looked at Kathy, who frowned at the next statement.

"As you know, we believe that he'll stop bombing if his manuscript is published."

He raised his eyebrows at Kathy and continued.

"In my own analysis, the manuscript has 232 numbered paragraphs and then 8 pages of 32 footnotes. There's a diagram of symptoms resulting from what the writer calls 'disruption of the power process.' The paragraphs are divided into 27 different chapters with various themes. I've put together a glossary of terms and an index to guide us further."

Tony Muljat signaled with a familiar wave of his arm for attention.

"As you know, the manuscript references only four books and two magazines. The books are *The True Believer* by Eric Hoffer, *Ancient Engineers* by L. Sprague DeCamp, *Chinese Political Thought in the Twentieth Century* by Chester Tan, and *Violence in America: Historical and Comparative Perspectives* by Roger Lane. The magazines are *Scientific American* and *Omni*. Robin Shipman and I had a noted researcher look at these works and check for correlations or similarities.

"The co-editor of *Violence In America*, Ted Gurr, wrote a paper with a faculty member at the University of Illinois called 'The Conflict Process.' The Unabomber uses the term power process. In 1981, Gurr was a faculty member at Northwestern University. Gurr also wrote a book called *Why Men Rebel*. If you were to go to a public library, you'd find these books and Eric Hoffer's book, *The True Believer* almost around the corner from each other on the bookshelves. They're all about violence, aggression, and terrorism."

Kathy added a behavioral word.

"The Manifesto strikes me as autobiographical in nature. There are recurring discussions of psychological problems such as depression, low self-esteem, and lack of fulfillment. He talks about "problems in living" and "intellectual and psychological impediments." She nodded towards her colleague. "Fitz has collated every theme in the document, and I think it's telling that, although the title is "Industrial Society and Its Future," the most common topic is how children are raised and treated and educated."

This was interesting, and we considered it thoughtfully. Kathy always came up with something from another angle that helped take us out of our wingtips and put us in the bomber's shoes.

"What other themes do you see?" I asked.

"Besides children, he writes about feelings of inferiority, job requirements and conditions, industrial labor, psychological problems, alcoholism, sex, and love."

"How is this going to help us find this guy?" Freeman said. We were all thinking the same thing.

Kathy carefully searched for words to boil it down.

"I think he's had these views—strong views—for a long time. He's expressed them before, to someone. Someone will recognize him. Then, as we learn more about him, we'll be able to link these themes he writes about to events in his life. Then we'll know—behaviorally—that we have the right guy."

"After that, all we'll have to do is get some real evidence," Penny drawled. She grinned at Kathy while everyone laughed, and finally Kathy laughed, too. She and Penny were friends, and had been in the FBI during the same timeframe. Sometimes the two of them would close the door of Penny's office and confer on the best way to navigate through the male-dominated environment of the FBI.

∞ ∞ ∞

Maggie Stringer was a star in the ranks of the Counterintelligence analysts in San Francisco, and we'd grabbed her away as soon as we could when I started beefing up our analytical cadre on UNA-BOM. Her dad had been an agent, and Maggie's long tenure in San Francisco as well as her peerless intellectual gifts soon made her indispensable to us. She and her longtime analyst sidekick, Lee Hayden, went through a vast list of scholars who might be able to help us put the Manifesto further into focus. Maggie narrowed it down to several dozen academic luminaries, whom, in late fall 1995, we decided to invite for a two-day conference to discuss the Manifesto from their different perspectives.

We held the conference at the Pan Pacific Hotel on Post in San Francisco, where we also put a number of them up on the government dime.

A little before 9:00 in the morning, Tony, Joel, Max, Fitz, and I were plying the assembled group with coffee and pastries in the hotel conference room while we waited for the last of their number to arrive. No one had heard from L. Sprague DeCamp, the author of *Ancient Engineers*, since he'd boarded the plane for San Francisco. FBI agent Vicki Woosley, who was assigned to greet him at the airport and get him to the meeting at the Pan Pacific, called me and said in a mystified tone:

"I'm at a phone bank at the airport, and there's no sign of him. His plane arrived but when everyone got off, I didn't see him . . . Wait . . ."

Her voice faded as she leaned away from the phone, and then came back, but she sounded just as mystified as before.

"Um, well. He's about a hundred yards away, but I think it's going to take us a while to get there," she said.

I was a little mystified myself until Vicki finally arrived with the distinguished author. L. Sprague DeCamp took the tiniest of steps as he maintained an upward, proud posture, and during the conference we all learned to take things at his pace rather than ours. His mind was far more agile than his body, and it was interesting to meet him.

We acted as moderators during the free-wheeling discussions that ensued for the next day and a half. We planned to try to steer the conversation in certain directions, if necessary; and, at the end of the conference, we planned to seek a consensus from them on a profile of the Unabomber based on their review of the manuscript.

We should have known that consensus was a pipe dream in a group of academics. But after a while, some common themes emerged.

"Most of the paper expressed ideas popular in the 1970s, but aren't widely promoted now. They're hardly studied either."

"*Chinese Political Thought* is from 1971 and was never extensively used, even then."

"You can look at almost every page and find a paragraph that reflects 1970s arguments that were anti-Marxist."

"The writer is not so much against government, but against technology."

"The ideology is from the 1960s to early 1970s."

"But the work has been updated with current references."

"He's making an appeal for academic respectability."

"From the language and concepts, it seems as though the manuscript might have been the basis for a term paper at some point in time."

"If he's published, he'll still bomb again. It may not be immediately, but eventually he'll bomb again."

"*Violence In America* was popular in the early to mid 1970s and used in sociology, political science, and criminology. I'm sure it was used at Northwestern."

"Whoever wrote the manuscript had ideas that were out there in the atmosphere at the time. They could have come from a variety of sources."

"I think he has a blue-collar type job."

"Maybe, but I think he wants to be a social scientist. He hates science. He hates technology. Statistically speaking, the manuscript could have been part of a graduate study program in the social sciences."

"He uses the word 'anomie' in paragraph 64. One would encounter this word in sociology, anthropology, or in a political science course."

"The study illustrates an multidisciplinary background. He learned a little about a lot of things."

Criminology professor Eric Hickey from Fresno State University had the last word before we asked the scholars to take a break and form a consensus—if they could—on the bomber's profile.

"He certainly doesn't want academic criticism of his work," he said.

Hours later, they presented their findings. The manuscript was well written, as a possible doctoral thesis in the 1970s. It was likely to have been presented to a professor for review and might be recognized by that professor. The writer became aware of the books mentioned in the manuscript during his early college years. The books would have been used in the 1970s at Northwestern and the University of Chicago. Gender-specific language in the manuscript dated it to the 1970s, because after the early 1980s non-gender-specific language was dominant. The writer had some higher educational background and seemed strongest in sociology. He had a secure job that required technical skills. He was isolated, about 45 years old, unconnected, and unpublished.

Several of us stayed at the hotel to talk for hours after the scholars left to resume their lives in educational institutions, writing books, or retirement. The latter sounded especially attractive to me, although I was only 45 at the time. Most of our guests had seemed to thoroughly enjoy their exercise with the UTF, but now we had to make sense of the information overload.

It was the one thing about UNABOM that never changed. What was important and what wasn't? What would help solve the case and what was irrelevant? Who could ever be sure?

Penny and I dropped Max off at his house around 8:30 p.m. Wondering aloud how we would ever be able to sort through so many puzzle pieces and find our way, we decided to stop at our favorite Chinese restaurant in downtown Danville. I called my wife, Joy, to see if she could meet us, but she had already eaten, the kids were getting ready for bed, and it was a school night. She wished us bon appetit.

Penny was great at helping me put perspective on the day. Her contagious laugh and happy-go-lucky demeanor made her a pleasure to be around, and I was delighted she had agreed to come and work with us on the UTF.

It was against Louis Freeh's "bright line" for FBI agents to drink alcohol while on duty. But Penny Harper and I have been out of the FBI for years now, so I have a confession to make. We ordered a bottle of wine and drank the whole thing during dinner.

That actually amounts to about 2 ½ glasses each, which is 3 times more than Director Freeh would have approved of. But after a day of dealing with academia and UNABOM together, it sure made everything clearer.

Documented Use of Disguises
by Theodore J. Kaczynski

"Pipes bought in a Junkyard, Utah Scrap Metal, at 900 S Street, some blocks to the west of West Temple, in Salt Lake City. When I bought these pipes, I gave the name Charles Kradnik, with no address. I was wearing silvered glasses, gum (chewing gum) under my upper lip (changing its shape that way), and a piece of wax in the left nostril, distorting it. I had to sign a receipt (with the name of Charles Kradnik), but I did it in such a way that I did not leave any of my fingerprints."

GX 18-2030, p. 47

"When I bought this pipe, I was wearing a bulky cloak, with a jacket inside, so I would appear heavier than I am; silvered glasses; a cap with a visor that covered my forehead; and kleenex inside my nostrils which expanded them; and my beard was darkened so it would appear almost black, or at least a very dark brown."

GX 18-2030, p. 48

"When I bought these stamps, I was wearing the same clothes, glasses, beard color, etc., that I described under number 20 above."

GX 18-2030, p. 48

"Bought at Kramis Hardware in Missoula; disguised; June, 1985;"

GX 18-2030, p. 47

"Springs. Bought at Coast to Coast, Missoula, Nov. 1990. The only disguise I was wearing were the silvered eyeglasses."

GX 18-2030, p. 48

"plus	minus
confuses them about hair	may make them suspect we're not from CA, hence track busses
removes their idea we have brown hair	may make them suspect suspect we wore wig
	may make them doubt false verbal clues."

GX 18-2041D, p. 23

"For instance, last Fall I attempted a bombing and spent nearly three hundred bucks just for travel expenses, motel, clothing for disguise, etc."

GX 18-2046A, pgs. 66-67

Government trial exhibit documenting Kaczynski's use of disguises when conducting any activity relating to his bombings.

10

MAKING THE CONNECTION

Sometimes we get lucky. The story that the UNABOM Task Force got lucky is what everybody heard after the capture of the infamous Unabomber. But it was a lot more complicated—and hair-raising—than the newspapers and magazines reported.

A careful Lone Wolf operating on his own, in a social vacuum, is devilishly hard to track. In the rare instance exemplified by the situation after the Oklahoma City bombing, luck and vigilance aligned when an alert state trooper stopped Timothy McVeigh on his flight from the crime scene in April 1995. In the same way, and after a string of bombings by his (one-man) "Army of God," Eric Rudolph was finally identified by a concerned citizen who noticed him walking in the opposite direction of a tide of people moving toward the scene of his deadly bombing of a family clinic in Birmingham in January 1998.

Every Lone Wolf, no matter how isolated he is at the outset of his mission, originates in a pack. In the McVeigh and Rudolph cases, family members and friends were contacted by law enforcement after they were identified. To determine motive and corroborate evidence from their past activities, their backgrounds, habits, haunts, and personalities were meticulously documented.

Every prosecutor needs as much information about a defendant as possible before he or she steps into the courtroom. The kind of painstaking care taken by investigators in developing and maintaining relationships with the families of defendants as well as those of victims is like gold in a courtroom.

Since 9/11, most of the public discussion about the failures of the FBI and other agencies has focused on their inability to "connect the dots" because of antiquated computer technology, large and unwieldy bureaucracies, and just plain bad communication between agencies.

In the FBI, this diagnosis has resulted in nearly a billion dollars spent on computer technology to try to tie together 12,000 FBI agents and thousands more analysts with all information from every FBI location in the United States and abroad. As many people have worked on this, and as hard as many have tried to achieve it, there is still no adequate, automated case file system that fully supports the FBI's massive responsibilities in counterterrorism and other areas.

But even if there were, it would probably make little difference in the hunt for a Lone Wolf. Since 9/11, the FBI has hired large numbers of young computer wizards who have been conditioned to believe that the answer to any puzzle can be found on a computer screen. Legions of these new young agents now sit at their desks searching information in cyberspace for the keys that will unlock unsolved cases.

But tracking the Lone Wolf is fundamentally a people business. No amount of computer expertise can equal the development of persistent, patient trust and respect between people. If an investigator can develop the right relationship with friends or family members—who also have a stake in the hunt—the results can be spectacular.

∞ ∞ ∞

Joel was working at his desk in early February 1996 when he heard an overhead page pleading for someone from the UTF to call the office operator. After the third plea, Joel activated his own private policy: if no one picked up after the third page for UNABOM, he picked it up himself.

On the line was Molly Flynn, an FBI agent in the Washington, D.C., Field Office.

"I'm the one who got the papers from that lawyer and took them to the Lab," she said.

Joel shuffled through suspect files while he listened. It suddenly dawned on him that he knew what this was about. Of all the people who could have picked up the call from Molly, it was an amazing piece of luck that it was Joel.

A few days earlier, Joel had a call from FBI agent Mike Harrison in South Carolina. Harrison knew an attorney in Washington, D.C., who had a client with some information about a possible UNABOM suspect. The client didn't want to be identified, but did want to provide a document to the FBI for comparison with the UNABOM Manifesto.

Joel contacted the FBI Washington Field Office, asked them to send someone to pick up the document, and then promptly put it out of his mind. He anticipated that the paper would add a few millimeters to the truckload of paper from the public that flooded into the UTF every week. We'd been deluged with phone calls and mailings since the publication of the Manifesto, especially since the reward for information leading to the arrest of the Unabomber was now $1 million.

We'd asked for it, and we were surfing madly through it, but the sheer volume of information was straining our capacity to review it. Joel, Penny, and I worried constantly that we'd miss the critical clue that would lead us to the Unabomber, because it would be hopelessly buried in all the stacks of mail and phone call reports. We all shared a persistent, nightmarish vision that we might actually possess information identifying the Unabomber, but wouldn't excavate it from the pile before the Unabomber killed again.

"I took the papers to the Lab," Molly continued. "The guy there looked at them for about two seconds and told me to forget it. But when I looked at this—I mean, I don't really know anything about the case, but I've read the Manifesto, and these papers look interesting to me. I'm sure you must have tons of things like this (that might be literally true, Joel thought), but I wanted to talk to someone on the task force, so I'd feel better about just letting this go . . . "

"Wait," said Joel. "You're talking to one of the UTF supervisors."

He told her that the Lab was just looking at the typeface for comparison to known UNABOM documents, not at the words themselves. He asked her to fax the papers to his attention.

"I promise you I'll personally take a look at them," he said.

Molly seemed greatly relieved. Joel was relieved to just get back to work evaluating the next set of promising UNABOM suspects. Thirty minutes later, the faxed document was on the corner of Joel's desk, where it sat for another few hours before Joel remembered his promise. It was about 6:00 in the evening when he began to look at it.

Ten minutes later, the 23-page essay lay in front of him, next to a copy of the UNABOM Manifesto. He sat back in his chair and took a ragged breath. "I don't know his name yet," he thought, "but I'm the first to know for certain that we've found the Unabomber. We're going to solve this case." He picked up the phone and called Kathy.

"What're you doing?"

Kathy chuckled dryly.

"Ahh, I'm working. What're you doing?"

He told her he wanted her to look at something and said he'd meet her at the Lyon's on the corner. It was one of the places we all escaped from the office to talk, and they were used to a lot of orders for pie and coffee from the UTF. He passed the document to her as the server poured the coffee. She raised her eyebrows, but then looked down at it and started to read it swiftly. Suddenly she stopped and looked up across the table at him. Her voice was tense.

"Where did you get this?"

Joel nodded at the document.

"What d'you think?"

Kathy took a deep breath, then looked back down at the pages on the table.

"Well, this is the first thing I've seen in a year and a half that's made the hair on the back of my neck stand up."

Joel nodded, and they pondered their next move. We'd just eliminated our latest, "best" UNABOM suspect after a grueling and contentious investigation. Half the task force was mad at me for shutting it down, and several of our noisier members were loudly proclaiming around the office that I'd failed to identify the Unabomber when they'd put him right under my nose and shown him to me. People were weary and angry for various reasons, and we were all looking forward to some time off during the approaching weekend to cool off before we dug back in. Joel and Kathy decided to wait until the next morning, a Thursday, to bring yet another UNABOM suspect to the fore.

The next day, Joel called me and asked me to go to lunch with them at Max's Opera Café at Van Ness and Golden Gate Avenue. The restaurant had become a mainstay in our constant plan to reassess UNABOM strategies, and many a suspect was eliminated while we quietly discussed facts and made decisions while dining there. Largely because of my own enthusiastic appetite, the core of Team UNABOM had been cemented together by eating out.

"Can't go today; Freeman just stopped by, and he and I are going to lunch in about an hour," I said.

They wouldn't let me hang up the phone.

"Just get out of it and meet us in the lobby, Terry," Joel said pointedly.

This kind of insistence was unusual for Joel, so I told the SAC something had come up, and I was skipping lunch. As I left the office, I stopped by Max's office and invited him along.

February days in San Francisco can be sunny and warm, with fleecy clouds in a bright blue sky. It was that kind of day as we walked the short block to the restaurant. The Opera Café served comfort food: massive servings of home made meatloaf, freshly prepared mashed potatoes with rich, brown gravy, steaks, pork chops, and salads that could serve two.

Kathy and Joel joined us after Max and I had ordered, and sat down across the table as the restaurant buzzed around us.

"We have a new suspect," Joel said.

He slid a copy of the essay across the table, one to me and one to Max.

"What's this?" I asked tiredly. Max shook his head and looked down at his plate. "After this last episode, people need at least a weekend of rest."

Joel and Kathy nodded carefully. Yes, everyone's tired. We've just eliminated the best suspect yet. Yes, UNABOM can wear you out, they seemed to say as they continued to nod quietly, still looking pointedly at the documents in front of us.

"We think this was written by the Unabomber," Kathy said.

Joel looked steadily at me.

Max was weary and annoyed.

"Well, I hope it is, Kath, I hope it is the guy, but it's just a stack of paper to me, and not evidence of anything."

Kathy looked at Joel.

"We shouldn't have brought it up here. They're not ready to look at it now."

A little stung by this, I glanced at the document and heard Joel say, "Terry, I know. Just take it home and read it, then tell us what you think."

Max jumped in again.

"This isn't evidence of anything. We need evidence. We have many better suspects in UNABOM than whoever wrote this essay. It's just words. You don't even know who wrote this. What can we do with this when we have other better suspects? We need evidence."

Max was the senior agent on the UTF, and had more experience in criminal work than any of us from the counterintelligence side of the house.

"I'll read it later," he said, tossing the essay aside.

From the corner of my eye, I saw Freeman walk into the Opera Café with George Grotz, the office media representative. I wanted to slide underneath the table but it was too late. Jim walked right over to me with a shark-like grin.

"So, you stood me up for the gang, huh? And didn't invite me to join you guys. Okay."

He laughed evilly as he and George walked to their table. I wondered what I would suffer for standing up the Boss, and then realized I didn't have a future anyway. I was assigned to UNABOM, and the road stretched long and hard ahead.

That evening, Max and I carpooled home, and we had no further dialogue about the essay. I was asleep by the time we were eastbound in the middle of the Bay Bridge.

Later that night, while my wife Joy was watching television and I was lying on the couch, I began to flip through the essay. A familiar phrase suddenly leapt out at me: "The sphere of human freedom."

I had read that in only one other document, or at least I thought I had. I jumped off the couch, faster than a kid at Christmas, and retrieved the copy of the UNABOM Manifesto that

I kept on my desk at home. Page after page, I fingered through the Unabomber's anti-technology diatribe, noticing other similarities before I found the same exact phrase used in a document written in 1971 by Joel and Kathy's new suspect, and given to agent Molly Flynn in Washington by an attorney representing a client who was worried that a family member might be involved in UNABOM. I felt my adrenaline surge. Energized beyond imagination, I looked over at my wife.

"Joy," I said, "I think we've found the Unabomber."

∞ ∞ ∞

The following Friday, Kathy, Lee Stark, and Jim Willson flew into Washington, D.C., during a blizzard. At the Hyatt Hotel a few blocks from FBI Headquarters, they prepared to meet with Molly Flynn the next morning. By this time, we had learned that our potential witness was a resident of Schenectady, New York—a social worker named David Kaczynski.

On Saturday, Stark, Willson, and Flynn met with David and his wife, Linda, in the office of their Washington, D.C., attorney, Tony Bisceglie. The agents were intrigued, but by the end of that long day they were not at all convinced that David's brother Theodore was the Unabomber.

In fact, it's safe to say that on that Valentine's Day weekend in 1996, only Joel, Kathy, Fitz, Tony, Freeman, and I truly believed the Unabomber had finally been identified.

Near midnight on Saturday, as they prepared for a second day of interviews, Lee told Kathy it had been a very uncomfortable day in Bisceglie's law office. David and Linda seemed very unsure they had done the right thing by contacting the FBI. As David gave them a number of letters he had received from his brother over the years, he said he was not sure his brother was involved in the bombings. He wanted assurances that Ted, if he was the Unabomber, would not receive the death penalty. Lee, a tall man with sandy hair whose grin was marked by a disarming set of dimples, told Kathy that the power in Bisceglie's office would be disconnected Sunday morning due to the blizzard, and reiterated that the atmosphere on Saturday had been chilly, whatever the weather.

"Okay," Kathy said. "We'll make it warmer here, then."

She called the front desk and arranged for a larger suite, ordered a breakfast table with tea, coffee, pastries, and fruit, and made preparations to host the second interview on Sunday morning. Before they quit for the night, she led the team through a preliminary evaluation of 45 letters from Theodore Kaczynski that David turned over to them during the Saturday interview.

Kathy was the most knowledgeable member on the task force concerning the UNABOM Manifesto and the other UNABOM writings that had been collected over the years. She was also thoroughly familiar with the extensive variety of academic and linguistic projects on the task force, having worked on some herself. So she was anxious to compare all of the language-related analysis with the letters from David's brother.

The handwritten letters and their postmarked envelopes were potentially critical pieces of evidence in the case. Now, in the hotel, the agents used gloves to handle them, preserving latent fingerprint evidence and the possibility of collection of hair and fiber evidence. Some of the letters contained references to chemicals that might correspond to explosive mixtures in the UNABOM devices.

The Montana postmarks on the envelopes were valuable for their comparison with the dates and places that UNABOM devices were either mailed from or left at by the bomber. Stamps on the letters could be compared with stamps on the mailed devices. The letters themselves could be compared with other known writing samples from Kaczynski's brother for similarities as striking as those in the 1971 essay he'd written.

At about 8:00 the next morning, Kathy teamed up with her colleagues, awaiting the arrival of David and his wife, Linda. They were ushered into the suite by attorney Tony Bisceglie, a short, personable man with a sharp, keen gaze and thick dark hair. He wore black cowboy boots with his impeccable Washington suit.

Bisceglie nodded as he shook Kathy's hand while glancing at the table of coffee and pastries. He smiled briefly, then turned to his clients.

David Kaczynski was a tall man with wide, but slightly stooped, shoulders and a gentle face. His eyes were soft with concern and evident pain. Even before he spoke, he conveyed a deep sorrow at the situation, as well as a resolve to deal with it. His voice was as gentle as his face.

Linda, a professor of Philosophy in Schenectady, New York, was a petite woman with large, dark eyes and a wary expression. Unhappy to be in the room, she sat rigidly in the chair and carefully told Kathy an absorbing story.

Linda said she had never met Theodore "Ted" Kaczynski, but was aware that he had voiced great opposition to her marrying his brother. She knew Ted's views about the evils of technology, and of his withdrawal from his family over the years. From David, she knew a considerable amount about Ted's personality and pre-occupations. All this led her to closely examine an article about the UNABOM case in the Paris, France, edition of the *Herald Tribune* while she was on sabbatical there in August, 1995.

The article said the Unabomber was a loner, most probably from Chicago, had an association with Salt Lake City, and had spent time in Northern California.

"Ted's originally from Chicago," she remembered thinking, "and of course he was in northern California when he was at Berkeley."

The *Tribune* article was accompanied by excerpts from a document the news media was calling the "UNABOM Manifesto." When David joined her in Paris for the last part of her trip, she told him about the article and excerpts.

"It sounded like Ted, what I knew of his beliefs," Linda related. "The article said the entire manuscript was going to be published. I knew I wanted David to read it, in case Ted really was involved."

Shortly after they returned from France, the *Post* and the *Times* jointly published the UNABOM Manifesto, but paper copies of it had been snatched up so quickly there were none left by the time she persuaded David to read it. They went to a library and looked it up on the computer. She watched his face change after he read only a few paragraphs.

He saw what I saw, Kathy thought, the same words, the same phrasing. She turned her attention to David, who listened carefully as Kathy established her goals for the interview.

"We need to know as much as possible about your brother," she said, "so I'll be asking a lot of questions about your experiences and perceptions as you grew up together, what Ted was like at various ages, what his interests were, what his relationships with other people were like."

During the long and detailed discussion that ensued, David said repeatedly that he hoped his own cooperation would eliminate Ted as a suspect.

He described his brother as a troubled and solitary person who, as he grew up, became increasingly abusive and accusatory of their bewildered parents. Ted had been alienated from the family for a long time, and David had last seen him in 1986. He detailed Ted's lack of friends, his moody behavior, and his increasing fury at what he called the "technological society." He described the tragic circumstances of their father's suicide after a diagnosis of terminal cancer in late 1990. With evident pain, he said that Ted had appeared indifferent to the tragedy, and made no attempt to travel to Chicago for the funeral. Kathy leaned forward as he wiped tears from his eyes.

"Now, that was hard to talk about," she said quietly. "A lot of this is hard to talk about, and we know that. You need to take a break, so we'll stop for awhile."

David and Linda stood up and left the suite for a walk outside. Bisceglie joined Kathy on the hotel balcony and lit a cigarette.

"That was well done," he said, and turned to face her. "We're going to have to talk about what you're going to do next. I know how these things can go, and we have to make something clear. There will be no operational use of my clients in this investigation."

"We'll certainly address that, if you like," Kathy said politely.

Bisceglie was a high profile, accomplished attorney who had befriended an FBI agent named Mike Harrison when they met in connection with another Bureau case.

At the end of 1995, an old friend from law school, Susan Swanson, had called him from Chicago, where she was a private investigator, and asked if he would represent her friend, Linda, and her husband in their contemplated contact with the FBI. Bisceglie called Mike Harrison, who phoned a colleague at the Washington, D.C., Field Office. It was that colleague who had directed Molly to pick up the 1971 essay from Bisceglie.

When everyone returned to the suite, Kathy turned her attention to Ted's letters to David. The handwriting on the letters was clear and distinct. One of the letters, postmarked in the mid-1980s, asked David to check suppliers and prices on sodium chloride. Sodium chloride had been used with other chemicals as part of the explosive mixture in some UNABOM devices.

In another letter, there was a reference to *Ancient Engineers* by L. Sprague DeCamp. The book was one of several quoted in the UNABOM Manifesto. Yet another letter referred to a book by the French philosopher Jacques Ellul, *The Technological Society*, a book Ted very much admired and had recommended to David. *The Technological Society* was quoted several times in the UNABOM Manifesto.

None of the postmarks on the envelopes ruled out the possibility that Theodore Kaczynski was the Unabomber, since none of the postmarks conflicted with the dates of UNABOM mailings anywhere in the United States.

While Kathy mentally logged the information she was gleaning from the letters, she concentrated on David, her eyes locked on his. The other agents took detailed notes.

David explained their context, when and how the correspondence was conducted. He described his own relationship with his brother. He had idolized Ted, seven years his senior, and had always admired him despite the difficulties he caused in the family. When David and Linda married in the summer of 1990, Ted had angrily severed relations with David almost entirely. For the past six years, he heard from Ted only if he needed money, or wanted to reiterate his contempt for the way his younger brother was living his life.

David had deliberated long and hard about contacting the FBI. He was terribly worried that if the FBI thought Ted was the Unabomber, his brother might meet the fate of those barricaded at Waco and Ruby Ridge when an assault was made on his mountain cabin in the Montana forest. At the same time, if his brother was somehow involved, David's own compassion for the victims and their families made him determined to ensure that he did everything possible to prevent any further loss of life.

"I have to do something, but I have to protect Ted as much as I can," he said. "And I will do everything I can to help you to eliminate him as a suspect in these crimes."

As Kathy brought the interview to a close, David reminded her that he had more letters from Ted at his own cabin in southwest Texas.

"I have a lot more letters there," he said. "I've kept nearly every letter Ted ever wrote me. And my mother has more letters and other things of Ted's." He looked at Bisceglie and back at Kathy.

"I don't want my mother contacted," he said firmly. "She's not to be approached without me, not until I agree to do it and I'm to be there with her."

"And I want to reiterate," Bisceglie added, "that my client will provide you information but will not contact Ted Kaczynski for you or act as your agent in any way. We'll have to get this in writing."

Kathy accepted the conditions on behalf of the task force. Regarding the retrieval of additional letters from David's cabin in Texas, David was unhesitating.

"I can meet you next weekend," he said.

As they got up to leave, David's eyes held no less sorrow than when had he entered. Kathy glanced at Linda and thought she knew what she was feeling. Linda had to be wondering what they had gotten themselves into. Kathy sent a silent message of support Linda's way. Trust us, Kathy thought. We're going to do this right. But she herself wondered if it were true. A lot of things could go wrong when different agendas—even within the same agency, let alone a multi-agency task force—collided in a major case.

∞ ∞ ∞

The following Friday afternoon, after a hectic week back in San Francisco working with the text of the letters and briefing us further on the interviews in Washington, Lee and Kathy flew to El Paso, Texas, to rendezvous with David and make the long trek to his cabin in the southwest Texas "Badlands."

They were both senior agents, but had widely varied backgrounds. Lee had been a career Army officer. He had joined the FBI in the early 1970s after recovering from critical injuries he received during an assault by the North Vietnamese Army after the 1968 Tet Offensive. One of the best White Collar Crime investigators in San Francisco, Lee had many successful convictions under his belt. Kathy had also left the military to join the Bureau in 1978, but since she specialized in Soviet counterintelligence, she'd had little to do with helping U.S. attorneys make cases in federal court. Since they worked on "opposite sides of the house" in the Bureau, they might otherwise have never worked together, but they turned out to be a good team in dealing with the most important witness ever in the UNABOM case.

David Kaczynski had just finished a grueling week working at a residential facility for troubled teenagers, and would ordinarily have been looking forward to a weekend at home with his wife. Now, however, he was walking off a plane at midnight at the El Paso airport, met by Lee and Kathy, and ferried to their hotel where he slept a few hours before they had to leave on their Badlands road trip.

At 6:00 Saturday morning, Kathy and Lee blinked blearily at the young El Paso agent who strode energetically into the hotel lobby. With great animation, he proclaimed they would be driving south to the Big Bend Wilderness in a "brand new Chevy Suburban." After they all piled in, he grinned, gunned the engine, and they sped out of the parking lot. When they reached the highway, he took off at an average speed of 100 miles an hour, chattering the whole while about a recent assignment he'd had in Haiti. Muttering occasionally to himself about the strain on the new engine, Lee clung during the whole ride to the shoulder strap in the front passenger seat, casting disbelieving looks at the driver. Lee had withstood assaults from the North Vietnamese army and countless dicey arrest scenarios in the FBI, but he'd rarely been as concerned as he was now about whether they'd make it to their destination in one piece.

In the back, David and Kathy had a long conversation about Ted. There was a constant, faint hum from an El Paso Division aircraft that kept an eye on them. The FBI had reports of bandits along this road, who reportedly preyed on tourists and ran guns and drugs between Mexico and the United States, and we weren't taking any chances with this witness.

Kathy repeatedly reassured David that the plane was standard operating procedure, but the drone of the plane's engines hung over most of the drive. David had spent a good part of his life in the Texas wilderness areas, had hiked and lived alone there, and these armed FBI agents were acting as if they were a stagecoach about to be overrun by bandits. But he accepted the circumstances with as much calm as he could muster, and he was committed to getting more of the letters his brother had sent him. He told Kathy it had been a while since he'd visited his cabin, and despite the circumstances, he was looking forward to being there.

By afternoon, the Suburban was crawling like a beetle over steep, rutted and rocky terrain, at a top speed of two or three miles per hour. There were few structures in the area, which was a good distance from the highway, and the only sounds besides the car's engine were calls from birds wheeling overhead. David finally indicated a stopping point, and they all walked towards a small structure well off the road.

David's cabin was clean and neat, flooded with sunlight, its outside eaves painted a bright pink. There were shelves of books and colorful rag rugs on a clean floor. David smiled and nodded as Kathy speculated that the pink eaves had been a contribution from Linda. He went to a trap door outside and opened it, retrieving the letters from Ted he had stored with other materials in an underground space.

As Lee sat at a table outside and began cataloguing the newest group of letters, David brewed Kathy an herbal tea on a small propane stove in the kitchen. They sipped their tea while David walked quietly around his property, checking to see if things were in order. He may have been trying to pretend this was just another visit to the cabin, that the FBI was not here poking around in the private retreat he had built himself and that was so precious to him. Kathy watched him, sympathizing with his discomfort. Strangers with guns had invaded the quiet lives of the Kaczynski family, and his older brother was in terrible trouble.

"I know this is difficult for you," she said. "We don't want to intrude more than necessary. We'll walk away and leave you alone here for as long as you like. When you're ready, come back to the car and we'll leave."

As they drove away from the cabin, David looked back with apparent resignation. At that point, neither Kathy nor Lee nor anyone else on the UTF had seen the Montana cabin Ted Kaczynski had lived in for most of the past 25 years.

But David had seen it, had helped buy the land for it. He knew what it looked like: a dark, brooding structure in the Montana woods. Kathy would wonder later, when she first walked up to it while the Evidence Response Team searched it in April, at the contrast between Ted's gloomy Montana retreat and the bright and earnest outlook suggested by the cabin with pink eaves that David had built in southwest Texas.

∞ ∞ ∞

Kathy and David talked at length many more times before we arrested Theodore Kaczynski without incident on the morning of April 3, 1996. On that day, Kathy tried desperately to reach David and his family before they were besieged by the media and barricaded themselves in their home. When she finally got him on the phone, the press had already begun their onslaught. David hung up on her in fury and anguish at what he considered was a broken promise to keep his cooperation—which he had pledged for the public good and to protect his brother's life—confidential.

Nearly two years later, in late 1997, David, his mother, and their attorney, Tony Bisceglie, arrived in the packed U.S. District Courtroom of Judge Garland Burrell in Sacramento for one of his brother's many pretrial hearings. Bisceglie and Kathy had greeted each other a few minutes earlier, and Kathy had asked the attorney to give David her best wishes for him and his family.

Now David looked to where Kathy sat, on the prosecution side of the courtroom. He got up from his seat and walked into the aisle as Kathy, a member of the federal team that had run down and was now prosecuting his brother, got up and went to meet him. In front of an astonished crowd, the brother of the Unabomber gave the FBI agent who had so much to do with his brother's capture a warm hug.

Since 9/11, the FBI has spent almost a billion dollars striving to build a computer system that will help its agents perform more efficiently and communicate more broadly in "connecting the dots" that will forestall future terrorist attacks on American soil. But law enforcement is more about people than it is about technology. The hug that David and Kathy shared was priceless. The friendship they established endures to this day, a lasting lesson in the importance of trust and respectful, professional relationships in the war on terror.

Mathematics Assistant Professor
Theodore Kaczynski, U.C. Berkeley

Kaczynski's 1990 Montana
driver's license photograph.

11

THE TERRORIST IN THE WOODS

FBI agent Dave Weber crawled on his stomach to within 200 yards of the cabin.

He was alone, in deep snow, and his movements were stealthy in the winter quiet.

A Montana native, Weber was the perfect choice to reconnoiter the cabin. He was as at home in a business suit testifying in court as he was now, in winter camouflage in the middle of the Helena National Forest. Dave and I were First Office agents together in Portland in the late 70s, where he was selected as the office Firearms Instructor. When he came to San Francisco, he'd taken the position full time, at the same time acting as SWAT Team Leader and Defensive Tactics Coordinator. During his years on city streets, he'd kept his woodsman skills sharp, and now he was back in the forests of his boyhood, hunting the most dangerous quarry he'd ever been up against.

We needed confirmation that the "Hermit of Baldy Mountain," a local reference to Theodore Kaczynski, was holed up in his cabin.

Sweat prickled Dave's face and neck under his layers of winter gear as he made the slow and cautious climb to a concealed location above the cabin. Temperatures had risen as high as 45 degrees during the day, and Weber grew concerned as he watched melting snow pouring from the roof of Kaczynski's cabin.

An early end to winter could make things even more complicated for us. If the snow melted, the Unabomber would be far freer to resume his attacks. Dave anticipated that Kaczynski's survival skills were likely to have been so developed that he might slip out unnoticed, taking one of the many back trails he must have found during his long years in these woods.

The tang of burning alder wood floated through the trees from the cabin below. Dave noted the time and checked the sky. The early dark of winter approached, and he knew the sweat on his skin would turn to flecks of ice within the hour, despite the earlier heat of the day. It was February, and there were many snows to come. For now, he'd gotten the information he'd climbed up here for: the subject of the only UTF search warrant—still being drafted in San Francisco—was in his cabin and under surveillance.

The UTF had established a permanent lookout at the Sportsman's Motel on State Highway 200 that ran east to west through Lincoln. FBI agents Candice DeLong and John Gray, who had transferred to San Francisco from the Chicago UTF, were assigned a single, critical task. There was one bus stop in Lincoln, and it was in front of the motel. Together, Delong and Gray kept it in sight, and monitored travelers from Lincoln who took the Rimrock Trailways bus that departed once a day for Missoula and Great Falls, Montana. From there, multiple connections were available to Greyhound Lines and travel to locations outside Montana.

Agents were dispatched to a forward command post in Missoula, while another team was sent to Salt Lake City. If Delong and Gray saw Kaczynski get on a bus, Max would contact us in San Francisco, and one of several contingency plans would be implemented.

All of the plans had a common denominator. At some point, Freeman and I would have to make a decision to either stop and detain Kaczynski, or wait to learn more about what he was doing.

Stopping him too soon would alert him to our presence before the search warrant was finished. What if he was on a "dry run," and carried nothing connecting him to UNABOM? We'd lose all our advantage, and we wouldn't be able to hold him. Any evidence in the cabin would swiftly disappear, if he hadn't gotten rid of it already.

But if we waited too long, Kaczynski might disappear along some wilderness path, on his way to another target. Surveillance under the best of conditions is an art, not a science, and we all knew it. Without a warrant, even if we stopped him to prevent him from killing again, we'd risk losing our chance for a successful prosecution in the UNABOM case. What about justice for all of the UNABOM victims over eighteen years?

From mid-February to April 3, 1996, the tension was constant and excruciating as we raced time, the weather, and eventually the news media to prevent the Unabomber from striking again.

∞ ∞ ∞

Working in a wilderness environment posed one unique challenge after another. After he arrived and got things set up, Max called to give us a progress report on his small expeditionary force in Helena and Lincoln.

"We can do some of the things you asked us to do, like discreetly check hotel records, find out if the books mentioned in the manuscript are available in local libraries, and things like that, but we have a real problem in those mountains around Lincoln. We can't communicate with each other once we're up there."

There were no communication relay links around Lincoln, and communication was critical for our operation. Freeman and I had met with the SAC in Salt Lake to brief him on our interests in Lincoln, and two agents in the Helena office were brought into the case.

"We'll see if Salt Lake can help out," I said.

"Won't do any good," Max said. "I've talked to Tom McDaniel in Helena. He says they've tried for years to get communications links up that way, but it's never worked out. The mountain peaks towards Lincoln are thousands of feet high, and the forest is rugged."

We fell silent. There was no way we could get this done if we couldn't communicate with each other in time. Cell phones were clunky and unreliable in 1996, especially in the mountains. If Kaczynski climbed on a bus, he might as well be on the far side of the moon.

"How do you feel about getting Bill Hagle up there to give it a try?" San Francisco had one of the best Electronic Technicians— "ETs"— in the FBI: Willis "Bill" Hagle.

"Send him," said Max. "He'll probably need someone else to conduct a survey. Weber can help him. I can, too, for that matter."

"He'll be on the first plane out tomorrow morning."

As I signed off, Jim told Max we would let the SAC in Salt Lake know what we were planning. We doubted he would much care.

While the UTF presence was quietly growing in western Montana, the Salt Lake FBI and the Hostage Rescue Team were deployed in large numbers in eastern Montana in a standoff with the Freemen Militia. For quite a while, that situation provided us great cover. FBI agents travel armed, and it would have been even more difficult for us had we provoked curiosity at the dozens of agents we were eventually sending on numerous flights to Helena. As it was, they assumed our people were joining the FBI contingent dealing with the Freemen.

Montana State Highway 279 moves past the airport in Helena north through Canyon Creek, passing Stemple Pass Road before coming to State Highway 200. Southwest on State 200 is the way to Lincoln, which is cradled in the center of the Helena National Forest. Central Montana is blanketed with birch, alder, and pine canopies that make up a continuous series of national forests. The Deerlodge, Lolo, and Lewis and Clark National Forests pick up where the Helena leaves off.

Theodore Kaczynski's cabin sat on one and one-half acres four miles south of Lincoln and one-half mile east of Stemple Pass Road on Canyon Creek. He purchased the land in 1971 from Butch Gehring, who operated a sawmill nearby, and built his 10- x 12-foot wilderness house up a draw and at the rear of a clearing against trees supported by rocky cliffs. The house had no electricity, no running water, no gas or propane, and no plumbing.

In a state where no city's population exceeded 100,000, Kaczynski found a spot isolated even by Montana standards. Millions of secluded acres were his backyard, his lab, and his classroom. Most of his needs were met through fishing and hunting near his home. Montana lakes and streams boast brown, brook, rainbow and cutthroat trout, whitefish, catfish, salmon, walleye, grayling, bass, and perch. There were deer, elk, buffalo, bear, and mountain lions in the same wilderness as wild turkeys, grouse, pheasant, and partridge.

Mountains rose to 8,000 feet, and snow covered the ground for months at a time during most winters. The only way to access the highest points was by snowmobile. Throughout the Helena National Forest and in the vicinity of Lincoln were over 400 miles of snow-mobiling trails. We would later learn that the sounds and disruptions of snowmobiles were a much-hated intrusion into the quiet retreat that Kaczynski had called his home for 25 years.

Max and Dave met Bill Hagle and his assistant, Rick Ethridge, at the airport and briefed them on everything they knew about Montana. It was cold and turning colder. A snowstorm was forecast for the mountains around Lincoln. Snow mixed with rain was the backdrop for most of Hagle's stay.

I thought Bill was the best ET in the FBI. He was in his fifties, lean and spry. His talent was equal to his dedication, which was limitless. He told Max that he'd wait out the bad weather, no matter how long it took. Max grinned darkly at him as they drove him to a Super 8 motel.

"If the weather turns bad here, it can stay that way the rest of the winter."

The next day, they drove up to Lincoln, and Bill learned to drive a snowmobile. Since Dave Weber was one of his instructors, he learned to tear around fast. His other instructor was Jerry Burns, a forest service officer who knew the snowmobile trails intimately.

But their mission involved driving off the trails. Bill gripped the handles of the snowmobile until he couldn't move, and his body ached from the constant assault of the icy wind. A cold rain continually lashed his eyes. Just when he felt he couldn't hold on any longer, the three of them would stop and climb the final 100 feet to the timberline on foot. There, Bill checked ridges covered in snow and ice to see if he could build a communications network of repeaters throughout the area. The deep snow concealed the near-vertical angle of the repeated climbs, and eventually he was too exhausted to continue.

It was getting dark and they were on their descent when Bill lost his balance on the snowmobile. He was thrown into the wet snow, and kicked clear of the machine, watching in horror as it kept going, slowly at first and then faster and faster until it lurched up and then plunged over an embankment, out of sight.

"I could have been on that," he muttered, as Weber and Burns ran up to him.

They all shook their heads in disbelief. They walked over to the drop-off and saw the tail end of the snowmobile drifting peacefully in a snow bank 50 feet below. Dave looked up at Bill.

"What d'you say we get out of here and over to the Marysville Steak House?"

They'd completed their survey, and Bill was confident he'd be able to rig the area with a communications system that would serve the UTF.

"Yeah," said Burns. "We can come back and fish that out of there in the Spring."

Marysville, an old mining town off State Highway 200, was about a 30-minute drive down from the mountain. There was nothing fancy about the building's façade, but they were cheered by the warm interior, as well as by the sight and smell of grilling steaks from the back porch that faced the mountains. The bartender greeted them with a friendly shout as they stepped through the door. Besides, it was time to celebrate. Within days, Hagle would have his entire San Francisco ET crew relocated to the western Montana mountains, and the UTF would have an electronic leash around the Lone Wolf's lair.

∞ ∞ ∞

No one should have been out in this cold, but Butch Gehring had a sawmill to run. He was used to the cold. Standing in front of him, Max Noel wasn't. Max grumbled silently to himself as the icy wind cut through his inadequate jacket and trousers. His hands were like ice, and he shivered as mixed snow and rain fell from the sky and blew off the trees. He gritted his teeth as they began to chatter, and forced himself to attend to every word Gehring said about the hermit on Baldy Mountain.

"I've know him for years. Keeps to himself. Moved to Montana and has pretty much never left that cabin."

Max had told Gehring, who had sold Theodore Kaczynski property adjacent to his sawmill in the 1970s, that the FBI had questions about a hazy issue from years before that involved federal taxes on Kaczynski's land. He was happy to talk to Max as long as it took, and he seemed to have no problem with the weather. Curious, though, how this FBI guy danced around in one spot while he asked his questions.

Every time Max tried to jot down some notes, his government pen froze. He shook it and hit it against his leg, but it was hopeless. The writing pad was soaked anyway, with snow, ice, and rain.

"I feel sorry for him," Gehring said. "He's alone. Doesn't have any job that I can tell." He gazed up at the sky in leisurely reminiscence. "I told him I had some work for him once. I didn't expect much, since the work involved numbers and such. I don't think he's had much schooling."

Max listened while he struggled with the frozen pen and tried to cover his notepad with his coat. It only made him colder.

"I wanted him to work on my ledgers. I figured it'd take some considerable amount of time. He agreed to do it, came over, drank down a beer without stopping for a breath, and then settled in and straightened out all my records in no time. I was surprised. He's pretty good with numbers. After that, he never came back to ask for more work, and I never thought to ask him again to help out."

Max thanked Gehring and walked quickly back to his four-wheel drive. So the guy was pretty good with numbers, he thought. Starting the engine, he had visions of a double shot of espresso, extra hot.

∞ ∞ ∞

The end of the Montana winter was in sight. The sun was higher in the sky each day, and the streams and rivers outside of Lincoln were rising as the snow on the ridges began to melt. The frozen crust of the ground was replaced by a watery mixture of melting ice and dirt, which made a thick putty that stuck to our boots.

Soon, the door to Theodore Kaczynski's cabin would open.

Now we pulled out all the stops. We needed evidence that Kaczynski had traveled outside of Lincoln, and Montana, and it needed to correlate with the postmark dates on the letters we'd received from David. We needed to corroborate the web of behavioral evidence with solid information about as many of Kaczynski's activities as we could.

Paul Wilhelmus and ATF Agent Mike Grady started knocking on hotel doors in Helena. They began with the types of places they figured Kaczynski would be most likely to stay.

They hit pay dirt immediately. The manager of the Park Hotel identified a Theodore Kaczynski who had rented a room at the hotel 31 times between April 1980 and October 1995. Incredibly, he still had the paper records documenting each visit, as well as the check in and out dates. The information was sent overnight to a UTF analytical team in San Francisco, where a timeline was being prepared.

The bomb to Percy Wood, president of United Airlines, was mailed from Chicago on June 3, 1980. Kaczynski was in the Park Hotel in Helena for two days on three occasions in April, May, and August of 1980.

A bomb was placed at the University of Utah on October 8, 1981. Kaczynski was at the Park Hotel on November 9–10, 1981.

A bomb was mailed from Provo, Utah, on April 23, 1982. Kaczynski was at the Park Hotel a month later, on May 12 and 13.

In Chicago, David Kaczynski told Kathy and Lee that when his brother returned to Chicago from Montana in 1978, he traveled by Greyhound bus.

An agent team found three bus drivers from RimRock Trailways who identified photographs of Kaczynski as a passenger who had traveled between Lincoln and Missoula during 1995. Further, they discovered that connections could be made in Helena and Idaho Falls to travel to the San Francisco Bay Area on Greyhound Lines. It took 25 hours to get from Helena to Sacramento, 28 hours to get to Oakland, and 28 ½ hours to get to San Francisco.

Agents checked libraries for the book titles mentioned in the UNABOM Manifesto. The University of Montana in Missoula, Montana State in Bozeman, Carroll College, and the public library in Helena all had most of the books in editions referenced by the Unabomber.

Twenty four hours before we served the search warrant, Max took a break from his arrest plan when Jim and I gave him the green light to interview the librarian in Lincoln.

She described Kaczynski as a frequent user of the library, where he "conducted his research." Sometimes she assisted by ordering books and periodicals for him. She recalled ordering "tons of stuff" for Kaczynski on the author of *Ancient Engineers*, L. Sprague DeCamp, and she told Max that Kaczynski hopped on buses and traveled much more than most people knew. She spoke of Kaczynski's visits to Chicago or Detroit, California, or Colorado. Max noted to himself that her recollection of the time frames for these trips correlated with several UNABOM events.

In San Francisco, the affidavit for the search warrant of Theodore Kaczynski's cabin was growing in credibility, as a result of the intensive investigation in Montana joined with the behavioral and linguistic evidence gleaned from the Manifesto, Kaczynski's letters to his brother, and the essay he'd written in 1971.

In late March, Max listened as Jim and I made one of the final, significant decisions that led us to the Unabomber's door.

Since assigning Max and his small team to Montana in February, Freeman and I had rotated in and out of Helena on a regular basis. By teleconference between Last Chance Gulch and San Francisco, we kept each other updated on the overall status of the investigation.

David Kaczynski told us his mother, Wanda, had just moved from the Kaczynski family home in Lombard, Illinois, to Schenectady, New York. He told Kathy that when he'd helped her move, he'd seen "things of Ted's," including a large wooden chest his mother had kept that held many of his brother's things. It was from this chest that David had retrieved the copy of the 1971 essay he'd first made available to us in February.

Meanwhile, Molly Flynn contacted David's attorney, Tony Bisceglie, who then had a lengthy conversation with his clients about the need to tell Wanda Kaczynski about her son. David made the painful decision to tell his mother about his suspicions of Ted, and that he had contacted the FBI.

From Helena, I called Jim in San Francisco.

"Kathy and Lee are leaving for Albany on March 22nd. They'll hook up with Molly Flynn and coordinate with Bisceglie on the possibility of interviewing Wanda about Ted."

Freeman balked. He wasn't happy with Kathy at the time. While she, Lee, and Molly were in Chicago meeting with David during preparations for his mother's move, he had told her to ask David to write a letter to his brother.

"Boss," Kathy said, "We promised him we wouldn't use him operationally."

Jim's reply colored the air a little blue, but Kathy held her ground. He eventually agreed, but he wasn't going to have Kathy in charge in Schenectady. Now he growled a little as he gave me my marching orders.

"You're going with them. I need to know that we're managing David the right way. So get on the same plane. I'll fly to Helena while you're gone."

We finished by reviewing the latest forensic findings of the FBI Lab, including the status of the transfer from Los Angeles to northern California of the bomb disrupter designed by Sandia National Laboratory in New Mexico, and the progress of the linguistic comparisons of the UNABOM manuscript and other known UNABOM writings with the 1971 essay. Fitz was back in San Francisco after a stint at Quantico, and I assigned him a team of analysts to complete the assessment for inclusion in the search warrant.

I raised my eyebrows and exhaled in relief as I hung up the phone. Max had followed every word and looked at me a little wide-eyed.

"I thought we were busy here," he said in a disbelieving tone. "I had no idea so much was going on in so many different places."

I smiled.

"We have the evidence, Max. It's only a matter of time."

Panoramic view from area near Butch Gehring's sawmill, Lincoln, Montana.

12

THE TREASURE CHEST

We flew into Schenectady in a fever of expectation. Kathy, Lee, and I met Molly Flynn, who'd driven up from Washington, when we all checked in at the hotel.

After over a month of meeting David Kaczynski on weekends in Washington, D.C., Texas, and Chicago, we were finally on his home turf. As Freeman had insisted, I was with them; but unlike him, I had little worry about Kathy's relationship with David. Jim and Max suspected that Kathy had become too close, too sympathetic to David, and might not be representing the government's interests as vigorously as she should. But I knew Kathy, and we'd had long discussions about our meetings with David. I thought the nature of her interaction with David was a large part of why we were now in Schenectady, ready to meet with his mother and obtain the final bits of documentary and other evidence that would put a bow on the unique search warrant affidavit being assembled in San Francisco to search Kaczynski's cabin in Montana.

As she always did, Kathy called David soon after she arrived. And as he always did, David carefully asked her the question he always asked her when she called to initiate another meeting.

"I'm assuming that, since we're meeting again, you haven't yet uncovered evidence to eliminate the possibility that Ted is involved in this case?"

Kathy gave a version of the same respectful reply she always did.

"No, we haven't eliminated Ted as a suspect. So we need to proceed further."

This time, things were even more tense than usual. David was anticipating telling his mother about his suspicions of Ted and his own discussions with the FBI. He was hoping to secure her cooperation in granting us access to possessions of Ted's that she had kept over the long years of his estrangement from the family, in the large wooden trunk she'd had transported with her household goods in the move from Chicago. Kathy knew David was dreading the encounter with his mother, who he'd described as proud and defensive about her oldest son, and who, he anticipated, would be extremely angry with him for his own actions. He agonized that he'd lose the love and respect of the last family member he had contact with, and the pain in his voice was evident over the phone.

"Would you be free to come to our hotel in the morning?" Kathy asked. "We'll discuss where we are with the investigation and get your views on how best to proceed with the interview of your mother."

He agreed, his tone calm but solemn. Kathy thought again about what a remarkable person David Kaczynski was.

He'd never had to come forward. He could have dismissed his wife's suspicions about his brother, whom she'd never even met. He could have left the 1971 essay in the trunk in Chicago with the rest of Ted's things, and no one would ever have known. His brother would have been left alone to lead the solitary life he craved, and the private grief of the Kaczynski family would never have been intruded upon by the FBI, or trotted out into the public domain in the media furor that would follow Ted's arrest.

But David did come forward. He chose to do the right thing when it was the hardest thing for him to do. And Kathy, who knew to her core that Ted Kaczynski was indeed the Unabomber, knew also that David was walking into a whirlwind that she would be unable to prepare him for. She knew it, but she couldn't prevent it. All she could do was try to walk into it with him as much as she could.

That evening, Lee, Kathy, Molly, and I had a quiet and reflective dinner in the hotel dining room. Only a few weeks ago, the UTF had been running full speed ahead, vetting hundreds of suspects, pursuing thousands of leads, connecting puzzle pieces that kept forming the wrong picture, and believing that everything we were learning was bringing us one step closer to identifying the Unabomber. A few of us had believed that publishing the UNA-BOM Manifesto could bring him into focus for us. The past few weeks of nonstop travel, analysis, meetings with David, and discreet investigation in Montana had been a blur. We were a little dazed by the recent, swift developments in the case—but we were ready.

We joked a little about the fact that Freeman had ordered me to come and chaperone the "David K" team in Schenectady. Lee's eyes twinkled as he recalled for us the phone call they'd gotten from Jim when they were in Chicago.

"I was listening to her say, 'But Boss, we promised,'" he said, looking at Kathy with a grin. "And I told her to give me the phone, but, before I could say much, he started hollering so loud that all I could say then was, Yes, sir!"

Molly had been in the Chicago hotel room when this talk with Freeman occurred, and she nodded emphatically at me as we all laughed, indicating that's exactly what had happened. Lee looked at me appraisingly.

"I'm glad it's you, Terry. You're one of us."

I smiled back at him. He'd made it easy for me to explain to all of them my thoughts about the role I would play in Schenectady.

I had decided not to meet David during the trip. I would let the team do their interviews with him and his mother while remaining at a distance, able to evaluate the information they developed from an objective viewpoint.

On a good day, forming a useful and productive bond with someone who provides critical information in a case is an emotionally draining and time-consuming experience. I had faith in the relationship Kathy, Lee, and Molly had established with David, and I told them so. I told them I'd stay out of their way in Schenectady as long as they kept me fully apprised—by phone—of their progress.

They weren't unanimous in their opinions about the case. Of the three of them, Lee was the most skeptical about the identification of Theodore Kaczynski as the Unabomber. After all, he'd excelled in bringing white collar criminals to justice. For years, he had lived in a world of handwriting exemplars, dated inks, forensic examinations of bank accounts, accounting by the numbers of each entry in a register, and overseas bank accounts fattened by fraud. He, like Max—with whom he'd worked for years in the Hayward office of the San Francisco Division—was driven by the search for hard evidence. It had to be explainable to a judge and a jury, and it had to show direct connection of a criminal with his crime.

Molly had been trained in the law before she became an FBI agent. And when it came to proving a case, she had much the same attitude as Lee. When the three of them had met with David in Chicago, they'd also gone to brief the Chicago UTF on the new subject San Francisco had surfaced in the case. Even though it had been Molly whose interest had first been stirred by the 1971 essay she'd picked up from Tony Biseglie's office, she wasn't convinced that Theodore Kaczynski was the Unabomber.

If Lee and Molly were skeptical, the Chicago UTF and their management were downright hostile. I knew Kathy had gotten yelled at pretty thoroughly during a meeting with the group of agents who had worked the case on and off for years, and who were adamant that they had UNABOM suspects far better than a hermit who'd lived in the Montana woods without electricity or plumbing for 25 years. She also sat through a withering barrage from the Chicago front office, when she briefed the doubtful SAC and his assistant, who stood over her while he made a forceful speech that we in San Francisco were "crazy" if we thought someone with no access to power tools or a foundry could have made the UNABOM devices.

Now, at the hotel in Schenectady, Lee pushed away from the dinner table and gestured for coffee. He looked at me and shook his head gently, saying slowly in his deep voice, "I just don't know. It seems like we still don't have much real evidence tying this guy to UNABOM."

Kathy and I exchanged glances. We knew there was a lot of opposition to our convictions about Theodore Kaczynski being the Unabomber, even from key UTF members like Lee. It was hard for him to defend us to the rest of the UTF in the contentious atmosphere that had grown up in the face of this new, most controversial suspect, especially since he wasn't himself convinced that we had the Unabomber identified. I decided to make my case to Lee as if I were telling it to the judge who would sign our search warrant.

"I think we have a lot of evidence. It's a different kind of evidence. In this case, it's a combination of the unopposed timeline, tellingly similar language, and themes in the writing, and a thousand little pieces here and there that add up to one thing: Theodore Kaczynski is the Unabomber."

Kathy leaned forward and spoke earnestly to Lee.

"And tomorrow, we'll find some of the final pieces we need to put it all together."

The next morning, I paced in my hotel room while waiting to hear from Kathy, Lee, and Molly on the results of their meeting with David. I later learned that David had again raised a critical issue. If it developed that his brother had actually committed the UNABOM crimes, he said, would the federal government agree to waive the death penalty in response to David's own cooperation in his capture?

Kathy knew she was risking a jump into quicksand. She wasn't the attorney Molly was, and she hadn't taken hundreds of cases to court like Lee. But she knew that she was the one who owed David an answer. She summarized her response to me later, in front of Lee and Molly.

"I said that I'm an FBI agent, not a prosecutor, and that I wouldn't be the one making that decision. I did tell him that we would communicate the facts of his cooperation and assistance to us to those who would make that decision in the future, and that it would be an important consideration in the decision."

Lee nodded. It would be vital for the eventual prosecution to ensure that no promises about this issue were made to David, even though he wasn't the subject of the case and he wasn't on trial.

By noon, Lee, Kathy, and I were in a rental car, headed to a hoped-for rendezvous with Wanda Kaczynski at her new home in Schenectady, about a 45 minute drive from our hotel. Molly drove her Bureau car. When we'd arrived two days earlier, the dry cold weather had hit us Californians hard, but at least the sun was shining. Now, the day-time sky had turned dark, and rain and possible thunderstorms were on the way. The heater blasted away inside the car as we went over our plan. Checking our watches, we knew that David would be arriving at his mother's house to begin breaking the story to his mother that her oldest son might be the Unabomber.

We parked around the corner from the address, and Kathy called Tony Biseglie. Amazingly, although the attorney was in the middle of the woods on a ski vacation in Vermont, they were able to connect. Biseglie said he'd just spoken to David, who'd readied his mother for our visit. We were cleared to go.

David's eyes were sad as he answered his mother's door, but the tears he'd just dried were from relief. His mother had listened to his story with disbelief, but in the end she had comforted him, saying that he had done the right thing. Now the tiny woman stood and welcomed three armed FBI agents into her new home. She offered them tea, and then told them she understood what they were there for. She told them she did not believe for a moment that her son Ted was guilty of any crime, but, like David, if she could keep anyone else from being hurt by the UNABOM crimes, she would open her house to the FBI.

Sitting down with Lee and Kathy in the living room, 79-year-old Wanda Kaczynski sat with dignified courtesy and sipped her tea as she discussed her oldest son. She validated much of what we had already learned from David about Ted's early years, and described his entry into Harvard at the age of 16.

"He was so young and so lacking in social skills. It was always hard for him to make friends. I think he grew even more isolated while he was at Harvard."

David listened intently, keeping his mother's emotional and physical state in mind as Kathy and Lee ticked through the elements of Theodore Kaczynski's development over many years. Meanwhile, Molly recorded an inventory of some 90 items they ultimately removed from Wanda Kaczynski's home that afternoon. All were instrumental in pointing to Theodore John Kaczynski as the elusive Unabomber.

There were letters written to Wanda by Ted, copies of cancelled checks showing money she had given him, and several essays Ted had written over the years. There was the chest full of his belongings that had been abandoned when Ted left the family home years earlier. Wanda queried him about it at one point, and he told her he didn't want any of the contents so she could do with it as she wished. She kept everything. The chest had remained closed and untouched during the move from Lombard, Illinois, to upstate New York.

Inside was a carbon copy of the 23-page essay written by Ted in 1971 that David had provided to the UTF in February. Molly dutifully recorded it on the inventory form of items acquired.

Another item was a letter Theodore Kaczynski wrote to the editor of *The Chicago Daily News*, dated December 14, 1969. The letter began, "The stricter gun control laws recommended by the U.S. Commission on Violence are a case in point." In 1968, President Lyndon Johnson had formed a commission to address the escalating violence that marred American society. Among its members were notable scholars Milton Eisenhower, Eric Hoffer, and James Q. Wilson. The commission produced a report, *The History of Violence in America*, which was referenced in the Unabomber's manuscript. Several other letters, copies of those sent to editors of newspapers in the Chicago area and various magazines, discussed technology and liberty. Molly carefully correlated all of them, studying each line as she made recordings in her growing inventory log.

Wanda's cancelled checks told a story that none of us had anticipated. Between May 1985 and July 1991, she sent Ted close to $14,000. David had sent him $1,000 in November 1994 and $2,000 in February 1995.

Over the previous ten years, Theodore Kaczynski had lived a wilderness lifestyle with no apparent income. In fact, he'd also been living off the approximately $17,000 provided by his mother and brother. Both David and his mother were horrified when they learned that several of the monetary gifts coincided with the timing of UNABOM events. Travel and delivery of bombs in the spring and winter of 1985 appeared to have been funded by $1,200 he had received from Wanda during that time. Another $620 came just two months before the 1987 attack on Caams Computer store in Salt Lake City, with a bomb carved from the same two-by-fours as the device that had killed Hugh Scrutton of Sacramento, California, in December 1985.

In November 1994, Ted had appealed to David for $1,000 a month before Thomas Mosser was murdered in his New Jersey home by a bomb mailed from San Francisco. When he asked for another $2,000 in February 1995, Ted wrote David that, if this didn't help him with his unfinished business, then nothing would help. Two months later, a bomb mailed to the California Forestry Association killed Gilbert Murray.

We had thought David's face could show no greater sorrow than what we had already seen; but this was a huge blow, and it registered. This gentle man and his mother, in an effort to reach out with help to their angry and estranged family member, had unwittingly funded the terror campaign that had shattered the lives of so many other families all over the country.

One of the most chilling documents found in the chest was a story drafted by Ted titled, "How I Blew Up Harold Snilly, by Apios Tuberosa, a pseudonym for T. J. Kaczynski, 463 N. Ridge, Lombard, Illinois, 60148." Kaczynski described how he mixed up a batch of chemicals and gave the finished product to a high school classmate. The story read:

> When I was in high school I took a course in chemistry . . . my rather specialized home collection of reagents; powdered aluminum, powdered magnesium, powdered zinc, sulfur, potassium, nitrate, potassium permanganate . . . in suitable combinations these things are capable of exploding. One day in the laboratory, having finished my assigned experiment early, I thought I might as well spend the extra time pursuing my favorite line of research . . . a mixture of red phosphorus and potassium chlorate seemed promising. I did not know at the time that it is the red phosphorus in the scratching surface of a matchbook, together with the potassium chlorate in the match head, that makes a match light so readily. I later found that the mixture is extremely sensitive to friction and practically impossible to work with.

Later, as we read and re-read the Harold Snilly story, Kathy and I looked at each other in amazement. The first six UNABOM devices contained powdered aluminum, potassium chlorate, and match heads. All were mentioned in the article.

As the hours passed by, Wanda Kaczynski became pleasantly engaged in conversation with the agents she met that rainy afternoon. She had read articles about the Unabomber that described him as a loner who was anti-technology. She leaned forward and spoke earnestly to Lee and Kathy.

"People like my son Ted are vulnerable to suspicion. He likes to live alone, likes privacy, is an environmentalist, and he deplores the excesses of technology," she said.

Molly wrote the quote down, word for word.

Wanda told the agents it would be wrong and unfair to target Ted because of his lifestyle, but then said, "If it is him who is doing these terrible things, he must be stopped."

She described a visit she and her husband had made to Montana in the mid 1980s. Ted had just completed a root cellar, the entrance of which was visible from his front door, about 150 feet from a creek that ran through his property. David had already told us about the root cellar, and Wanda's account, added to his, contributed to the search warrant affidavit being drafted in San Francisco.

She said she had given Ted a portable manual typewriter during the same period, and remembered that he would have had access to another portable and one electric typewriter at the family home in Chicago in the late 1970s. She was certain that Ted was living at the family home from August or September 1978 until late 1979. He had a job at the Prince Castle Restaurant Equipment Division while he was there. She remembered walking with him to the local commuter train station when he left to return to Montana.

The third UNABOM device, the bomb that misfired in the cargo hold of American Airlines Flight 444, was mailed from the Chicago area in November 1979.

Several hours had passed by the time the interview with Wanda Kaczynski neared its end. Molly made sure of her inventory of items taken from what had turned out to be a treasure chest of information and evidence for us. We now had additional typewritten letters from Theodore Kaczynski, which the FBI Lab would later say—just as they had with the 1971 essay—did not match any of the known typewriting samples of the Unabomber.

Once again, it was the content rather than forensics that was key. We had a constellation of personal items, the "How I Bombed Harold Snilly" story, and a vivid account of Theodore Kaczynski's life from Wanda that augmented what we had obtained from David.

I watched the agents walk down the stairs to where I waited in the car, flapping my arms to keep warm while I alternated between country tunes and rock oldies on the radio. I had left the area only once, when I scouted an Italian restaurant in the area that looked promising for the hearty dinner I knew the team would appreciate. Each of them was carrying a large box, and I felt a surge of optimism when I realized they'd hit the mother lode.

Later, Kathy and I took a look at some of the new evidence. One of the undated, handwritten letters from Ted to Wanda Kaczynski immediately caught our attention. After writing about his concern that privacy and freedom were both eroding in the United States, Ted wrote:

"We will be sacrificing some of the materialistic benefits of technology, but there just isn't any other way. We can't eat our cake and have it, too."

In the UNABOM Manifesto was the phrase, "Well, you can't eat your cake and have it, too."

We were certain that the long hunt for the Unabomber was over.

```
        HOW I BLEW UP HAROLD SNILLY
                    by
              Apios Tuberosa
              (Pseudoym for:
               T.J. Kaczynski
               463 N. Ridge
               Lombard, Illinois 60148)


When When I was in highschool I took a course in chemistry.
There was only one aspect of the subject which interestedmme,
as any chemist could have seen from a brief inspection of my
rather specialized home collection of reagents:  powdered alumin-
num, powdered magnesium, powddred zinc, sulfur, potassium nitrate,
```

Story written by Kaczynski in his youth, obtained from the home of his mother, with her consent, in Schenectady, New York, in 1996.

13

CAPTURE

Agent Turchie," Judge Lovell said.

I was jolted from my voyage through UNABOM time and space and back into the present.

"Have you served any other search warrants in the UNABOM case on any other suspects?"

"No, sir," I replied. "In fact, our Assistant U.S. Attorney in San Francisco has kept a sharp eye on that. He didn't want any issues with search warrants being used as an investigative tool, since that would call any later warrants into question at prosecution."

I looked at Bernie Hubley, the Assistant U.S. Attorney in Helena, for support, and he cast an approving expression my way, as if to say, "Good answer."

"These word comparisons and the language study are something I've never seen before," said the Judge. "Collectively, with all of the other information, they make a compelling argument for the search warrant.

"But let me ask you: on December 10, 1985, the Unabomber placed a device in a Sacramento parking lot, killing the victim who picked it up. However, it says here that you identified in your Montana investigation that Kaczynski made a walk-in deposit at a bank in Missoula, Montana, on December 10, 1985. How could he have been in Montana and California at the same time?"

"Yes, sir. That's right," I said. "Here in Montana, we found a deposit slip indicating that Mr. Kaczynski made a walk-in deposit in the Missoula bank on that date. It was the only information we developed in our 18-year timeline that appears to contradict the possibility that Kaczynski was the Unabomber.

"But that bank says that, at that time, they were changing over their computers, and they suspect that the slip might actually be inaccurate. We're continuing to look into it. I wanted to include it in the search warrant so you would know we had developed at least one piece of information that, on its face, seems to alibi Kaczynski for at least one UNABOM event."

The Judge cast a satisfied glance at me, nodded, and reached for his pen.

"I find that this search warrant contains more than ample probable cause to justify a search of the cabin of Theodore Kaczynski," Judge Lovell said.

Then, he looked at me sternly.

"Now, if this *is* the Unabomber, you go arrest him!"

As Bernie and I left the Federal Building, we shared a victorious handshake, and I told him I'd see him later that night.

"Good luck, Terry, " Bernie said. "To all of you."

Before I left Helena for the two-hour drive to Lincoln, I called Freeman to let him know Judge Lovell signed the search warrant. Jim gave the order for everyone to move into their positions. By noon, he gave the final green light to move against the cabin, just minutes before I pulled into the parking lot of the Seven-up Ranch just a few miles from Kaczynski's cabin.

∞ ∞ ∞

The tiny wooden cabin sat in a small clearing still frosted with snow. Blue sky filtered through a heavy canopy of green pine, birch, and alder. Wood smoke curled from the cabin's chimney.

For a final day before the months—years—of commotion and turmoil to come, it was quiet in the clearing. To Theodore Kaczynski, it must have felt like many other mornings he'd spent in the 25 years since he had built his cabin in the forest.

In 1971, it took just two weeks to build. Dark and unpainted, it now looked forbidding, but it was still solid. When we had it hauled away later that month, it would impress the workmen with its sturdiness. We stowed it in an airplane hanger at a Montana air force base to keep it from the souvenir hunters who soon thronged the clearing where it had stood for a quarter century. If we hadn't, it would have been torn apart in the public frenzy that was to sweep Lincoln after April 3rd, 1996.

The unpaved road that led to the cabin passed Butch Gehring's sawmill and eventually turned into a narrow foot trail. One of two small windows looked out from the cabin over the trail, minimizing the likelihood of anyone arriving unnoticed. No electric power lines ran to it, and there was no running water except for a nearby stream.

Dozens of federal agents were hidden in the woods around the cabin. They were there for two reasons: to keep the public—and the media—out, and to keep Kaczynski in. They shivered in their tactical gear as they waited for the search warrant to be served on the cabin, and while they waited, they wondered. What would happen when the Unabomber was cornered? Was the cabin one huge booby trap, wired to explode if he sensed his capture was imminent?

We worried about the risk, but CBS news had given us no choice. Dan Rather had called FBI Director Freeh personally to say they had information Theodore Kaczynski had been identified as the Unabomber. Freeh appealed to Rather and his colleagues to allow us 24 hours to finish and serve the search warrant on the cabin before they descended en masse on the small town of Lincoln, Montana.

I'd secured Judge Lovell's signature on the search warrant just a couple of hours before. In the 18 years since the first attack, it was the only search warrant ever served on a UNABOM suspect. Now we raced to preserve the evidence we hoped was in the cabin, and it was a race against time. Time, the media, and the chance that the Unabomber himself might already know we had found the location of his long hidden lair.

I drove up from Helena to Lincoln with the signed warrant. Freeman had already moved the tactical teams into position. I had just pulled into the parking lot of our Lincoln command post, several miles away, when he green-lit the move against the cabin.

"Just get him out of the cabin, Max."

Jim knew the stakes. In addition to the fact that we were all worried about a failsafe device that Theodore Kaczynski might have rigged at the cabin, Kathy had pledged to David Kaczynski that the FBI would protect his brother and get him out of the cabin alive. David had trusted Kathy's assurances that this wouldn't turn into another Waco or Ruby Ridge, and that the UTF would do its utmost to ensure that his brother would not be harmed.

Max nodded at Jim and looked at his small team. Paul Wilhelmus stood by, quiet and ready. Next to him was Tom McDaniel, a tall, burly man in a cowboy hat and blue jeans, wearing a leather jacket and boots. Tom was the senior agent in the small office the FBI had in Helena. He and Max hit it off immediately. They would appear together with Paul on magazine covers all over the world after they escorted Theodore Kaczynski to the Helena County jail the next day.

Forest Service Officer Jerry Burns stood to Tom's side. Burns knew the area well. He was also acquainted with Ted Kaczynski. Burns was one of a handful of people we'd confided in after the initial deployment of Max's team to Montana in February. McDaniel had recommended him to Max as someone in the area they could trust.

Burns supplied the plan of approach. He had spoken to Kaczynski several times about property boundaries, and he knew the "hermit of Baldy Mountain" was very keen to protect his interests and his property. Burns told Max that he could introduce the team as surveyors who wanted a look at Kaczynski's land. The objective would be to disguise as long as possible that the men who'd come to visit were federal law enforcement officers, and their own safety was at risk if they were discovered before Kaczynski was out of the cabin.

The team started down the road, away from the Gehring sawmill. Their boots crunched in the remaining snow. They didn't say much, and during their quarter mile trek the air seemed to grow increasingly still. Just minutes later, they came to the long slope that marked the way to the property. At its bottom stood the silent cabin. They glanced at each other and started down the slope. When they neared the clearing, Jerry Burns, lanky in his green uniform and wearing a cowboy hat, called a greeting to the cabin door a few yards away.

"Ted! There's some survey guys here who need to look at your property."

No response.

They walked slowly towards the door, and Burns called again.

"Ted! They're just here to look at the land!"

The door to the cabin opened halfway. A lean, shaggy-haired figure with skin darkened by smoke from his wood stove poked his head out to peer at them. Burns walked up to the door and asked Kaczynski to come outside. His hair was so coated with soot that it stood out from his head as he cocked it to look at Burns.

"I need to get my coat," Kaczynski muttered.

He started to turn away and the door began to close behind him. They couldn't let this happen. If Kaczynski really was the Unabomber, he might have a bomb ready to detonate inside the cabin in the event he was cornered. Burns reached with both hands into the doorway and grabbed Kaczynski, pulling him out of the cabin with such force that the two men tumbled to the ground. Kaczynski began to struggle, and Max pulled his .9mm pistol and trained it on the suspect, shouting at him to halt. Tom McDaniel took a big step forward. He bent down, encircled both Burns and Kaczynski with his long arms, and the struggle subsided.

As Kaczynski was handcuffed, the team began to breathe more easily. He walked without comment between them to a nearby cabin, where they sat him down and silently laid out in front of him several items tying him to the UNABOM crimes. They hoped for some response or acknowledgment: a glance of curiosity or anything else that might signal his willingness to talk to them. He said nothing. He showed no reaction. When they asked him directly whether he wanted to talk to them, however, his response was clear.

"I'll talk about anything except the case," he said.

Max began chatting with him about how he had lived in the woods. Outside the temperature began to drop, and ATF Agent Mike Grady worked nervously to start a fire in the cabin fireplace. After multiple attempts produced nothing but a trail of smoke that rose and curled in the room, Kaczynski looked at Grady and politely recommended that he open the flue.

Max held out a copy of the search warrant affidavit and told him that the FBI was authorized to search his cabin. He then asked a slow, careful question.

"Is there anything in the cabin that could harm anyone?"

"No," Kaczynski said in a calm voice, looking directly at Max. "Am I under arrest?"

Max told him he was being detained until we determined the situation in the cabin.

"Can I see the search warrant?"

· Max held it up to him, and Kaczynski scanned it rapidly. He looked back up at Max.

"I want to talk to him, this agent," he said. "Terry Turchie."

"Maybe later," said Max.

Meanwhile, a large-scale search operation had begun under Freeman's and my direction. The select members from the San Francisco FBI SWAT team, who had spent long hours in the snowy woods before Kaczynski's door was open, emerged from their posts. They'd been prepared to intercept any attempt by the Unabomber to escape through the trails over the Continental Divide that could have led him over the Canadian border.

Jim and I oversaw the entry of U.S. Army ordnance experts to check the grounds outside of the cabin and throughout his property for hidden explosives and booby traps. They moved in on the cabin and the root cellar as the Evidence Response Teams stood by. Everything had to be done in phases, slowly, deliberately, and with exquisite caution. Evidence had to be preserved, and the search teams had to be protected. Even though our Lone Wolf had been captured, his lair remained incredibly dangerous.

At the same time, we knew it was only a matter of time before we were deluged by the media. In the UTF command post at the Seven-up Ranch, televisions were blaring and a rapid series of phone calls were already coming in. Soon we saw the familiar features of FBI Media Representative, Rick Smith, who announced to the world from San Francisco that the infamous Unabomber was in custody. The news rocketed around the globe, since the case had become a source of fascination for an international audience as its drama and mystery had grown over the years.

We had guarded our secrecy as closely as we could before serving the search warrant. Agonizingly for David, his wife, Linda, and for David's mother, Wanda, we'd been unable to risk letting them know in advance. Now the media descended like a tornado on the Kaczynski home in Schenectady.

Still in San Francisco, Kathy, finally given the okay to notify David, made an urgent call to upstate New York. While she tried to persuade him not to turn on the television, it became obvious it was too late. In wild grief and anger, David cursed and hung up on her.

As the media barrage intensified, television and radio reporters and talk show hosts joined print journalists outside David and Linda's home in Schenectady. It was soon apparent there had been a leak in the investigation, and David's cooperation with the FBI, which had always been to ensure his brother's safety while protecting the lives of others, was now known to the media. The media didn't see it that way, and that's not how they portrayed it. A radio disk jockey from New York set up a microphone on the lawn and screamed to his audience and anyone within hearing distance that the Unabomber's brother had turned him in to the FBI.

Molly drove up from Washington to Schenectady, determined to try to help the family. David and Linda were huddled with a bewildered Wanda, barricaded in their home, when they heard a knock on their back door. It was Molly, and they let her in. She'd spoken to Kathy, and she knew what had happened. When she started to apologize on behalf of all of us, words failed her and she burst into tears. Incredibly, all three went to hug and console her. She later told us that, to avoid the media, she had crept through neighborhood backyards to get to their back door. Now she composed herself, and told the family we'd been unable to contact them before the search warrant was served. She assured them that Theodore Kaczynski was safe and no one else had been harmed. Concerning the leak about David's involvement with us, there was nothing she could say. In the end, we'd been unable to control the desire of someone in the Department of Justice to enhance their own feelings of importance by feeding a juicy morsel to the press.

∞ ∞ ∞

Jim and I drove past the mailbox with the name "T Kaczynski" on Stemple Pass Road. We took the dirt road that led past Butch Gehring's house and sawmill, and stopped where the dirt turned to impassable mud and rock. Max walked up to us from the cabin where Kaczynski sat in handcuffs. We all shook hands, congratulated each other on a safe operation thus far, and then Max shook his head while he told us about his conversation with Kaczynski.

"He wants a copy of the search warrant affidavit. And he wants to talk to you, Terry."

"Thanks for the warning," I smiled.

Max had spent the whole day without his standard fuel of coffee and espresso, but he was more amped up than I had ever seen him. The adrenaline in his system would keep him awake for days.

He led us down the steep and muddy path to the seasonal cabin that had become our makeshift detention center. When we rounded the corner and came through the door, we came face to face with the former Berkeley math professor turned Lone Wolf who'd eluded justice for so many years.

His hands were cuffed behind him. His clothes were grimy and tattered. The material of his trousers, literally rotting away, hung from his legs in shreds. He looked from me to Jim with apparent calm as Max rather formally introduced us.

"Theodore Kaczynski, this is Jim Freeman, Special Agent in Charge of the FBI in San Francisco. And this is Terry Turchie, the agent in charge of the UNABOM Task Force."

Jim and I nodded in acknowledgment. A copy of the warrant rested on Kaczynski's lap.

"Are you the Agent Turchie mentioned in the search warrant?"

"I am," I said.

"Would it be possible to get a copy of the statement of probable cause that supports the search warrant affidavit?"

He sounded like a seasoned defense attorney. I smiled mildly at him.

"Not now. A copy will be provided to you and your attorney at a later and more appropriate time."

"Thank you," he said.

He averted his eyes and seemed to withdraw into a private space. I was amazed by his composure, especially since I knew he had been taken by complete surprise. Agent Don Sachtleben, an experienced bomb technician who worked for Pat Webb's Bomb Squad in San Francisco, had glanced briefly inside the cabin after the Army bomb techs declared it clear. Don had seen in one glance that the cabin was a bomb factory. Actual confirmation was left to the old master. I walked with Pat to the door, where we stood while he made a long, searching appraisal of the small room and its contents. As we backed away, careful not to contaminate the scene, the seasoned and normally sarcastic Webb blinked rapidly, as if he couldn't quite believe it. Then he looked at me, and I saw tears streaming down his face.

"It's him," he said, a slight quaver in his voice. "It's the Unabomber."

That's what we'd been waiting for. Based on the solid expertise and long experience of both Webb and Sachtleben, Jim and I told Max to advise Kaczynski of his rights and transport him to the Helena jail.

∞ ∞ ∞

Getting the Unabomber safely out of his cabin was just the prelude to the critical next chapter in the case. There was no time to celebrate; the job was far from over. Reporters flocked to the scene as bright yellow evidence tape was strung in front of the road that led to Butch Gehring's property. The quiet piece of land that sheltered Theodore Kaczynski's anonymity for so many years was now a crime scene. The UTF mission now was to locate, identify, and remove everything in the area related to the UNABOM crimes.

U.S. Army explosives experts scoured the property for buried explosives, booby traps, and other concealed dangers Kaczynski might have left behind in the event he was ever taken. The tactical teams turned their attention to securing the area from intruders.

San Francisco's Evidence Response Team sprang into action. Shuttling supplies from a landing near Gehring's sawmill, they made dozens of trips in an All-Terrain Vehicle moving hundreds of clear plastic envelopes, lined writing pads, pens, pencils, magic markers, evidence tape, exhibit envelopes, and a vast assortment of evidence containers to the Forward Command Post. Waterproof tarps were positioned to protect the scene from rain and snow.

Closer to the cabin, the lines of evidence tape marked a narrow access route to the cabin door, where agent Jay Colvin was the gatekeeper. San Francisco had one of the first full Evidence Response Teams in the FBI, and they trained law enforcement officers around the world. Now they conducted one of the most methodical and significant searches in FBI history. For the next two weeks, they moved carefully in and out of the cabin like a line of ants, logging their evidence in with Colvin and returning for more.

UNABOM devices were our most immediate concern, but there were other dangers. Mountain roads coated with unevenly melting ice and snow sent agent Rob Dugay's SUV over a cliff, but he crawled out unscathed. A team of agents watching over the perimeter was surprised one morning by a mountain lion that stood between them and their car, curiously observing them and then disappearing into the woods. Pat Webb, already plagued by a chronic back problem, slipped on the ice and needed to be airlifted from the forest floor to a Helena hospital.

But the gravest threat was a live bomb. We'd been prepared for this, and on the second full day of the search, our preparations were put to the test. Wrapped in shiny aluminum foil and stashed underneath Kaczynski's bed was an explosive device ready to wrap for the mail. The search came to an immediate halt. Legions of agents with assignments that took them close to the cabin were moved out of the area. Sandia National Laboratory in New Mexico had designed and built the bomb disrupter for just such an event, and the word went out to the U.S. military to transport the disrupter to Montana.

Don Sachtleben began coordinating the removal of the bomb from the cabin. The device was gently drawn from underneath the bed. Robotic arm extensions carefully placed it into a container. The container was transferred to a small caterpillar, and Sachtleben began the slow journey down the dirt logging road with the explosive package. Watching from a distance, we were sweatier than Don. It took an hour to move a few feet. Sachtleben drove the delicate cargo to the machine made especially for UNABOM called the Pan Disrupter. It was staged in an open field about a quarter of a mile from Kaczynski's cabin.

Like an astronaut docking the shuttle with the NASA space station, Sachtleben steered the tractor until it delicately engaged the Pan Disrupter. After he off-loaded the bomb, the machine quickly went about its mission. X-rays of the package confirmed it was a live device, and photographs were taken as evidence. Then, as we all held our breaths, a small detonation disarmed the bomb for good.

When the FBI Lab ultimately opened the package, the bomb's working parts were removed. Inside was a fully assembled switch identical in every way to another switch found inside Kaczynski's cabin. These two switches were identical to switches found in debris at earlier UNABOM crime scenes. Forensics didn't lead us to Kaczynski's cabin door, but forensics and careful advance planning sealed his fate.

∞ ∞ ∞

Max sat with Kaczynski in the back of an SUV, while Wilhelmus and McDaniel rode in front. Jim and I followed in our own four-wheel drive. We'd been wise to put analyst Lee Hayden in charge of logistical support in Montana. Besides handling all hotel and flight arrangements for the agents and analysts who were streaming into Helena, he'd rented every available four-wheel vehicle in western Montana for us. Traveling the rutted dirt roads studded with ice on the way to the cabin required special equipment, and for the time being every SUV in our hands was unavailable to the media. Reporters and crews from all over the country and some from overseas were lining up at car rental counters at the airport. It bought us a little more time to secure the scene, and we needed every minute of it.

As we crossed the Continental Divide and started the long descent towards Helena, the mobile phone buzzed in our car. Jim answered, and an excited voice on the other end said the Director wanted to talk to us. "Justice is telling the Director we have no grounds yet to arrest Kaczynski," said the voice. "They say we never consulted with them to see if there's probable cause. He wants you to get a Material Witness warrant to hold onto him until we figure out what to do."

Just as Louis himself came on the line, the phone connection evaporated. Jim and I looked at each other, then shrugged. We had the Unabomber, in the car in front of us, in the company of three veteran federal agents. We'd take that as a win, for now.

By the time we got to Helena, however, phones were ringing off the hook. Jim's face was increasingly grim as he talked to the Director. DOJ and the FBI Lab were not persuaded that we'd had any legal basis for placing Kaczynski in custody and removing him from the vicinity of his cabin. I was on another line with Bernie Hubley, who'd sat in Judge Lovell's courtroom with me that morning. After I'd given him a rundown on the problem, he said in an urgent tone, "Get Freeman off the phone and meet me in my office right away."

I passed Jim a note, whispered loudly, and finally resorted to making gruesome faces at him before I got him to hang up. He started to discuss the call, but I rushed him over to Bernie's office instead. Max and Paul had Kaczynski in another room, and were plying him with milk and Snickers bars. They'd been with him since noon, and it was now close to 9 p.m.

Tom Mohnal had arrived in Helena, and came at once to Hubley's office. Don Satchleben had driven over from Lincoln. Bernie, Jim, and I rounded out the group. We went over the facts, and Bernie questioned Satchleben hard. He decided there was ample information based on Satchleben's experience and observations that we could hold Kaczynski and indict him for possessing bomb-making paraphernalia.

I called Howard Shapiro, who was working in the Strategic Operations Center at FBIHQ. It was past midnight in Washington, D.C. Howard told me what the problem was. The same DOJ attorney who was assigned to the case after Jamie Gorelick's memo was telling everyone in Washington, including Director Freeh, that the UTF had no probable cause to arrest Kaczynski. Someone in the FBI Lab, who obviously didn't have the facts, was making the same argument.

I carefully went through each fact with Shapiro, and gave him the detail Bernie was getting from Sachtleben. Howard listened without interruption, and then put our dilemma to bed.

"It's obvious that Louis and I were given bad information. I'll let him know you've got probable cause for the arrest. Go ahead, Terry."

And Kaczynski went to jail.

Twenty-five months later, after weeks of pretrial hearings in Sacramento that constituted legal combat between Kaczynski's defense counsel and Bob Cleary's UNABOM prosecution team, Theodore John Kaczynski pled guilty to 13 bombing offenses. He also acknowledged that he was responsible for 16 bombings that occurred between May 25, 1978, and April 24, 1995.

∞ ∞ ∞

Kaczynski was born and raised in Chicago. He traveled to Salt Lake City from Montana by bus to place or mail four of his bombs. For two and half years he taught mathematics at the University of California at Berkeley, just yards from Cory Hall, the site of two of his bombings. He took a course called History of Science in his freshman year at Harvard University, a course of the same name and discipline referenced in the letter the Unabomber sent to Professor James McConnell at the University of Michigan in 1985. Kaczynski earned his Ph.D. in mathematics from that same university.

Since the early 1970s, Theodore Kaczynski had used various forums to rail about the dangers technology posed to society. He talked about it, and he wrote about it. The UNABOM manuscript was the culmination of his lifelong work and beliefs.

And he was angry. We found over 30,000 pages of his writings in his Montana cabin, along with the bomb he'd been ready to mail. Among his writings were these prophetic words:

> Since committing these crimes reported elsewhere in my notes I feel better. I am still plenty angry, you understand, but the difference is that I am now able to strike back, to a degree . . . My first thought was to kill somebody I hated and then kill myself before the cops could get me. (I've always considered death preferable to life imprisonment.)

Forensic Psychiatrist, Sally Johnson, who Judge Garland appointed to examine Kaczynski's mental state for competency, diagnosed him as having long suffered from paranoid schizophrenia. Furious at this finding, Kaczynski tried to fire his attorneys and refused to accept a diagnosis of mental illness as the cause of his career as the Unabomber. He pled guilty to avoid being characterized as " a sickie," during the trial.

On May 4, 1998, Theodore Kaczynski was sentenced to spend the rest of his life, without the possibility of parole, at the Federal Super-Max Penitentiary at Florence, Colorado.

I wasn't at the hearing when he was sentenced. I was in the mountains of western North Carolina leading the fugitive hunt for America's newest Lone Wolf serial bomber: Eric Robert Rudolph.

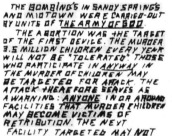

Rudolph Fugitive Task Force Headquarters Andrews, North Carolina, 1998: timeline and mock-up of supplies Rudolph took with him into the Nantahala Forest.

Army of God letter written by Eric Robert Rudolph.

14

THE NEXT AMERICAN TERRORIST

During my clerical years in Washington, D.C., I earned a Master's Degree in Public Administration. Compared to UNABOM, that was like a weekend seminar.

After years of fruitless efforts by law enforcement all over the country to catch the Unabomber, we wrote a new playbook. Our two years of intensive and innovative investigation, critically augmented with an ongoing psychological collaboration, had led to a bloodless arrest and a guilty plea from the most notorious domestic terrorist in U.S. history. Director Freeh issued a statement after Kaczynski's arrest, calling our work "the most complex investigation ever conducted by federal law enforcement."

I knew the Director was pleased with my work. I was happy about it, too. I'd learned a tremendous amount, and Kathy and I had begun to develop an integrative way of combining effective management and leadership with ongoing behavioral analysis. I didn't realize that I would need to immediately apply the lessons I'd learned in UNABOM to the hunt for the next Lone Wolf.

In 1996, America hosted the Summer Olympics in Atlanta, Georgia. One balmy night, a massive explosion ripped through the crowd of partygoers in Centennial Olympic Park. A deadly bomb concealed in a military Alice Pack had detonated beneath a park bench.

Security was tight at the Atlanta games, except in one area. There were no backpack searches or metal detectors in Centennial Park. Olympics organizers had overruled law enforcement advice, and wanted to provide one venue of free access for the public to celebrate that summer.

A new Lone Wolf found this useful. His bomb was made from three metal pipes filled with smokeless powder, capped with end plugs and 8d masonry nails for shrapnel. A Big Ben alarm clock and 12 volt battery provided the timing and ignition system.

Before the blast, the Atlanta Police Department received an anonymous call.

"There is a bomb in Centennial Park," said a garbled voice. "You have ten minutes."

Letters from the "Army of God" claimed credit for the bombing in letters to the news media. Over the next year and a half, three bombings followed.

An abortion clinic in Atlanta was attacked in January 1997. The bomb contained 24 sticks of dynamite, 4d flooring nails, and twisted iron wire. It was built on steel plates inside metal ammo cans, using a Baby Ben alarm clock and D-cell batteries for the ignition and timing systems.

In February 1997, a bomb was placed at a gay nightclub in Atlanta. When emergency personnel and law enforcement responded to the scene, a second device detonated. It was clearly meant to kill and maim the first responders. More letters from the Army of God claimed credit for the blasts.

On January 30, 1998, off-duty police officer Robert "Sandy" Sanderson was on security duty at a Birmingham abortion clinic when he leaned over a device triggered by remote control from a stealthy figure watching him only yards away. Officer Sanderson was killed instantly.

People from all over the area ran towards the blast. In the tumult, a young student at the University of Alabama saw a curious sight. While a steady stream of people ran to the scene, one man walked calmly away from it. The student decided to follow him and was able to jot down the license number of a pickup truck with out-of-state license plates as it sped from the scene. The truck was registered to Eric Robert Rudolph of Topton, North Carolina.

The identification of Eric Rudolph sparked one of the most intensive fugitive searches in the history of the United States. Several days after the Birmingham bombing, he was traced to a mobile home on Cane Creek Road in Murphy, North Carolina. When Federal agents converged on the scene, the screen door of the trailer swung open in the cold wind. Another Lone Wolf had vanished into the wilderness.

With Theodore Kaczynski on his way to the Supermax in Colorado, I had been ready to leave Sacramento and return to San Francisco. So much for making plans. One morning in early March, my wife read an article in the local newspaper to me. I was being sent to Atlanta to coordinate the multi-jurisdictional fugitive search for Eric Rudolph, and Director Freeh had promoted me to Inspector. The FBI Director also sent his trusted assistant, John Behnke, to Atlanta, to coordinate the massive investigation into all of the bombings.

As encouraging as it was to have an identified suspect, the FBI was already under assault for its handling of the earlier Centennial Park bombing. Leaks to the news media had identified a security guard at the Olympics as a possible suspect. FBI executives, buoyed by support from the profilers at Quantico, had zeroed in on Richard Jewell.

During the summer of 1996, as Kathy and I were preparing to move to Sacramento with the UNABOM prosecution team, Fitz had called from Quantico about the Olympic Park bombing.

"They think they have their man," he said. "He fits the profile."

We were concerned at this news, and it turned out our concerns were justified. Richard Jewell had nothing to do with the Olympic Park bombing. Director Freeh himself had taken the Congressional rap for the decision to treat Jewell as the primary suspect.

Two years of public criticism and bitterness with the Jewell affair spilled over into the early days of the bombing in Birmingham. The U.S. Attorney in Alabama didn't want to concede any authority to his counterparts in Atlanta on the Southeast Bomb Task Force. The FBI in Atlanta was convinced that Rudolph was the serial offender responsible for all four attacks. The FBI in Birmingham was certain that Eric Rudolph was responsible for the cold-blooded killing of Officer Sanderson. They were unconvinced he was responsible for the Atlanta bombings and didn't want their case polluted by the goings-on in Georgia. The FBI in Charlotte was keeping a wary eye on the Federal agents streaming into western North Carolina, along with armed law enforcement officers from the Georgia State Bureau of Investigation. It was tense, to say the least.

One of nature's prevailing themes in law enforcement is that an action by the FBI in a bombing case will trigger an equal and immediate reaction from the ATF.

When I arrived in the area, Don Bell, an Assistant SAC from the ATF's Charlotte Division, greeted me. An affable southern gentleman, Bell had been sent to western North Carolina by his boss, my good friend from his days with the UTF in San Francisco, Mark Logan. Logan must have known that Don would be a perfect complement to my own personality and skill level.

Don knew the South, and he understood the people who lived in Murphy, Topton, and Andrews, the small mountain towns that Rudolph called home. He knew his ATF agents from Asheville, only an hour's drive away, and had good relationships with the local law enforcement agencies in the area. He even knew how to use a laptop computer that he carried with him everywhere he went. We were allies from the start.

"We need a new strategy and a different organizational structure," I told him. "The first thing we have to do is bring some consistency to this fugitive hunt."

I thought of the early days of UNABOM during the first assessment Don and I made of the situation.

Agents were rotating in and out every five days. No records were being maintained of leads being covered, and there was no ongoing analysis of interviews of people in the community. If there was a pattern to the information they were developing, there was no way we were in a position to detect it.

The fugitive search was being run from a nearby National Guard Armory, located at the opening to a large meadow and with mountains on either side of the road. Agents circulating in and out of the place were sitting ducks for ambush by a Lone Wolf who had already killed one policeman. We needed better security and better office space at the outset.

"Okay," Don said. "You dictate the strategy, and I'll type it out on the computer." He looked wryly at me.

"But make it fast, I'm hungry."

I wondered aloud how I could be so lucky. Don was an expert laptop jockey, as well as someone who appreciated three square (large) meals every day, with dessert. We saw just about everything through the same lens, and we trusted each other implicitly.

On April 1, 1998, in a small conference room at the Country Hearth Inn in Andrews, we laid out our plans to 18 FBI, ATF, and Georgia State Bureau of Investigation (GBI) agents who had either volunteered or been volunteered by their agency to serve for 90 uninterrupted days in the Nantahala outback. Don and I had decided that 500,000 acres of National Forest land would become the primary search area in our fugitive hunt for Eric Rudolph.

Getting to this point hadn't been easy. ATF Headquarters in Washington, D.C., had balked at Don's request for 90-day assignments for the ATF agents. His response to his Headquarters was masterful.

"Okay," he told them, "If we don't fill the slots, the FBI will be happy to send an additional six of their guys to help."

The ATF agents came for 90 days.

We divided the group into nine teams of two agents each, regardless of the agency they came from. We selected FBI Supervisor Bill Lewis from Atlanta and ATF Supervisor C. J. Hyman from Asheville to jointly supervise the investigators. Don and I included Charles Stone and others from the GBI alongside the teams.

We solidified as a team that morning, dismissing the conflict that swirled between our agencies in other jurisdictions and focusing our attention on Eric Robert Rudolph. Our strategy was simple, and it was also something I'd learned during the hunt for the Unabomber. The teams would be assigned to geographical areas surrounding the perimeter of the massive forest, conduct hundreds of interviews, and carry out hundreds of additional contacts so that the locals could get to know the Federal agents and put a face with a name. They would track the fugitive, while simultaneously developing evidence to connect him to the bombings in Atlanta and Birmingham.

Joel Moss joined the fugitive search in mid-May. I had been trying to convince the new San Francisco SAC to allow Joel to work on the Rudolph case from the first day I arrived on the scene. John Behnke and I finally made a private appeal to Director Freeh, and Joel was on the next flight out.

He began work on a variety of projects. His supervisory status gave him the stature to assist Lewis and Hyman. At the same time, it allowed him to navigate through the FBI bureaucracy to get the additional personnel and resources necessary to further the fugitive hunt. Joel helped Don and me anchor the fugitive search with an analytical team, as we had in UNABOM. We transferred several data loaders and analysts into Andrews, where they began a massive effort to put all fugitive lead results into the Bureau's Rapid Start database. We sorted the information into priority categories, and we established a UTF-style list of fact, fiction, and theory related to Eric Rudolph and the fugitive search.

We now had an investigative strategy customized to the area, an implementation plan centered on the fugitive's own habits and haunts, and an unorthodox organizational structure that provided the flexibility we needed to deal with any situation. Our search for our new Lone Wolf went from zero to sixty in days. But there was one more issue we hadn't yet addressed.

When we arrived in Murphy, C. J. took Don and me to meet Cherokee County Sheriff Jack Thompson. A colorful lawman who knew every square inch of his county, Thompson didn't stand on ceremony.

"A police officer was killed in Alabama. All you Feds come storming into Cherokee County looking for Rudolph, and no one ever comes to tell the police or the Sheriff's office what's going on. We know this place. We could help, but now everyone's really upset. It's like you don't trust us."

He was right. Don and I looked at each other knowing he was reflecting what every law enforcement officer in the area felt. I decided to plead guilty.

"We made a mistake. Help us undo it. We'd like any Sheriff's office or police department that wants to be represented on the fugitive hunt to join us."

The Sheriff gave me a wary look. His tone changed.

"Well, everybody makes mistakes. I accept what you said, I don't know about how others might feel. And then there's the matter of money: how would we pay to put an officer on the task force?"

"We'll pay for it, Sheriff. There's money for that."

After that, Sheriff Thompson and Larry Payne, the Murphy Police Chief, hosted a meeting at the county courthouse. Sheriffs and police chiefs from the surrounding jurisdictions showed up. Don and I made our pitch to them, and Charles Stone showed them mock-ups of Rudolph's bombs, describing how they worked. We revealed sensitive details of the investigation and asked that they consider being equal partners in the search. Within weeks, in one form or another, two dozen agencies formed the core of the search for Eric Rudolph. During the entire year I spent in North Carolina, none of the information we shared with all of the other Federal, State, and local agencies was ever leaked to anyone. They never violated our trust.

The strategy paid off immediately. A local resident was able to place Rudolph in Atlanta during one of the bombings. Agent Jim Eckel from the Atlanta FBI struck up a friendship with Rudolph's former sister-in-law, who spoke freely about statements Rudolph had made in the past. She told Eckel that if Rudolph were ever pursued, he'd use the north-to-south Appalachian Trail and the east-to-west Barton Trail to stay ahead of his hunters and hide out in the woods until they tired.

On one of his solitary sojourns, Rudolph had disappeared for over two weeks into the forest. He told no one where he had been. ATF Agent Steve Gillis researched historical U.S. Geological Survey records and developed the "cave and mine" initiative. Gillis spearheaded searches in hundreds of locations spread out over the Nantahala Forest. An FBI data loader from Savannah, Warren Thompson, implemented a massive Rapid Start effort, spending long hours and often seven days a week collecting, updating, and retrieving information to be analyzed.

Don and I held morning strategy meetings over coffee and pastries at the Bradley Inn, a bed and breakfast behind our command post. It was owned and managed by Jo and John Paul Jones, who moved from Atlanta to help bring life and commerce to the charming little town of Andrews. The Bradley played a pivotal role in our ability to deal with the stress and strain of long days and changing seasons with no sign of Rudolph. When Director Freeh flew into Andrews for a one-day briefing, Jo Jones hosted a lunch in the quaint dining room of her upstairs residence. The Director signed her guest book, "Louis Freeh, New York," then walked outside and told a horde of press he had no doubt the search was properly concentrated in the mountains. When ATF Director John McGaw followed Freeh, he was hosted to a similar lunch and then promptly told the waiting media that he thought Rudolph was dead.

As the Fourth of July neared, Don and I made plans to use FBI and ATF SWAT teams to start from Murphy, where Rudolph's truck had been found, and Topton, where he had grown up, and hike through the forest until they met in the middle. The distance was about 20 miles, as the crow flies. By taking the same routes that Rudolph had to take, we hoped to generate leads as to his whereabouts and more ideas about how to find him. But we ran out of time. A week before the forest search started, Rudolph emerged at the house of a family friend, hidden down a long driveway from the main road and concealed by the hills that surrounded it.

Rudolph asked the friend, who owned a health food store in Andrews, to give him food and a truck, so he could transport the supplies to a mountain hideaway. The man refused, and then spent several days thinking about what to do. Meanwhile, Rudolph returned to the man's house and took food, supplies, and an old pickup before disappearing once again into the forest. The store owner called Kenny Cope, a local deputy who was working with the fugitive task force. Cope contacted the ATF agent assigned to the area, who promptly found me in my office in Andrews. Don had returned to Charlotte for the weekend to visit his family, so I headed out with the agent to meet with the store owner and Cope.

George Lynch, a U.S. Forest Service law enforcement officer, found the abandoned pickup truck at a campground a few miles from the store owner's house. Lynch had the reputation as one of the best trackers in the forest service, and his persistence delivered the prize. Less than 48 hours later, every hotel, motel, inn, and bed and breakfast along a 20-mile stretch of U.S. Highways 19 and 74 was filled with SWAT teams, additional investigators, and reporters from network news affiliates. Appletree Campground near Topton became the forward base for the swelling fugitive task force. Tents, generators, and helicopter launch pads appeared overnight. Trailers housing hunting, cadaver, and explosive-sniffing dogs staked out parking spaces near the creek. Duke Blackburn, commander of the Georgia Department of Corrections, took responsibility for perimeter security of the campsite, and brought his dogs and highly disciplined officers to the job.

The fugitive hunt had begun to look like a military exercise, but Don and I were determined to keep control of it. Our small force of 20 hunters had turned into a well-armed camp of 200 tactical agents, including the FBI's vaunted Hostage Rescue Team and the ATF's comparable National Response Team.

Because things were going so well, I almost forgot about the UNABOM lessons I'd learned in dealing with diehard traditionalists in the FBI. I soon needed to review them.

I had selected ATF Supervisor C. J. Hyman to coordinate all of the tactical strategy. Each morning at 6:00, he briefed patrols before they set out in search of Rudolph. At night, C. J., Don, and I evaluated what we'd learned and discussed priorities for the next morning.

FBI Headquarters made it clear that it was unacceptable in their view for an ATF supervisor to give directions to FBI SWAT teams, directly or otherwise. In a separate phone call, they told me they were going to send more SACs to North Carolina to help me, just like they'd done at Waco and Ruby Ridge.

I cringed inwardly at the comparison with those events, and I certainly didn't need a lot of team owners instead of players. I looked to Freeh for support, and he intervened. C. J. stayed in the job, and I didn't have to carry bags for a stream of SACs from around the country.

Other Bureau officials pressed us to arrange a polygraph of the healthfood store owner, whom Joel had been interviewing and building a relationship with for weeks. They were convinced he'd been harboring Rudolph. We disagreed. Giving this witness a polygraph would send a bad message to the small community: "Come forward with information, and we will arrest you." It wouldn't help us. The Director backed me up, and the polygraph wasn't administered until Rudolph's defense team insisted on it years later. He passed it with flying colors.

Last known address of Eric Robert Rudolph on Cane Creek Road, Murphy, North Carolina.

Campsite for the hunters of fugitive Eric Rudolph, 1998.

15

THE ANDREWS CAMPAIGN

We had several potentially explosive episodes during our time in Andrews. The touchiest of these involved the controversial former Army Special Forces officer Bo Gritz and Randy Weaver, the survivalist and white separatist whose wife and son were killed during the deadly siege at his property in Ruby Ridge, Idaho, that also claimed the life of a U.S. Marshall in 1992.

GBI's Charles Stone had run into Gritz at a convention in Atlanta, and asked his thoughts about Rudolph. Gritz's response was to rally his followers and show up in Andrews with Weaver to deal with the locals and find Rudolph before we did. A small army of searchers accompanied them.

FBI Headquarters made it clear that the FBI should stay away from Gritz. But how could we avoid a potential tragedy by ignoring it?

Charles and I waited in the lobby of the hotel for Gritz to pick us up and drive to his compound. Three cars buzzed into the drive-thru: a lead car, an SUV carrying Gritz and his driver, and a chase car. Charles and I jumped into the middle car, and it sped away without slowing down. Gritz sat in the passenger front seat and turned around to extend his hand. He operated like the military leader he considered himself to be, and he made it clear he was in charge of his followers. Charles exchanged pleasantries in his Georgia good-ole-boy manner and lessened the electrical charge in the atmosphere between us.

"Colonel Gritz, this is Terry Turchie, the FBI commander here on scene I told you about."

"Good to meet you. Thanks for seeing us today," Gritz said.

He seemed to be satisfied with our interaction thus far, and I almost relaxed a little during the short ride to his parking lot command post near a hospital in Andrews.

The place was abuzz with men dressed in blue jeans or military fatigues huddled in small groups and drinking coffee. A variety of pickup trucks and SUVs with out-of-state license plates were parked throughout the area in no particular order. As our caravan appeared, they stopped their chat and watched as we pulled up to an older trailer that had been towed into place overnight.

Gritz climbed quickly out of the car and led us into the trailer.

"We'll be using this as our Command Post for the search," he said as we got seated inside.

Before I'd left for the meeting, I'd been deliberately sketchy with FBI Headquarters about the details. All I knew for certain was that Gritz was in town, and he was accompanied by dozens of unknown militia types, so it was vital that I met with him in a calm and reasoned manner. To do anything less was asking for trouble.

As Gritz spread open a detailed map of the area on top of a small desk, into the trailer walked Randy Weaver. We shook hands, and Weaver introduced his own entourage of two younger men. Then all of us sat down and turned our attention to Bo Gritz.

"We have information from our Intelligence Unit that Rudolph is hiding out here."

He pointed to an area of the Nantahala Forest that we had searched several times during the first month and found nothing.

"Our plan is to interview our sources of information again and to dispatch a number of men, led by me, to this location and wait for him to hook up with us. Once that happens we'll assure him that he will be safe and then lead him out of the forest to a waiting attorney. What we need is for you, Terry, to assign an agent to our patrols so that we have seamless communications all around. That way, you and I can be sure that there'll be no mishaps."

Gritz stopped and looked at all of us, then focused his attention on me. I felt a strange sense of relief as I watched Weaver nod in agreement. It seemed that no one in the room wanted another tragedy like Ruby Ridge or Waco. I cleared my throat to speak.

"Colonel Gritz, I can't place FBI or ATF agents with your patrols. There are a hundred reasons why that's not going to work for us. What I can do is tell you I have no problem with you searching the area you're pointing at. I'll make sure that none of our patrols are there at the same time. Each day, we need to communicate with each other about where you're going to be so we can continue to steer clear of one another. Charles Stone from GBI will be your point of contact. I understand what you're trying to do. I also think you're well aware of what we have to do if we find Eric Rudolph. So, with that said, let's try to make this work and not bring any new problems to these beautiful mountains."

Gritz moved to his feet, and Weaver did the same. They seemed to be going out of their way to appear non-threatening.

"Deal," said Gritz. "Nice meeting you. Thanks for coming."

We all shook hands, and Charles and I were driven back to our hotel. Several days later, a local newspaper reporter called me.

"Bo Gritz and his guys have set up camp at a vacant campground near the Bob Allison campground, where Rudolph disappeared. He's put up armed guards and he's told local residents they aren't allowed to enter. He said you approved it. Did the FBI approve Gritz to take over a public campground?"

I laughed out loud.

"What do you think the answer is? And while you're thinking about it, you can also tell Colonel Gritz he knows better."

"Still, what are you going to do about it?"

"Not a damn thing. Why don't you talk to the local Sheriff."

Bo Gritz, Randy Weaver, and their ardent supporters left the western North Carolina mountains seven days after they arrived and never returned. Rudolph and the fugitive task force continued their game of cat and mouse.

∞ ∞ ∞

July in North Carolina is stifling. The daytime searches started early and ended by mid afternoon before the heat of the summer sun scorched the earth and the searchers. But we were making progress. Atlanta residents with summer homes in the mountains called to report suspicious break-ins. Typically, a handful of books, medicine, food stuffs, socks, boots, and size 34 men's underwear were missing. At least two healthy dogs within a one-half mile Topton area radius died mysteriously. We had an autopsy performed on one of them; the cause of death was antifreeze poisoning. Rudolph had boasted about poisoning dogs with antifreeze.

A U.S. Army search expert visited with us and confirmed that an entire army could hide in the kudzu-covered forest, and we would miss it on the walk-over. Kathy traveled to Andrews with forensic psychiatrist Dr. Park Dietz, where they reviewed the results of our search. They told us they believed Rudolph was hiding out in the forest, where he felt comfortable, safe, and in control of the environment. We didn't have him, but we had him cornered, and I was conditioned by UNABOM to fight the long fight.

But by mid August, international terrorists had struck U.S. Embassies in Kenya and Tanzania, and the FBI was overwhelmed. Resources were diverted to assist in evidence collection on the African continent. The fugitive search in North Carolina competed for manpower and money to sustain the hunt. Before the rainy season, we relocated the task force from the Appletree Campground to an empty furniture warehouse in Andrews.

On November 11, Veteran's Day, eight rifle shots penetrated the walls and doors of the new command post. An agent inside the warehouse felt a puff of air as two rounds flew within an inch of his head. The shooters escaped, speeding down the road in their getaway car. Later that night, a beam of laser light was directed at a task force helicopter flying over the Andrews High School. A local militia leader picked up the man with the laser, and a SWAT team pursued them until they stopped in front of the police station on the main street of town.

FBI agents interviewed the two men until well after midnight as other militia types gathered outside, facing off the SWAT units. The night was hot, and it was getting hotter.

Don and I went to the police station and confronted the militia leader with the shooting at the task force command post. He denied any knowledge, claiming the laser light incident was not connected. He stuck to the story that he and his companion had nothing to do with any shooting.

After he calmed down himself, our militia leader agreed to quiet down his rowdy colleagues outside the station. He also agreed to give us a 306 rifle at his house, since the casings from the scene were 306 caliber.

Don and I told the SWAT team to stay at the station, and the militia leader told his friends not to follow us. Although their blood was up and they didn't think it was safe, SWAT did as they were instructed. The militia types weren't as disciplined.

Their leader lived down the street and around the corner from the police station. As our car came to a stop, he ran into the house before Don and I cleared the first step on the front porch. He slammed the screen door behind him and disappeared, yelling over his shoulder, "You guys can't come in here, remember!"

Don and I looked at each other. Maybe this hadn't been such a good idea after all. It was pitch black, almost 2:00 in the morning. The task force compound had been attacked hours earlier by unknown assailants. The militia was all over town and keyed up about the detention of their neighbor. And we'd told this militia leader that we trusted him. We'd agreed that he was telling the truth and wasn't involved in the shootings. It was all a big coincidence, and he and his friend had been in the wrong place at the wrong time. Now we stood alone on his front porch while we waited for him to bring us a 306 caliber rifle.

We weren't alone for long. Suddenly, from the darkened street came the sound of car doors slamming shut, and loud voices split the silent night air. From a hedge close to the property line, a rowdy figure jumped up from the side yard and onto the front porch, landing right where Don and I were standing. Threats started coming from every direction. We were surrounded by at least a dozen militia members.

"You Feds aren't welcome here,"

"Get your asses out of this town."

"Rudolph is innocent, but the government is killing babies."

"San Francisco is full of queers."

When I glanced at Don, he wanted to smile. He knew what I was thinking. Why did they always have to bring up San Francisco like that? Both of us tried to maintain a calm outward demeanor that gave no indication of our real alarm.

"You know why we're here. We're here to find Rudolph. When we find him, we'll leave."

The chorus continued, but the crowd seemed to become calmer as we waited and talked, even if we were in each other's faces the whole time. The rowdiest, mouthiest guy was a fellow they all referred to as Six Pack. He didn't get the nickname because he worked out. He wasn't even from North Carolina.

"We don't believe you Feds," he roared as he looked at his colleagues. "You can't be trusted."

I looked right at him.

"Our SWAT team stayed put. You didn't. We're standing here with a whole gang of you. We're the ones who are alone. How can you feel that we're a threat to you?"

Just then, the door swung open and our militia leader thrust a 306 rifle in our direction. Don grabbed it on the run, and we bade farewell to the assembled crowd, returning to the SWAT team waiting on Main Street.

"Jeez," said Don as he checked the magazine on the rifle. "I'm glad to be getting out of there. I think that's the dumbest thing I've ever done."

"Yeah," I said. "Well, it's been several hours since the shooting and things seem to be calming down. Maybe we aren't as dumb as we think we are." We looked at each other and laughed. We knew we'd been lucky.

Forty-eight hours later, one of the FBI agents assigned to the fugitive search reported that a family he had befriended in his geographical area of our "surround the forest" campaign had given him some information that might be helpful. On the night of the command post attack, they heard a car speed past their house. At the moment they looked out the window, they thought they saw someone toss a rifle out of the car.

We searched the weeds and brush in the area but never found a rifle. Using the witness description of the car, we came up with the names of several local rowdies who had criminal records and who had been in and out of jail for numerous offenses.

At first, the investigation into the assault on Federal officers was assigned to the Charlotte FBI office, but I eventually convinced Headquarters that it needed to be solved quickly, and that our task force member, John Behnke, would be a great choice to work it. Two years later, the group went to jail. The initial information provided by local citizens helped to make the case, along with the initiative John used to bring the case together. My old friend and ally from UNABOM had come through again.

∞ ∞ ∞

The shooting and the laser light incident caused more stress and strain between the task force and the Andrews community than at any time since the visit from Gritz and Weaver. We were helped through it all by a relationship we had developed months earlier with Pastor George Simmons of St. Andrew Lutheran Church. Pastor Simmons had invited Don and me to attend monthly meetings that all of the clergy held in his church basement. We saw it as a way to connect with the local population through the network of churches throughout the area. The idea was to avoid problems and build trust. When it turned out that the guy who'd wielded the laser was a member of one of the local congregations, they asked for our help in keeping him from going to prison for assaulting Federal agents. They assured us that he was normally a decent citizen. The local Assistant U.S. Attorney arranged for a pretrial diversion, and the matter was settled to everyone's satisfaction.

By March 1999, Joel and I had been in North Carolina for a full year. We asked Director Freeh to send us back to San Francisco. Don had returned to Charlotte and decided to retire from ATF. C. J. was transferred to ATF Headquarters in Washington, D.C. Bill Lewis took over the role of providing consistent leadership to the task force members who remained in Andrews.

The FBI's fugitive hunt continued, but at a reduced level. Meanwhile, in Kenya, Tanzania, and other overseas locations, the Bureau became more entrenched in the fight against al Quaeda and Osama Bin Laden. Four more years passed. But Eric Rudolph never placed another bomb and never killed or harmed anyone else.

In the summer of 2003, Rudolph was arrested by a young Murphy police officer. He had come out of the forest to scavenge for food at a dumpster behind a grocery store.

As we'd predicted, he had never left the area. He had never been harbored by a local citizen. His bombings had never been part of any conspiracy. He was a Lone Wolf driven deep into his woods by a fugitive search task force modeled on lessons learned when I'd run the last UNABOM Task Force.

On April 13, 2005, Eric Rudolph wrote:

> The next year (1998-1999) was a starving time. Hunted and haggard, I struggled to survive . . . After so many years ducking and hiding and eating crappy foods, you tend to let your guard down, and this is what led to my capture in Murphy in 2003.

Eric Robert Rudolph in a ballistic vest, on his way to court in 2003.

Searching a cave in the Nantahala Forest.

16

LESSONS LEARNED

You learn from both your mistakes and successes. In running the multiagency task forces that hunted Lone Wolf Terrorists in Montana and North Carolina, I had lots of learning opportunities.

Traditional law enforcement organizational structures often don't work well in a highly complex investigation. This tenet is a hard pill for traditionalists in all agencies to swallow because tradition is part of loyalty in law enforcement, the same as it is in the military. Within my own organization, I was often viewed as reckless or naive, and I heard constantly from SACs and supervisors in other offices as well as FBI Headquarters that what I was doing was not the way the FBI does things.

Every headquarters element will concentrate on centralizing control. The problem in a complex case with new and challenging elements—like hunting a Lone Wolf Terrorist—is that centralized control can stifle creativity and imagination. Luckily for me, the Director trusted me and Jim Freeman to make the plays on the field. As a result, we were able to move on a dime. In UNABOM, that translated into solving a 16-year-old serial bombing case in 24 months.

In the Rudolph case, the stamp we put on the fugitive search in North Carolina outlasted the active attention span of the agencies involved—including the FBI. The impact of that first year in Andrews and on Eric Rudolph himself served to drive the Lone Wolf so deep into the woods that he eventually succumbed to hunger ("the starving time") and dropped his guard enough to be cornered by a lone police officer on patrol.

In UNABOM, Director Freeh effectively became the SAC, Jim Freeman the squad supervisor, and I was the case agent. This was heresy to my colleagues and to the FBI management structure as a whole. But it meant that we had the ability in a case that involved multiple jurisdictions all over the country to assess any situation, develop strategies, coordinate a plan of attack, and then implement it in minutes rather than days or weeks.

∞ ∞ ∞

Even before we had the UNABOM Manifesto, we used the Unabomber's own words against him. With no DNA, no fingerprints, and no trace evidence that could be used to track him from the crime scenes to his lair, his words were all we had to link him to his deeds. We had constant opposition to this—even from some of our best people—because the gold standard of evidence in a courtroom is physical evidence. We ran out every lead, but when the physical evidence dried up, we didn't stop there. With no DNA, no fingerprints, and no connection to the victims, we focused on finding the Unabomber by publicizing his word usages, phrases, and content to the public at large. Our strategy led us to a place Theodore Kaczynski never dreamed we'd find: his safehouse in Montana. The cabin was a treasure trove of evidence. Why? Because he'd been careful never to compromise himself by leaving any physical evidence at his crime scenes that would lead us there. He never thought we'd find him.

During the search of the cabin, we found more words that were critical evidence: thousands of pages of handwritten notes, daily journals, and an autobiography. He had shelves of notebooks that precisely detailed the experiments he conducted during the years he'd evolved his bomb designs. He'd converted hundreds of pages into a mathematical code, which we were able to break only because we also found two codebooks he used as his "keys." The coded information also outlined the painstaking effort he went to in order to deceive law enforcement. The following passage is typical:

> A while back I obtained 2 human hairs from the bathroom in the Missoula bus depot. I broke one of these hairs into two pieces, and I placed one piece between the layers of the electrical tape I used to wrap the wire joints inside the

package. (See Fig. 14). The reason for this is to deceive the policemen, who will think that the hair belongs to whoever made the device.

Kaczynski's native instinct for caution and self-preservation was sharpened during his 25 years in the wilderness. This notation, found on a label on pipes stored in his cabin, is a further example of the care he took to conceal his true identity:

> Pipes bought in a junkyard, Utah Scrap Metal, at 900 S Street, some blocks to the west of West Temple, in Salt Lake City. When I bought these pipes I gave the name Charles Kradnick, with no address. I was wearing silvered glasses, gum (chewing gum) under my upper lip (changing its shape that way), and a piece of wax in the left nostril, distorting it. I had to sign a receipt (with the name of Charles Kradnick), but I did it in such a way that I did not leave any of my fingerprints.

There was nothing this Lone Wolf found too difficult to do in order to maintain his image as the solitary and self-sufficient woodsman other citizens of Lincoln, Montana, took him to be. We were amazed at what came out of the cabin. There were chemical mixtures and jars of shrapnel on shelves he'd hung on the inside walls; a thick, wooden workbench and a storehouse of tools; a pair of tennis shoes he'd modified by affixing a smaller pair beneath the soles to leave tracks smaller than he would otherwise have made; the gray, hooded sweat-shirt and sunglasses the Salt Lake City witness had described in 1987; stores of metal and wood that would link forensically to UNABOM devices. Crammed into a loft area were boxes of materials linked to many of the bombs, as well as the typewriter used to produce the UNABOM Manifesto. We found a carbon copy of the letter he had sent to Dr. David Gelernter at Yale University, complaining about people with advanced degress not being as smart as they think they are and people without a college degree not counting. The hand-written note on the copy explained, "this will make them think I don't have an advanced degree."

He had detailed plans of how to dispose of incriminating evidence away from his cabin—never implemented, since he never saw us coming, despite what CBS and other news media might have planned in breaking the story after Kaczynski's identity was leaked to the press. He'd needed no workshop or foundry, no electricity for power tools; he'd cast his own metal, and formed his devices out of found materials. He even constructed a working pistol ("I plan to use it as a homicide weapon"). Under his bed, we found a live bomb ready to wrap and mail.

∞ ∞ ∞

I learned the critical importance of selecting the right mix of people for the job, with skills and experience levels that complement each other. It was brought home to me once again, as it was during my earlier days supervising Squad 12 in San Francisco, that sometimes the right people aren't the "stars" of the office, but a maverick, nontraditional mix with an innovative bent. It's been my repeated observation that the agents with the best reputations in an FBI Field Office are often more socially popular than they are productive. This makes sense, of course, and in a purely social sense you don't expect the most amusing rascals in the office to also be the workhorses. But as I said earlier, my advantage was in selecting for UNABOM talent that had proven itself to me earlier in my career, despite what reputation they had with the office as a whole.

I bucked tradition all over the place in both UNABOM and the Eric Rudolph fugitive hunt by picking the right people for tasks despite what agency they came from. We were stronger when we worked together as one team, not as individual agencies with differing agendas.

∞ ∞ ∞

Perhaps the most critical partner on our team was the American public. We demonstrated clearly the importance of communicating necessary information in an organized way to bolster public awareness of the words of the Unabomber. And individual acts of public responsibility and attention to duty have demonstrated time and time again to be the key to defeating terrorist acts.

After the April 1995 attack on the Murrah Federal Building in Oklahoma City, the fate of Timothy McVeigh was sealed when an alert State Trooper stopped him driving away in a car with no rear license plate.

Two witnesses actively contributed to the identification of Eric Robert Rudolph as he sped away from the scene minutes after murdering Officer Sanderson in Birmingham in January 1998.

In 1999, a U. S. Customs agent followed her instincts and detained Algerian Islamic Jihad member Ahmed Ressam as he tried to enter the U.S. from Canada to attack Los Angeles International Airport, among other targets.

David Kaczynski and his wife knew from repeated UTF press conferences that there were geographical clues to the Unabomber's identity: his origin in Chicago, association with Salt Lake City, and familiarity with the greater San Francisco Bay area. When coupled with the familiarity of the words and themes of the UNABOM Manifesto, they made the painful decision to contact the FBI.

In all of these instances, acts of domestic or international terrorism were prevented or solved due to heightened individual awareness. When Kathy completed her 2001 study for the FBI's Counterterrorism Division, "The Lone Terrorist, the Search for Connection and Its Relationship to Societal-Level Violence," she concluded that education and outreach and the raising of terrorism awareness by law enforcement agencies at local, state, and Federal levels would pay huge dividends in the terror war.

Even small investments of time and energy in public awareness by law enforcement agencies can potentially prevent deadly terrorist attacks. In August 2006, for example, British authorities attributed their success in thwarting a terrorist plot to bomb ten trans-Atlantic flights to the United States to a tip from a worried member of the Muslim community who reported general suspicions about an acquaintance. That tip led to the arrest of 19 people who were 48 hours from conducting real-time tests of bottles of liquid explosives that could be detonated by electronic signals from cell phones or iPods.

∞ ∞ ∞

In UNABOM and during the hunt for Eric Rudolph, we usually found ways to work around FBI Headquarters, balancing the good things they could offer while keeping them from controlling the investigation. This didn't make us very popular at the Hoover Building, and as a result, the UNABOM case is unheralded within the FBI.

In any criminal, counterintelligence, or counterterrorism investigation, however, FBI Headquarters has a significant role to play. FBIHQ supported the UTF with equipment, budgets, agents, and analyst transfers. The Profiling Unit ultimately agreed to assign a fulltime Quantico profiler to the task force and delivered Jim Fitzgerald to assist Kathy. Eighteen years of FBI Lab efforts with the forensic evidence in the case may not have led us to the Unabomber's lair, but when the door to the cabin was finally opened, there was a mother lode of evidence inside that validated the Lab's assessments over the years, and sealed Theodore Kaczynski's fate in court.

∞ ∞ ∞

We demonstrated that although every investigation is different, a successful outcome often depends on a few simple formulas that will work every time.

Be consistent, and keep the pressure constant.

Interview as many people as you need to, even if it's thousands, to develop pieces of information that will pull the puzzle together.

Stick with the facts, and accept that there will be dozens of dead-end avenues and coincidences that are irrelevant to the solution. Don't try to force-fit the pieces of the puzzle.

At the same time, encourage creativity and imagination with reference to the facts, and reward ingenuity and dedication.

When your team is bored out of their minds by looking at the same data over and over again, give them a break. Then have them look at it again.

∞ ∞ ∞

It isn't the intention of this book to recount in excruciating detail everything that happened in the long quest to identify the Unabomber, or during the five-year hunt to find Eric Rudolph. It would take hundreds of pages and frustrate the reader as much as both cases frustrated the investigators for so many years (although that would lend a hint of virtual reality to the story).

But there is merit in making certain the taxpayer knows that we left no stone unturned. And credibility is the rock that anchors American justice when it is blown by the turbulent winds of terrorism.

To give you an example of how much more went on in the UNABOM case that I haven't mentioned, here are some of the long roads we drove to their dead ends:

When we reviewed the evidence and reinvestigated each of the UNABOM crimes, we found a student at Northwestern University whose mother worked for the professor listed as the return addressee on the first UNABOM device in May 1978. That student eventually went on to Rennselaer Polytechnic Institute, where one of his professors was the addressee on the same device. Despite the coincidences that appeared to link him to the case, we eventually eliminated him as a suspect.

A Phillies cigar box housed the May 1979 device, which was left on a table in a graduate room at Northwestern University. It was wrapped in brown polka dot paper. We traced the paper to a Sears store in the suburbs of Chicago, and determined all locations in the United States where the rolls of paper were distributed. The paper had no other connection that we ever found to UNABOM.

Tom Mohnal at the FBI Lab traced wood fragments found at some of the crime scenes to specific types of wooden pallets and passed the information along to Max. By the time he finished running out the string, Max had identified and interviewed the primary wooden pallet "experts" in the country, learning all he could about how they were manufactured, where they were distributed, and who may have purchased them. Since Kaczynski's materials often consisted of scrap, the wood was never traceable.

FBI Lab examiners consulted with senior scientists at Lawrence Livermore National Laboratory, enlisting their expertise in reviewing some of the UNABOM forensic evidence. Aluminum end caps subjected to quantitative analysis offered insight into the potential source and type of industrial aluminum used. Solder analysis held the promise of identifying the source and distribution range. Wooden screws, springs, and the way wire was twisted in some of the devices could possibly be traced to the source, region of the country, and manufacturer. Preservatives in the wood could reveal region, and markings on the wood might indicate other hobbies or interests such as model railroads or guns.

After an initial review of the energetic materials (ammonium nitrate, aluminum powder, potassium chlorate) used in some of the UNABOM devices, Lawrence Livermore offered a preliminary opinion that the bomber didn't have any professional understanding of the materials he used. They believed he must have selected them based on experimentation, and probably pretested the devices before using a version of them.

When Kaczynski's journals were reviewed, there were detailed notes of his "experiments" and his frustration over failures. He wrote this concerning the bomb he placed in a hallway at the University of Utah in October, 1981:

> Last fall I attempted a bombing and spent nearly three hundred bucks just for travel expenses, motel, clothing for disguise, etc. aside from cost of materials for the bomb. And then the thing failed to explode. Damn. This was the firebomb found in U. of Utah Business School outside door of room containing some computer stuff.

Upset over the failure of the first bomb, Kaczynski tried again. He placed a device in a break room at Cory Hall at U.C. Berkeley in July 1982, and later wrote:

> According to newspaper, vice chairman of computer sci. dept. picked it up. He was considered to be out of danger of losing any fingers, but would need further surgery for bone and tendon damage in hand. Apparently pipe bomb went off but did not ignite gasoline. I don't understand it. Frustrated.

When we reinvestigated the February 1987 bombing at the Caams computer store in Salt Lake City, we determined a witness had seen a red Spyder Fiat leaving the scene after the bombing. It was never located.

Joel took the lead to track down the Fiat. He traveled to the outskirts of Salt Lake City, climbing over junkyard wreckage and through piles of scrap metal in a quest to identify the whereabouts of every Spyder Fiat ever owned, driven, or junked in Utah since the bombing. FBI agents in New York City acquired owner registration information on every individual who had purchased a Spyder Fiat of a particular vintage. The office in Salt Lake painstakingly located and eliminated every owner on the list until one day, through a local car dealership, they found a construction worker who recalled in great detail that he had been working at the strip mall where Caams was located on the day of the bombing. It had taken nine years, but the red Spyder Fiat had been eliminated as relevant to the identity of the Unabomber. At the very least, the Unabomber wouldn't be using the mysterious Fiat as an alternative theory in court.

In June 1993, the Unabomber sent a letter to *The New York Times* in which he provided a nine-digit number for identification, "so no one else can appear to speak in our name."

It looked like a Social Security Account Number, so we identified its holder. He had been incarcerated in California prisons most of his young adult life. When we talked with him, he didn't remember getting a Social Security number. He had never worked a day in his life, and wouldn't have needed one. Eventually, he recalled losing his wallet in the parking area of a Sacramento theater that had closed long since. When we drove to the empty lot where the theater once stood, we saw in the distance the rear parking lot for Rentech Computer Store, where the Unabomber had killed Hugh Scrutton in 1985.

Despite this, after the search of the cabin was complete and all the Unabomber's writings extensively reviewed, it appeared that his choice of the number had been random, with no connection to the missing wallet. Another strange UNABOM coincidence.

PART II

UNMASKING THE LONE AMERICAN TERRORIST

17

THE KACZYNSKI PAPERS

"I need you on the task force, Kathy."

Although he looked sincere, I knew Terry was also trying not to gag on his vegetarian entrée in front of the other patrons at the Millennium Restaurant in San Francisco. It was just after Halloween in 1994, and he'd taken over the UNABOM Task Force the previous April.

From 1988 to 1990, I'd worked for Terry on Squad 12, the Soviet Bloc Counterintelligence Squad. He and his relief supervisor, Joel Moss, had become my close friends in the two years we worked a fascinating espionage case together. During that time, I'd started graduate studies in clinical psychology, and Terry let me have my head in doing behavioral analysis on our subject, a puzzling human being who was also a foreign spy under deep cover in the United States. The case was a success, and to my delight, so was my psychological assessment.

Also in 1988, I'd been chosen by my mentor at the Behavioral Science Unit at Quantico, Dick Ault, to join a small team that traveled around the country interviewing people convicted of espionage; most were still in prison. Dick was one of "The Nine," the first—legendary—group of FBI profilers that also included *Mindhunter* author John Douglas. Because he had a special interest in counterintelligence and counterespionage, Dick was unique at Quantico.

Most profilers, like Douglas, were interested in crime scene interpretation rather than hunting spies. In the 1990s, the FBI still saw itself as primarily a criminal investigative agency. The big cases involved organized crime, major offenders, and white collar crime. In the Bureau, the National Security Division was known as "the other side of the house." Behavioral work mostly concerned serial killers, arson, and other types of violent crime. When counterintelligence (CI) needed a profiler, they had Dick Ault to call on.

But in 1993, Dick retired from the Bureau. This left the National Security Division, responsible for both CI and counter-terrorism at the time, without a behavioral profiler.

To fill the void, they selected six of us—Dick's recommendation—from the Field to "replace" Dick. Then they hired him back as a contractor to work with us. We were styled as the Behavioral Analysis Program (BAP) in the FBI, while, by this time, the original criminal profiling group split off from the Behavioral Science Unit at Quantico and was renamed the Investigative Support Unit. (This move was largely because the word "profile" had taken on unsavory references after allegations of racial profiling by law enforcement.) We "Bapeteers" worked cases as usual; but when we were called, we jumped on a plane and regrouped either in Washington, D.C. or at a Field office that needed behavioral assistance of one sort or another.

For two years, I worked CI cases all over the United States with Dick and the other agents on BAP. We clued case agents into the personalities of their subjects, advised them on undercover scenarios and interview approaches, and generally had a fantastic time sticking our (always invited) noses into everybody else's cases. I was lucky. Although I was still assigned to San Francisco, where I had just finished my doctoral curriculum in psychology, I was able to participate in the biggest espionage and counterintelligence cases in the country without being assigned to either New York or Washington, D.C.

Now, I looked at Terry across the lunch table and tried to contain my excitement. I'd watched him—and then Joel—become absorbed that year in the challenge and mystery of the longest unsolved serial bombing case in the FBI's history: UNABOM. I listened to them talk about the endless puzzles in the case, the long investigative roads that seemed to go nowhere, the mind-boggling coincidences that drove seasoned criminal investigators from the case year after year. I appealed to the Assistant Special Agent in

Charge for CI in San Francisco, expressing my fascination and my sure conviction that I could help the team. He was dismissive.

"They have behavioral people already, Kathy," he said, shaking his head. "I need you to run CI analysis and coordinate what Maggie Stringer and the other analysts are doing for the CI squads. Leave the UNABOM case alone."

From time to time, Terry would ask me a "hypothetical" question that obviously related to UNABOM. I'd run with it, but I kept the brakes on. He never asked me directly, and I never asked him about coming to the UTF. I knew he was frustrated with both Field profiling reps on the task force, but I didn't hear it from Terry. Office scuttlebutt was that they were on the outs. Secretly, I fantasized about joining the profiling reps in their mission, healing the breach, and working the most mysterious case in the FBI as part of their team. It never occurred to me that I'd get there on my own.

"You know I'm intrigued by this case, Terry," I said. "But the Investigative Support Unit is responsible for criminal cases. I'm not a profiler."

He shook his head in annoyance.

"No, you're in the BAP. I know what you can do—you proved it on Squad 12. You're also a team player, and I need that. I need to be able to rely on someone to be there for the agents and analysts when they develop suspects. I need fresh eyes on this. So . . ." He cocked his head. "Will you do it?"

"I'm already there," I grinned.

Terry abandoned all pretense of eating his delicate vegetarian feast (I think he and Joel went to Burger King afterward) and clapped his hands, rubbing them together in a characteristic gesture that I knew from experience meant, "Let's go!"

And so I joined the UNABOM Task Force.

I knew it would be a unique and challenging experience. What I didn't know was that it would be the beginning of a new body of knowledge and expertise in dealing with a kind of offender not really known or understood before then: the Lone Wolf terrorist.

During the next three and a half years, I absorbed everything I could from the work that was ongoing in UNABOM, as well as what was then known about serial bombers. It wasn't much. There were episodic accounts and case histories, notably the "Mad

Bomber" case in New York in the 1940s and 1950s, which sparked the interest of the first FBI profilers in the art of profiling itself. "Mad Bomber" George Metesky placed 30 bombs at public places—mostly theatres—and mailed angry letters about his grievances against the Edison Electric company for 16 years before psychiatrist James Brussell contributed a psychological profile that astonished detectives when it fit Metesky as neatly as the buttoned, double-breasted suit Brussell accurately predicted Metesky would be wearing when they arrested him.

Terry had asked Quantico for a study on serial bombers, but they'd never gotten around to it. I'd received a bundle of handwritten notes and articles on serial bombing cases from them, as well as a general serial arsonist profile. I started to dig into what else I could find at the same time I began working on UTF projects like content analysis of the book *Ice Brothers*, which concealed the UNABOM device that exploded in 1980.

I was instantly fascinated by the case. The shadowy figure behind the 16 years of bombing events was a complete cipher. He'd left no real clues, no keys to his identity; we didn't even know what "FC" stood for. We had a whiteboard on the wall covered with dozens of attempts at decoding "FC," much of which was unprintable in public reports.

Because Quantico hadn't conducted the serial bomber study Terry had asked for, their profiles were largely based on what was known about serial offenders in general, and serial arsonists in particular. The resulting UNABOM profile, which was updated several times from 1980 to 1993, concluded that the Unabomber was likely to be a white male between 43 and 53 years old, with a "varied employment record" that would reflect research and/or teaching positions. He was seen as highly intelligent, deliberate, patient, imaginative, and technically competent. He would be an avid reader of current affairs as well as a variety of other areas such as history, psychology, and science and technology. He was also likely to be a loner with poor interpersonal skills, who wanted revenge for wrongs done to him and recognition and credit for his "work."

As Terry noted earlier, the usefulness of a further updated profile for the UTF was significantly compromised when his two San

Francisco Field reps concluded that the professor who was the first victim in the UNABOM case in 1978 was the Unabomber. Combined with the lack of physical evidence leading to any geographical area—let alone any individual—this predisposition ran the agents on the hunt into a brick wall.

My joining the hunt wasn't designed to come up with a new profile. I was to look at everything again and try to work with Quantico to develop our knowledge of serial bombers as well as evaluating everything we were learning by continually re-investigating all UNABOM events and communications over the years. We also wanted Quantico to consult on a range of new suspects being developed as we went along. This was Terry's game plan, and it was evolving into a new way of integrating behavioral analysis with management and leadership in a case that we would develop over the next seven years.

This approach began to gel when Jim "Fitz" Fitzgerald came from Quantico to work with me. Fitz was a new profiler but a seasoned investigator.

∞ ∞ ∞

After Theodore Kaczynski was arrested, Fitz, Lee Stark, and I joined Terry and the rest of the UTF in Montana to get ready for the next phase of the case: getting a conviction in federal court.

When we arrived at the Helena airport, we grabbed one of the last four-wheel drives and drove up into the mountains. At about three in the afternoon, we arrived at the rustic hotel, and surprisingly good restaurant, at the Seven-up Ranch. Most of all we wanted to get to the cabin, but we knew we'd have to wait in line. Joel came to meet us and took us inside, where we sat at one of the long tables near a fire in the dining room. Suddenly, the doors banged open and in strode Terry and Jim Freeman. Both grinning.

"We're going to make you famous," Freeman said.

He swung a leg around a chair and he and Terry joined us at the table. Terry was having even more of a hard time than usual sitting still. An avid hiker, he looked far happier in his mountain gear than in his business suit. It had been a couple of days since the arrest and the beginning of the search, and they had already found the live bomb under the bed in Kaczynski's cabin. The search had slowed to a cautious crawl; but before it did, they'd found a manila envelope with the word "Autobiography" scrawled across it.

"We haven't had a chance to look at it," Jim continued, "But it's only part of hundreds—maybe thousands—of other writings we found in notebooks on the shelves."

"You've got your work cut out for you," Terry said. There was a twinkle in his eye as he grabbed a sandwich from the tray one of the ranch staff had just put in front of us. "But we can't let you see it yet; it's evidence. We'll have to set up a way to copy everything first."

Fitz, Lee, and I looked at each other, then back at our fearless leaders.

"When do we start?"

They laughed and got up from the table.

"Get ready and we'll get you out to the cabin," Terry said. "You need to see it before it's empty, although it looks like it's going be a long search."

They left as Joel came back into the room and then led us to his Jeep. It was coated with mud almost to the hood, and when we started the drive to the cabin, I saw why. After we were through Lincoln proper, it was all mud and melting ice on Stemple Pass Road. We fishtailed a little in the slurry as Joel gave us a tour during the 40 minutes it took to drive the few miles to the search headquarters.

Dozens of 4x4s and a couple of large trailers were parked in a big field adjacent to Butch Gehring's sawmill, and there were deep ruts in the mud leading up a long rise into the forest. When we got out of the Jeep, Joel nodded towards the trail.

"We walk from here," he said. He seemed more relaxed than I'd ever seen him. In the city, Joel was always in a suit and usually wore a calm, even impassive, expression. Here in the cold and fresh air of the Montana high country, he was in jeans and muddy boots, and his eyes were shining. I grinned at him and punched his shoulder.

"You like it up here, don't you?"

He grinned back.

"Interesting place," he said. "Let's go."

We began walking up the hill towards the trees. I knew most of the people who were busy all around us with various tasks, but I could hardly recognize any of them in their winter mountain gear. I thought about the day of the search when Max and his team had walked this trail in hushed silence on their way to meet the Unabomber. Smiling to myself, I thought how ironic it had been that Max and Paul Wilhelmus were the ones who'd first confronted Theodore Kaczynski. Neither of them had any real confidence that he was the Unabomber, and Max was astonished when he saw the soot-covered Kaczynski come out of the cabin.

"Is that what we've been chasing all these years?" he said to us later. "That's all I could think. It was unbelievable."

We reached the steep downward trail to Kaczynski's property and began to walk down to it. Evidence Response Team (ERT) people were everywhere, toting boxes of plastic-wrapped items all over the meadow where the cabin sat. Suzanne Alford, a petite Texan and one of my good friends among the female agents in San Francisco, waved as she walked by in rubber boots nearly as big as she was. The San Francisco ERT had a great reputation inside and outside the FBI, and Suzanne would soon be teaching evidence collection and preservation techniques in Indonesia and Bosnia.

As we walked up to the cabin door, I saw a loop on a string hanging to the side. It didn't look connected to anything, but it looked like it might have been.

"What's this?" I asked one of the young agents standing watch nearby. He walked up to it with me and we stared at it together.

"Don't know," he said. He looked at me curiously. I knew Pat Webb and the other bomb squad people had already been through this place, especially after the live bomb turned up under Kaczynski's bed, but we both looked at it with suspicion. Terry and Max had long worried that the cabin might be booby-trapped. Eventually, we both shrugged and turned away.

I walked inside. Fitz and Lee were already there; everyone else stepped out of the tiny room to let us have a look. Terry and Jim Freeman had agreed that it might be useful for the behavioral team to have a look at this Lone Wolf's lair before it was dismantled and its contents packaged for shipment to the FBI Lab in Washington.

A potbellied stove covered with soot stood to the rear center of the room. In front of it was what looked like a hand-crafted wooden folding chair. Behind a wall of wooden shelves were mason jars and oatmeal cartons and all kinds of other containers. All were hand-labeled with the names of chemical mixtures and collections of nails and other material usable as shrapnel. Sweatshirts and other clothing hung on nails to the left of the shelves, along with plastic bags of some soft material, shoes, and hanging pots. To my left was a high and thick wooden workbench, heavily used and stained. There was what looked like a drying rack hung up on the ceiling above the stove, and all around the room near the ceiling were shelves filled with books and three-ring binders.

The bed was at the right, toward the front of the room. It was a wood frame with storage underneath and a thin pallet on top, on which several blankets—they looked like army blankets—were folded. It was under this structure that the last UNABOM device had been found just a day or two earlier. The wall adjacent to the bed was coated with a dark stain that looked vaguely like the outline of a person. It turned out to be residue left from oil and dirt on Kaczynski's body, hair, and clothes that had accumulated over 25 years. Two rifles and a hunting bow hung on the same wall.

At the foot of the bed was a large wooden box that appeared to store firewood and kindling. To the right rear of the room, beyond the box, the shelves on the back wall did double duty as stairs to a square opening in the ceiling that led to a loft. The loft was packed with cardboard boxes and plastic bags of material, including the typewriter that the Lab would link forensically to the UNABOM Manifesto and letters to *The New York Times*, *The Washington Post* and The *San Francisco Chronicle*, among others.

Many of the boxes and other containers had additional markings on their labels that turned out to be codes that indicated how badly the contents might incriminate Kaczynski if they were ever found. As I looked at these later, I was completely fascinated by the insight they provided into the meticulous workings of Theodore Kaczynski's mind.

Although he had obviously never anticipated that he would ever be captured in his mountain hideaway, he'd been aware that, at some point, fate might catch up with him on one of his excursions outside Montana to either mail a bomb or send a letter. To control the level of damage a subsequent search of his cabin would cause him after such an arrest, he developed an intricate system of labeling incriminating materials according to a code that indicated how to destroy them:

Class 1. Hide carefully far from home
Class 2. Hide carefully far from home, but can be destroyed at a pinch
Class 3. Hide carefully far from home, but can be burned at a pinch
Class 4. Burn away from home
Class 5. Burn in stove, eventually
Class 6. Burn with glass jars
Class 7. Destroy (with glass jars)
Class 8. Treat to make safe
Class 9. Burn in stove, then dispose of remains
Class 10. Dump in trash far from home

He devised another level of classification that defined just how incriminating a given item might be to him. As near as we could figure out, since he has never spoken to anyone about his methods as far as I know, he labeled the most incriminating items "QQ," for "super queer," the next level of incrimination "Q" for "very queer," "R" for "moderately queer," and "S" for "slightly queer." The box that housed the typewriter, for example, was labeled "QQ." Finally, he noted when something was "B" (burnable) or "NB" (not burnable).

The intricate planning and exquisite caution that characterized Theodore Kaczynski's UNABOM career showed most clearly in every aspect of his writings. Nearly 40,000 pages in English, Spanish, and German came out of the cabin: notebooks, journals, coded materials, letters, and his autobiography. For me, this was the real treasure that came out of the search. Fitz, Lee, and I would soon extend our stay in Montana to examine it.

We walked through and out of the cabin under the watchful eye of agents on the ERT, who were alert to the danger of any contamination of what was actually a crime scene. Joel drove us back to the Seven-up Ranch, where we drew up a game plan on how to deal with the documents. By nightfall, we joined our colleagues for an amazing dinner of steak and huge lobster tail (salad for me), and several good bottles of red wine from the ranch cellars. As I went to sleep in a Lincoln motel room that night, I was dizzy with the prospect of what we'd discover about the mind of the Unabomber in thousands of pages of his writings.

We'd planned on spending only a day or two in Montana, but the next day over coffee Terry told us he had other plans.

"We're arranging to rent several office spaces in Helena," he said, "and one of them is going to be yours. Kathy, Fitz, I want you to coordinate getting each page of every one of the documents copied by ERT people in the next day or two. We have to get the originals on the Bureau plane back to the Lab in Washington, and we're not letting them go until we get copies."

We were at loggerheads with the Lab again. Jim Freeman took a hard line when told that all the evidence taken from the cabin was going to be scooped up by the Lab and taken back East.

"Once this stuff goes into evidence lockers at the Lab, we'll never see it again," he rumbled. "That's not gonna happen. This is our case, and our evidence. I'm not letting these documents out of our sight until every page is copied so we can analyze it."

That afternoon, Fitz, Lee, and I drove back down to Helena. Our Administrative Head, Sandy Figoni, had begun renting office space from delighted landlords all over Helena. It was the slow season, and the infusion of business from 50 or so extra people in town was good for restaurants and hotels as well as office managers. By the next day, the three of us walked up the stairs into what would be our own center of operations for the next two weeks. We called it "The Loft," and it was being rapidly furnished with desks, computers, and three large copiers that were soon in constant use.

Two agents from the ERT, Diane Kisabeth and Tracy Riley, had the dubious honor of handling and copying every single page taken from the cabin. For the task, they had to wear several successive pairs of cotton gloves while standing at the overworked copiers—which frequently broke down—for all of one night and day. They both glared at me from time to time at their bad luck in drawing this tedious duty, but I was too busy scanning the results to notice. After the initial copies were made, several sets of copies were made from those, and these are what occupied Fitz and me for the next two weeks as we sat in The Loft and entered the mysterious mind of the Unabomber.

I've said many times since that Theodore Kaczynski never had a thought he didn't write down. It was like striking gold . . . or water after a long drought. We pored over the pages for hours and hours each day, while all around us a dozen stenographers painstakingly key-stroked every word of each document into computers to enable further comparative analysis and provide a usable record for later use by the prosecution team. Luckily, Kaczynski's handwriting was fairly regular and possible for most of us to read, but there were many complications in this task. Many of the documents were in Spanish, and we had to import translators from FBIHQ. Then there were the codes.

Lee bent over the first of the codes that became available and put on his glasses. I eventually slid a chair under him. Using the code key that accompanied it, he began working it out. He printed the decoded text and read it aloud:

> May 1982 I sent a bomb to a computer expert named Patrick Fisver. His secretary opened it one newspaper said she was in hospital? In good condition? with arm and chest cuts. Other newspaper said bomb drove fragments of wood into her flesh. No indication that she was permanently disabled. Frustrating that I cant' seem to mako lethal bomb.

When Lee brought the paper to show Chief Prosecutor Bob Cleary at dinner that evening, Bob's eyes widened at the sight, and a huge grin appeared on his face. Even if Theodore Kaczynski never said an incriminating word to any investigator (and to this day, he never has), we knew these documents would seal his fate in court.

Copies of the codes and the code keys were sent to cryptanalysts at FBIHQ, who later told us that they might never have broken the codes if they hadn't also had the keys. Kaczynski was a mathematician and a genius, and he'd had time to devise some extremely intricate codes. Luckily for us, since he'd never seen us coming, we had his code keys. Many of the coded documents contained specific accounts of his bombing activities over the years, in great detail.

Lee eventually went on to other tasks, but Fitz and I stayed at The Loft. We each had a copy of all the documents, and we decided to read them in the same order so we could discuss them as we went. I was the faster reader, so I frequently outpaced Fitz and saw things before he did. I couldn't read fast enough. I was utterly fascinated. It was like entering Kaczynski's mind. Even though I hadn't yet put the writings in chronological order, I saw patterns in his thought that would lead me toward my future analysis of Lone Wolves.

Now, however, the hours grew long and we grew stiff in our chairs as the days passed and the work progressed. The sound of clicking keyboards was all around us as our diligent and long-suffering stenos put the mind of the Unabomber into computerized form. How Theodore Kaczynski would have hated the thought of that.

One day, I was reading a journal entry that took me into a surprising and bawdy aspect of Kaczynski's solitary existence. As I said earlier, he never had a thought—or performed an activity—that he didn't record on paper. This journal entry was a matter-of-fact discussion of his ability—due to his extreme flexibility—to gratify himself in a very intimate manner. I gave a start as I read this, and then peered over at Fitz, who was sitting with his glasses perched on the end of his nose and reading several pages behind me. I knew he hadn't gotten to this yet, and I decided to wait for his reaction. Sure enough, a few minutes later, we all heard a booming Philly accent exclaim:

"That's imPOSSIBLE!"

I threw my head back and howled with laughter, as startled stenos looked up all around us. Fitz looked over at me and his face reddened. I asked him wickedly how he knew that. We took a break and went outside on the walkway, where thin sunlight was trying to melt the snow from a most recent storm.

"This guy," Fitz said, shaking his head, "Jeez."

I reminded him, after we stopped laughing, about Max's recounting of the hours he'd sat with Kaczynski while DOJ attorneys in Washington argued about probable cause for his arrest. Eventually, he asked whether Kaczynski wanted anything to eat. Kaczynski politely refused everything Max offered him until he saw a Snickers candy bar. At the Unabomber's request, Max handed him the candy still in its wrapper, and watched in astonishment as—with his hands in cuffs behind his back—he unwrapped and ate the candy bar without any assistance.

∞ ∞ ∞

We worked at The Loft in Helena for a little over two weeks, and then we transferred the whole document operation back to UTF Headquarters in San Francisco to complete it. Within a month, thanks to tireless computer work by the steno force (looking back, I think we should have had a massage staff on call for them), I had many thousands of pages on the computer, and copies of the original handwritten documents they represented to refer back to when things didn't correlate.

A number of different people went through parts of the writings for all kinds of purposes. The Lab looked at the diagrams and chemical mixtures in the three-ring binder notebooks, where Kaczynski had meticulously recorded every aspect of his early experiments with making effective antipersonnel bombs. Other agents studied dated entries for comparison with UNABOM events over the years, finding in the coded material direct admissions—often boasts—about his successes, as well as laments about his failures to cause the destruction he'd intended.

I was probably the only one who read nearly every word of every document. For behavioral analysis to help the prosecution team, I had to know and digest every aspect I could find about how Theodore Kaczynski's mind worked. He had put it down on thousands of pages, and it was all there for me to read.

I was well suited to this work. Once at a family gathering, I noted jokingly that I was easily amused. My mother Helen nodded and said, "You are. You're very lucky that way."

My capacity for being easily amused was coupled with a native ability to read fast. This came in extremely handy, because although the writings of Theodore Kaczynski provided a startling amount of insight as to his personality, they also contained thousands of pages of what I came to call the "Porcupine Papers." He often wrote tens of pages about a single day's hunt for food, which wild greens he gathered to go with the small game he hunted, and the details of every day gathering and chopping wood or boiling water. There were many, many recipes for porcupine and other meaty fare, and many grisly depictions of how various other woodland creatures also ended up on Kaczynski's plate.

At the same time, he wrote long treatises to himself about philosophy, history, and political science. He wrote continuously about the abuses he'd suffered from society and from his family. He was adamant in his conviction that he had been severely emotionally abused and pushed by his parents, and wrote bitterly that they had turned him into a "social cripple" by skipping him two grades and sending him to Harvard at age 16.

At this writing in 2007, a long lawsuit filed initially by the media continues to plod through Federal court involving the question of who owns the UNABOM documents that came out of the cabin in Montana in 1996. Kaczynski himself provided the latest hitch in the proceedings early in 2007, when he filed a motion to prevent the government from redacting (censoring) the documents they may soon release that record his 18-year career as the Unabomber.

But those documents—the totality of which I alone plodded through ten years ago, the originals locked away since that time in FBI evidence vaults—ended up revealing much more to me than the story of the Unabomber alone. The months I spent reading, collating, and correlating them marked the next stage of the wider hunt that Terry and I would recognize only later was the most valuable contribution we ended up making to the field of counterterrorism in general: the unmasking of the Lone Wolf terrorist.

To me, the most striking thing about the documents from Theodore Kaczynski's cabin wasn't the searing and relentless anger they expressed. We knew he was angry. It wasn't in the obsessive care he took to conceal his identity, though that was really extraordinary; nor was it his capacity for enduring long frozen winters alone in his cabin.

What struck me most was the searing loneliness he continually expressed, and in particular, his tormented longing, expressed multiple times over many years, for a woman to join him in his voluntary exile from society.

Over and over again, Kaczynski wrote agonizing passages about his inability to understand or engage in normal social relationships with other people. Where women were concerned, he was utterly baffled, although he wrote of many attempts he'd made to both "learn about women" and to make efforts to establish contact with them.

He described being obsessed with one girl or another—all of whom were probably completely unaware of it—and sobbing hopelessly as he sat at his campfire in a new pair of jeans he'd ventured into Helena to buy to try to work up the courage to ask one for a date. He never did. His description of the only romantic kiss he ever exchanged with a woman he met at his workplace in 1978 during his trip home to work in Chicago sounds like an account from an educated Forrest Gump. The mechanics of kissing were alien and confusing to him, but he was determined to have more.

He confessed bitterly to never in his life having a sexual experience of any kind with a woman—with the exception of the kiss in Chicago. In his writings about 1978 and 1979, he lamented constantly about his obsession with this one woman, and he made far more entries in his journals about his longing for her than about the reason he came back to Chicago in 1978: to deliver his first bombs at the University of Chicago and Northwestern.

He tried repeatedly to figure out ways to break down the social barriers his peculiar personality—or his mental illness—continually imposed on him. He went back to the Bay Area in the 1980s (since he'd taught mathematics at U.C. Berkeley at the end of the 1960s, before he went to the Montana woods, he was familiar with the area), to earn some money doing odd jobs. While he was there, he joined Sierra Singles and wrote nearly one hundred pages about a girl he met on a hike. Twice he ran ads in Bay Area newspapers trying to interest some adventurous woman to come and live with him in the Montana wilderness. The last of these was an ad for "a squaw." He received replies (this was Northern California, after all); one he scornfully described as from "a horny bitch." He put several explicit excerpts from her reply in a typically savage and contemptuous letter to his parents (which we found in the treasure chest in his mother's apartment in Schenectady in 1996). And he never stopped condemning both his father and his mother for making him a "social cripple."

Because he wrote everything down, I was able to read accounts of his repeated failures to belong anywhere in society from his earliest memory. He was fascinated by his own character and haughty about his genius IQ, but he was bitter and withering in his self-condemnation of his failure in the social world. It was hard enough for him to make individual friends—he never really had any, and appears only to have really cared for his younger brother David early in their lives together—let alone participate in a group.

As much as has been written about Theodore Kaczynski since his arrest, this is something that very few know about him, because this aspect of his nature appears, for the most part, in writings from the cabin that have not been released to the public.

His defense attorneys were given summaries of significant parts of his writings prior to his eventual guilty plea, which helped convince them in their own minds as much as the opinions of defense psychiatric experts did that he had long suffered from paranoid schizophrenia. The court-appointed psychiatrist who examined him, well-respected forensic psychiatrist Dr. Sally Johnson from North Carolina, also reached this diagnosis after reviewing some of his writings and interviewing him in prison in Sacramento.

Neither Kaczynski nor his attorneys ever agreed to his examination by the two forensic psychiatrists hired by Chief UNABOM Prosecutor Bob Cleary: the formidable duo of Dr. Park Dietz from Newport Beach, California, and Dr. Phillip Resnick from Case Western Reserve University in Cleveland, Ohio. They had a summary I spent months writing in 1996 that excerpted in chronological order—in the order Kaczynski's life had taken—passages that expressed his inner world in the same detail that he described his life in the woods. I included passages from decoded and translated letters, journals, and diaries of Kaczynski's entire life. In some sense, written contemporaneously as they were to the events they describe, we considered that the writings from the cabin might actually provide the clearest portrayal of his intentions as well as his actions before and during his long bombing campaigns. For the same reasons, we considered that the "cabin docs" might represent the most accurate portrait of his personality.

In 1987, after a witness saw him place one of his bombs at the Caams computer store in Salt Lake City, Kaczynski appeared to have cautiously retreated to the woods to avoid any further risk of discovery. He didn't place or mail another bomb for over six years. Once again, his writings turned to his longing for social connection. This time, he determined to go back to the world and get a regular job, in a city or town environment he despised, in order to take a wife, have children, and lead a "normal life." Although he'd fashioned and unleashed twelve bombs by this time, maiming and injuring dozens of people and killing Hugh Scrutton in Sacramento in 1985, he wrote about leaving his bombing campaign behind. He wrote that he was growing older and would need more support. He decided to learn how to become part of society.

Except for the money he got from his mother and brother over the years to conduct his bombing forays, Kaczynski, for the most part, lived a life of determined frugality. He estimated that he only spent $350 or so per year on staples such as flour, sugar, and other items he couldn't hunt or gather himself. By 1990, three years since he'd placed his last bomb—despite his new ambition to become a "regular Joe"— he continued to develop his explosive devices so he could mail instead of place them in the future. He wasn't going to risk being seen by another witness, even in disguise. He documented numerous experiments in his notebooks, many of which required money for disguises and materials used in the bombs themselves.

But in the same year, he wrote that he paid $50 for an hour of psychotherapy from a female psychologist in a Montana town. This was a huge chunk of his yearly income. The reason? To learn how to become a regular citizen, take a wife, and raise a family.

For a while, his writings detailed his plans to follow the advice he was given in that hour. He knew he'd have a "period of adjustment." He speculated that settling down might help to calm the inner storms that had never been tamed by his endless study and dedicated life in the wilderness. He wrote that the Montana woods were being invaded by society anyway; that motorcyclists roared through the forest, and the drone of plane engines overhead never left him in peace. The wilderness was over for him, and his bombing campaign had been interrupted by the close call with the witness in 1987. He wrote about what kind of house he'd raise a family in and what kind of schooling he'd arrange for his children. He wrote about children indulgently but at a curious distance, as if they were an interesting kind of pet. He didn't seem to identify them with himself as a child, but he anticipated guiding them as they grew.

At some point in the early 1990s, however, Kaczynski's writings about this fantasized new life in society ended without fanfare or explanation. More letters were written to his brother requesting money. He began building his more evolved bomb designs, and he stopped writing about depression and loneliness. The Unabomber was back.

What happened to Theodore Kaczynski's final push to end his social isolation and become a part of society?

I wondered constantly about this, and read these later writings over and over looking for patterns. It was a mystery to me. Privately, I thought of Kaczynski as suffering from a variety of autism called Asperger's Syndrome, which is a high-functioning variant of the developmental disorder that doesn't include the difficulty with language that characterizes autism as a rule. I thought about neurologist Oliver Sack's description of patients with Asperger's Syndrome in his 1995 book *An Anthropologist on Mars*, about their skewed or nonexistent comprehension of social meanings and communications.

One day, I brought this up thoughtfully to the other two Musketeers as we sat in one of Terry's many favorite restaurants in San Francisco. I should have known it would bring out their inner nine-year olds. For a long while thereafter I had to listen to Beavis and Butthead-like comments about "assburgers," especially from Joel. The wackiness of my Bureau brothers, from my earliest days with Mossie, Pinhead, and Knucks (nicknames provided to protect their identities) to Terry and Joel, more than made up for never actually having any brothers when I was growing up. Yes, it does help to be easily amused.

I eventually collected my excerpts from the documents in the cabin, and other letters and writings from Theodore Kaczynski, into a 300-page bound volume, copies of which went to Terry and Jim Freeman as well as Chief Prosecutor Bob Cleary and the other prosecutors, Steve Freccero among them. We also made copies for each of our forensic psychiatrists, Drs. Dietz and Resnick. By the late summer of 1997, Max Noel and I took both of our psychiatric experts away from the offices and courtrooms where they conducted most of their professional lives and took them up to Montana, to where the Unabomber had lived and built his bombs—and his legend—for 25 years. They brought their bulky behavioral volumes with them.

Kaczynski commmmitted acts of vandalism wearing these shoes, which he fitted with smaller soles to disguise his footprints.

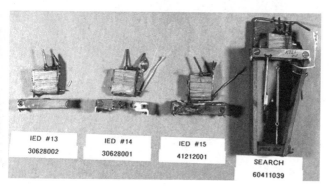

Three hickory bomb switches found at UNABOM crime scenes next to an intact switching mechanism found during the search of Kaczynski's cabin.

UNABOM disguise found in Theodore Kaczynski's cabin.

(A40)

95,73,70,18,33,95,45,62,38,28,85,43,17,82,
46,25,73,5,95,97,9,70,29,77,93,96,17,
32,22,44,54,68,40,64,79,11,33,93,68,38,
98,34,86,17,47,93,40,38,83,30,85,38,48,
49,52,62,72,29,19,78,23,13,94,56,36,76,7,
8,65,56,7,25,58,97,23,54,31,70,33,54,98,
2,36,30,96,79,41,99,60,5,65,37,77,85,58,
12,75,82,88,59,96,80,95,83,23,11,9,71,
73,62,46,42,20,43,89,16,40,95,29,40,49,
49,64,53,80,81,75,17,5,55,36,13,17,76,22,
40,7,56,18,64,20,63,24,52,89,2,56,53,
76,0,38,92,15,56,21,80,69,89,57,84,92,
5,25,93,98,91,68,51,42,88,54,41,74,1,
92,86,40,48,44,31,36,35,(33)32,93,38,
60,85,16,45,68,78,76,27,29,61,98,60,
52,60,53,28,65,74,22,17,49,29,58,50,54,
79,28,47,47,89,57,30,79,37,99,5,31,14,
61,84,23,54,84,36,96,24,21,60,8,98,5,5,

Kaczynski concealed admissions to some of his bombings in a methematical code that he created.

Typewriter used to type the UNABOM Manifesto.

18

BACK TO MONTANA

I first met Chief UNABOM prosecutor Bob Cleary while we were still working in The Loft in Montana. Terry and the Boss arranged dinner for a few of us with him at one of the local restaurants in Helena.

We were still in the middle of emptying and securing the cabin. Fitz and I were still surfing through thousands of handwritten writings when we took a break and joined the top UNABOM brass at the restaurant.

Bob Cleary was a coiled spring of energy with eyes that shone with intense focus and interest. When I met him, he immediately put me together with Fitz in his mind as the source of the behavioral work that had been done and was still ongoing in the case. He made it a point to come over to talk to me and shake my hand.

"Yeah!" he said enthusiastically, a big open grin on his bearded face. "Nice to meet you! You know that search warrant affidavit is the first one I've ever seen that was built primarily around behavioral information. That's fascinating. I look forward to working with you!"

Bob and his wife Peggy, both Assistant U.S. Attorneys, lived in Manhattan. At the time, Bob was First Assistant U.S. Attorney for New Jersey. After UNABOM, he was appointed to head the office. Bob's genial nature belied his intensity when he was at work, and he was always working. I could literally see his mind working behind his smile. I was surprised and intrigued by the effusive greeting he gave me, since behavioral work is done largely behind the scenes and is mostly forgotten in the heat of arrest scenarios and critical crime- scene searches. I remember, for example, one of our action-oriented UTF members bellowing the following while I stood near him in the San Francisco office in March:

"If you ain't in Montana, you ain't nowhere in this case! That's where it's all happening!"

I looked at him and wondered to myself how he thought the UTF got to Montana in the first place. But I wasn't surprised. Behavioral work moves inside and between minds, not visibly like a fast-moving case that involves sending hundreds of people on missions throughout the snowbound landscape of what was not so long ago the Wild West. Most people on the UTF had no idea what I did for a living, and there were quite a few who thought I didn't do much at all. They couldn't see it, and if I tried to show it to them and talk to them about it, their eyes were likely to glaze over and they might remember they had errands to run.

Terry knew and understood what I did, though, and so did Director Freeh. Now I was happy and a little surprised to find that Bob Cleary, who would take the government's case against Theodore Kaczynski into Federal court and before the public, understood it as well.

When it came to UNABOM, there was nothing Bob wasn't interested in. Although he'd had little experience with forensic psychiatry, he was eager to add to his expertise. We all knew there would be a strong emphasis on psychiatric issues. The physical evidence from the cabin was so overwhelming that Kaczynski's defense team had little choice but to rely on a mental defect defense. Despite their client being adamant that he was not mentally ill, they would need to explore every aspect of his life to corroborate their arguments on his behalf.

Because of that, Bob knew he needed to break out some big guns on the psychiatric side for the prosecution team. I watched him at the dinner table in Montana with a beer in front of him, joking with the troops while his mind ticked rapidly through the tasks in front of him. I saw that he was sizing up people around the table for their potential usefulness to him, and I was secretly gratified to realize that I was going to be one of his recruits. The excitement of working the UNABOM case with a tremendously talented team was going to continue for me, and I was on top of the world. I grinned across the table at Terry, whose cheerful, booming laugh made us all feel a part of and eager for the next challenge in the UNABOM case.

By the time Fitz and I got back to San Francisco in May 1996, Bob and the rest of the UNABOM prosecution team were setting up their cramped office space and getting their ducks in a row. Steve Freccero now sat in our FBI space more than he did in his upstairs office in the U.S. Attorney's office suite. Bernie Hubley came in from Montana, and Steve Lapham joined us from Sacramento. From DOJ Headquarters came a quiet and intense attorney named Doug Wilson, who was a whiz at preparing motions for the court and legal maneuvering between the West and East coasts.

Bob took on the psychiatric aspects of the prosecution himself, while he assigned critical projects related to physical evidence, witness interviews, and exhibits to "the Steves" (Freccero and Lapham), Bernie, and Doug. He already knew that the first forensic psychiatrist he wanted to talk to about joining the UNABOM prosecution was Park Elliott Dietz, M.D., M.P.H., Ph.D.

I knew about Park Dietz both from the news media and from my colleagues at Quantico. He was famous for his work in the gruesome Jeffrey Dahmer serial killer case, and had cut his forensic teeth in the arena of notorious cases when John Hinkley was tried for the shooting of President Ronald Reagan and several others in 1981.

Educated at Cornell, Johns Hopkins, and the University of Pennsylvania, Dr. Dietz was a full-time academic at Harvard Medical School and the University of Virginia Schools of Law and Medicine when he began working with the FBI. He had moved from Harvard to the University of Virginia in part to further his work with the Profiling Unit at Quantico, and he assisted them on numerous criminal cases where there were significant psychiatric issues. Over the years, his special ability to communicate complex concepts clearly and precisely to a lay audience had gained him a lot of admirers in law enforcement.

Forensic psychiatry is where psychiatry and the law intersect. Judges and attorneys from both the prosecution and the defense need precise information about the mental states and capabilities of defendants, whether they're mentally competent to stand trial and whether they have a mental illness or vulnerability that may have a bearing on the charged offense. Expert witnesses, like Dr. Dietz, have become critical members of both defense and prosecution teams in courts of all kinds in the United States and abroad. Dietz had a reputation with prosecutors as being magical in a courtroom. I saw a video of his testimony in the Dahmer case, where he clearly and calmly told the jury that Jeffrey Dahmer— killer and cannibal—was not insane, and then explained why. The jury found Dahmer guilty—and sane.

To me, there was nothing more interesting than finding out why people thought and behaved the way they did. I'd spent the last eight years studying clinical psychology on nights and weekends while I was a full-time FBI case agent, and everything I learned from the academic side added something to the way I did my work. The quality of my BAP team consultations around the country gained a perspective outside of counterintelligence and law enforcement that enabled me to look at a far broader picture than some of my colleagues who hadn't had formal psychological training.

In 1998, after the UNABOM case was over, I spent two years in a psychological internship with a State of California conditional-release program for mentally ill offenders and gained even more perspective. My interview experience was far broader than the other interns, who were mostly young psychology students who'd gone on to graduate school soon after their undergraduate education. We had a dynamic and unorthodox supervisor in Dr. Doug Korpi, a left-leaning U.C. Berkeley grad who took a chance on having an active-duty FBI agent participate in evaluations of people who were serving sentences at Atascadero State Mental Hospital for violent crimes.

But before that, I met Drs. Dietz and Resnick. I met Park Dietz first. In the summer of 1996, Bob Cleary and I went to Newport Beach in Southern California, where Park Dietz & Associates occupied a swanky office suite close enough to the beach to share its cool coastal breezes, even in summer.

I couldn't believe my good fortune. I knew agents who would have given anything to be in my shoes, consulting on his home turf with one of the biggest names in the forensic psychiatric world, and helping the Chief UNABOM prosecutor evaluate the usefulness of the Dietz operation for our case. It was a no-brainer, really; he had us at "hello." The intense interest Dietz had in the UNABOM case was obvious from the start, and Bob appreciated his ability to communicate complex psychiatric concepts in legal as well as layman's terms. Bob contracted with Dietz and his team on behalf of the Justice Department. For a year and a half, thereafter, I had a ringside seat as well as a place at the table while the best in the legal and forensic psychiatric business contributed to an impressive case for the prosecution of Theodore Kaczynski for the UNABOM crimes.

One of the first things Bob asked Park to do was to suggest another forensic psychiatrist of his own caliber to work with him on the case. Bob wanted depth on the team, and complete coverage in any event. I realized later that he also needed the synergistic effect of two psychiatric experts in dynamic dialogue. Park suggested several names, but his strongest recommendation was that we approach Phillip Resnick, M.D., who ran a training program for forensic psychiatrists at Case Western Reserve University in Cleveland, as well as consulting for either the defense or the prosecution in the same kinds of high-profile trials that Dietz & Associates handled.

Like Park, Dr. Resnick was a past president of the American Academy of Psychiatry and the Law. They were sometimes on opposite sides in court; and whereas Park was most frequently sought out as a consultant to the prosecution, Phil had nearly an equal number of cases where he'd also done work for the defense.

I had a good deal of exposure to both Dr. Dietz and Dr. Resnick during this intense pretrial period. They were a mesmerizing duo, who couldn't have been more different as individuals. But they were so keyed in to each other's expertise that they often seemed to communicate telepathically. They didn't rely on psychiatric jargon. It was like watching two martial arts masters whose game was so far above the rest that it looks effortless from the outside.

It became my job to translate contributions from Park and Phil as accurately as I could for the prosecutors and the UTF in general. I filled dozens of notebooks with nearly verbatim quotes from everything that came out of their mouths, either together or apart, in countless meetings, conference calls, and letters. I supplied Bob Cleary with a steady stream of memos that detailed their opinions and the progress of their work on the case.

They weren't physically with us much of the time. They both had businesses of their own, taught forensic psychiatric Fellows, and had homes and families in Southern California and Ohio. Bob and I either traveled to see them, or I spent long hours on the phone with one or both of them, covering yellow legal pads with notes and diagrams and assignments I drew based on what they needed to know. I also took continual questions for them from Bob, and did research for all of them in the UNABOM case files. I kept a steady dialogue going so that Bob Cleary didn't have to do it himself. He was managing the whole of the UNABOM prosecution as well as directing the psychiatric aspect of the case. He needed the help. It was challenging work, and I learned something every day. I was also conditioned to working long hours, nights, and weekends after two and a half years of intense investigation in the hunt for the Unabomber.

After Park recommended that we ask Dr. Resnick to join us, Bob and I traveled to Cleveland to meet him and discuss the case. The contrast between Dietz and Resnick amused us from the start.

After we met with him in Newport Beach, Park drove us for a gourmet lunch. His office suite was sunlit and spacious. Walls of bookcases held hundreds of accounts of sensational criminal cases like the serial killer Ted Bundy and the Menendez brothers, as well as psychological texts of all kinds. I drove a rental car down Highway One near the beach while Bob talked continually on his clunky government cell phone (he never knew the number, and we kept losing the signal). Park was a consultant for the *FORTUNE 500*, for television shows, and for entertainment and business figures who were being stalked or menaced in some way. It was a glamorous environment, to say the least.

When we reached Cleveland, Bob and I rented a car and drove to Case Western Reserve University, where we parked in an underground garage and walked through a maze of basement corridors to the office of Phillip Resnick, M.D. It was a tiny little room with two desks, one of which was used by the forensic psychiatric Fellows he trained. A scraggly little plant sat on the windowsill that I think looked out on a light well or something. Phil smiled and stood to meet us. He was as unassuming on first sight as he could be, and I was fascinated at the contrast between him and Park. We sat to talk, and Bob and I were quickly taken by the razor-sharp mind behind Phil's unprepossessing exterior. He had a whimsical sense of humor and a gentle air, but it was soon obvious that, like Park, Phil's mind operated effortlessly and at top speed. He already knew something about the UNABOM case, and he agreed to join the team.

At the end of the winter of 1996–1997, Fitz and I traveled to Cleveland to give Phil a suitcase full of information he'd requested. We walked back to the same little office, where the scraggly plant now baked in the frequent assaults from a tiny space heater that alternately grew red hot and then switched off noisily during our talk. The room was alternately icy and stifling hot. Phil, calm and apparently unaffected by the temperature, demonstrated during our conversation that he and his fellows had already spent long hours on UNABOM in the months since he'd started.

When we left, Fitz was driving us back to our hotel when I saw a big chunk of what looked like snow or ice (or both) ahead of us. I glanced over at him, sure that he'd change lanes to avoid it. He looked straight ahead, and I knew he saw it, so I didn't say anything until we hit it head-on and there was a huge crunch under the car. One of the tires blew and the wheel was badly torqued. We veered to a stop at the side of the highway. There was hardly any other traffic, so we weren't in any danger, but I looked incredulously at Fitz and watched him frown as I said what he knew I was going to say.

"I can't beLIEVE you hit that thing!"

Fitz grumbled and said something under his breath about how he thought it was "just snow." I pulled out my AAA card and called for a tow. When the tow truck showed, Fitz stayed in the car, sulking a little, while I went outside to talk to the driver. The "snowball" was a big rock covered with snow and ice. We got another rental car, but I gave Fitz such a ration about this that he's never forgotten it, and it's been a joke between us ever since.

I have always been amazed and intrigued by certain aspects of the male mind. I risk condemnation for stereotypy here, but I've had such long experience working and interacting daily with a mostly male workforce—first in the Air Force and then in the FBI—that I'm going to make an observation I hope won't offend any readers, or shock my colleagues in psychology with its chauvinism.

Joel Moss and I once drove out to the East Bay near San Francisco to do an interview. It was a sunny day in spring and there were wildflowers on the hills we drove through on the way back. I was enjoying the ride—it was nice to get out of the city. As we turned a corner, a big water tank came into view. I thought to myself, "Big water tank." Joel looked at it and said thoughtfully:

"I wonder how much dynamite it would take to blow that up."

I stared at him, and then we both laughed, Joel a little sardonically as he realized this would be something I would tease him about regularly in the future.

I think it's the differences in male and female perception that make a male/female interview team the best combination in both counterintelligence and in law enforcement. The integration of women agents into the FBI has greatly strengthened its ability to conduct increasingly sophisticated investigations, despite the fact that there are still a number of male agents in the FBI and in law enforcement in general who disparage the inclusion of women in investigative work. Psychology is investigative work. So are medicine, anthropology, history, science, and countless other occupations. It makes sense to use the widest combination of skills and abilities as possible in investigative work; it's more effective, and it's more rewarding.

Terry's appreciation of this fact has been the main driver for the development of our combination of a psychologically aware leadership and management style that has become our trademark. In all the years I've known him, I've never seen him do things the way everybody else did them just because of tradition. It never occurred to him that FBI tradition was important in itself, although to many in the Bureau, as in any law enforcement organization, tradition is sacrosanct. He respected tradition, but if it didn't work he moved forward, looking for a better way to do things, to move things along more effectively. In my opinion, this consistent and open-minded approach is the key to his success in

UNABOM, the fugitive hunt for Eric Rudolph, and nearly everything else he's done for over 30 years.

∞ ∞ ∞

After they were brought into the case, both of our forensic psychiatrists needed indepth information about Theodore Kaczynski and the life he'd lived. In the spring of 1997, Max Noel and I traveled with them to Montana for a week.

We followed the trail of the UTF as it had migrated northeast the year before. Our first destination, however, wasn't Helena or Lincoln but Great Falls, where the Unabomber's cabin had been moved for safekeeping to an empty hanger at nearby Malmstrom Air Force Base.

The wind whistled through the hanger as we got out of the car and walked in. Inside a dimly lit and padlocked enclosure sat the cabin, looking even smaller than it had in its forest clearing when I'd last seen it. Max saw to it that everything was accessible, and then led the way into the tiny structure.

I had a camera, but no flashlight, and we all peered around using the solitary light Max had brought. It was as dark as a cave, and still smelled vaguely of smoke. The woodstove was gone, as was everything else that had been removable; the only structure remaining was the wall of shelves at the rear that had held a startling amount of evidence and personal writings that had become as familiar to me as my own over the last year. By this time, whole passages from Kaczynski's autobiography, journals, letters, and other writings ran unbidden through my mind at all hours. I'd provided annotated and chronological excerpts for Park and Phil, and this was their first opportunity to see part of the environment that made the backdrop to Kaczynski's writings for over 25 years.

Park half-seriously proposed that he would take a sleeping bag and spend a night in the cabin alone to soak up the atmosphere. Clearly, however, this would be impossible. In addition to the dungeon-like atmosphere in the hanger, it was bitterly cold. I couldn't even imagine what the Air Force would think of a civilian—or anyone else, for that matter—camping out in a secure area on a Strategic Air Command site.

Both of our experts spent a considerable amount of time inside, however, and Max and I stepped out to let them conduct their review.

Max and I had worked together on UNABOM, but in diametrically opposed areas. He was all about physical evidence; I concentrated on my specialty: the mind of the Unabomber. Max was a good choice to show Park and Phil around Montana; he'd spent months supervising his team the year before in locations all over the state, and he'd already interviewed most of the people they now needed to talk to as they prepared their psychiatric evaluations and consultations for the prosecution team led by Bob Cleary.

We left the cabin in its silent enclosure and began the long drive to Lincoln. At the time, there was no real speed limit on Montana highways, and we fairly flew down the long stretches of road that led through an increasingly mountainous area.

I had warned Park before the trip about the rugged territory we'd be traveling, particularly around the cabin's former location. To my amazement, he showed up in Montana with a beautiful pair of tan boots that looked more designer than cowboy. "Forgot to mention the mud," I thought to myself. Phil—coming from Cleveland—wore practical garb; whereas, Park looked exactly like what he was: a Southern Californian in stylish and unsubstantial gear that would be sorely challenged by Montana weather. Although I'm also a Californian, the boots I'd bought for the trip were the ones I'd bought when Lee and I traveled with David Kaczynski to his own remote cabin in the Texas badlands the year before. I still have them, and they still sport the dirt they collected from both Texas and Montana in 1996. I decided never to wash them.

We arrived at the former UTF headquarters at the Seven-up Ranch. Since I hadn't stayed in the bunkhouse then, I had no idea what awaited us. There were no other guests, which was lucky, since each tiny room in the long one-story structure shared a single phone line to the outside world. I think Park and Phil were both a little stunned at this; their whole professional lives consisted of timely interchange and communication with their clients. They were uncomplaining and good-natured about it, though, as they were about everything during the trip. I think Max anticipated a lot more difficulty in fulfilling their requirements than we actually had; they were anything but prima donnas. But communication was a problem.

This was brought home to us very abruptly when we got a message from the ranch that Bob Cleary was trying urgently to reach his psychiatric team. Max led us into the little office at the ranch where a single telephone—with another phone line, fortunately— sat on an old desk next to an ancient thermal fax machine. We reached Bob, and he launched into a complicated story about a defense motion he'd just received that involved psychiatric issues.

"Can you send it to us?" Park and Phil asked after Bob gave them a summary. They turned to me to ask for the fax number. I looked at Max, who shrugged a little and shook his head, smiling tightly up at them.

"We can try," he said, glancing at me. One of the ranch staffers walked in with a smile that turned to a perplexed frown as we asked about the fax.

"How many pages is it?" she said.

"Thirty or forty," Park and Phil said together. She looked shocked.

"I don't know . . . we only ever have a page or two . . . it could take a while."

We assured her we'd be there as long as it took, and she set up the machine. I hadn't seen one like it in years. After 15 minutes or so, the first page started to crawl out of the opening, curling as it came, a little blurry and bright blue but readable. We realized we were in for a long campaign in the Seven-up Ranch office.

It was freezing in the little room, although the ranch staff seemed unperturbed; for them, the harsh winter was ending and it was nearly spring. We tenderfeet shivered and piled on coats and blankets. As the painfully slow little fax temperamentally coughed up its pages, it stopped several times, requiring careful attention pretty much the entire time. Park and Phil sat quietly reading while Max and I scouted rounds of hot coffee. I watched and read and took notes almost continually, and, as I did, I never stopped wondering at my own good fortune in getting this kind of exposure to the best in the business of forensic psychiatry.

I learned something almost every time Phil or Park spoke. I was satisfied that my doctoral study had prepared me to understand what they were talking about relative to psychological concepts and diagnostics, but I was thrilled that I was also getting an education in the law where it relates to psychiatry. I'd never had formal forensic psychology training, and working with them was turning out to be the seminar of all seminars. I marveled that I was also getting paid for having this ringside seat at what I considered to be the most fascinating aspect of working the UNABOM case. In retrospect, of course, it was also the basis for the larger issue of Lone Wolf terrorism that sparked the study Terry would commission from me years later.

We spent most of a week in Lincoln, where Max took us to every location Theodore Kaczynski mentioned during his long residence in the woods outside the town. Park and Phil interviewed sawmill operator Butch Gehring; this time Max didn't have to shiver outside in the cold while Butch told his story. They had a long talk with the librarian who'd provided Max with critical information before the search about Kaczynski's research interests as well as his movements in and out of the area using the bus system. I have a photo of Phil sitting at a child's desk in the Lincoln Library, his knees up close to his ears as he took careful notes. Max introduced them to a number of Kaczynski's closest neighbors, who politely said that nothing Kaczynski had ever done or said in 25 years had ever given them the slightest reason for concern that he was violent in any way.

The day before we left Montana, Max drove us down a long dirt road in the forest near Lincoln to meet a local resident who claimed to have had a special relationship with Kaczynski for many years. The FBI and journalists had interviewed Chris Waits numerous times; but if he turned out to have actually been someone in whom Kaczynski confided, forensic psychiatrists on the prosecution team needed to interview him as well. Although Waits later wrote a book about his contacts called *Unabomber: The Secret Life of Ted Kaczynski*, the discussion with Phil that day didn't illustrate any specific insight or knowledge on Waits' part that informed psychiatric issues on the case.

But it was interesting to meet Waits, whom Max had previously interviewed, and positively entertaining to watch the interaction between him, Phil, and Park. Waits was building a new house literally at the end of a road he'd extended into his property, above a picturesque ravine surrounded by thick stands of tall pines and other forest giants that obscured so much of the sky it seemed like twilight in mid-afternoon. He and his wife were living in a couple of trailers he'd moved onto the site, which they shared with a group of lively Shar Pei dogs who enthusiastically welcomed us to their camp. After Max introduced us and Phil prepared to interview Waits, Park started to drift around the area, at great hazard to his designer footwear. It was rugged terrain, but Park was curious about the ambitious way Waits was building his house. Max gave me a look.

"He could run into trouble around here, you know," he told me. "He'd better not stray too far from us—people get lost in these mountains all the time."

I looked over to where Park was disappearing into some trees and turned to follow him. Max called after me.

"Kath, don't make me come after both of you!"

By that time, Max was pretty tired of shepherding us city slickers, and he was impatient to get back to the "real work" of preparing for the federal trial of Theodore Kaczynski. I meandered around the area for a while with Park, who was utterly fascinated that someone would build a home in what he saw as savage wilderness, far from the wide open spaces of water and sky at his own base of operations in Southern California.

When I got back to the area, Phil was sitting on a camp chair that once again put his knees up around his ears, one of several around a well-used fire pit that Waits saw no reason to build a fire in due to what he must have considered balmy spring weather. As he and Waits began to talk, the dogs bounded over in delight and began crawling all over Phil as he struggled with his notebook and pad and tried to keep his big sheepskin-lined hat on his head. I began to pull the dogs off of him, but there were too many of them and they just came exuberantly back. Phil was utterly unperturbed. He calmly asked Waits a number of unhurried questions as the pack wagged and surged around him. I later learned that Phil has quite a few children and a big family in general, so I assumed his aplomb came from that as well as his professionalism. Park looked at the whole scene and shot me a wry glance, shaking his head. He was ready to say goodbye to Montana.

After Kaczynski pled guilty early the next year, Phil invited me to be on a panel that discussed the case at the October 1998 annual meeting of the American Academy for Psychiatry and the Law (AAPL) in New Orleans. Called "Unabomber: Madman or Misanthrope?", it was held before a large and interactive audience of forensic psychiatrists and law enforcement experts. Phil, Park, Chief Prosecutor Bob Cleary, Federal Death Penalty Resource Counsel David Bruck, and forensic psychiatrist Seymour Halleck, M.D., rounded out the panel.

For a little over three hours, we exchanged details of the psychiatric and legal aspects of the case with each other and the audience. It was lively; there was intense interest in UNABOM for many reasons, and forensic psychiatrists were fascinated with the idea that they themselves might be consulted on such a singularly unique subject.

Experts from the defense side on the panel were adamant that Theodore Kaczynski had suffered for years from a severe psychotic illness that rendered him incapable of knowing what was real and what was not. Park said pointedly that although he and Phil had not been permitted to examine Kaczynski himself, his thousands of pages of writings as well as the accounts of his behavior over many years argued against his being severely psychotic, and that although he appeared to have a serious personality disorder, he did not meet the criteria for a psychotic disorder.

Forensic psychiatrist Sally Johnson's evaluation for the court was extensively discussed. She had found Kaczynski to be suffering from paranoid schizophrenia. The court had asked her to render an opinion on whether the defendant was competent to stand trial, but she was compelled by her findings to go further.

What Dr. Johnson saw as a delusion on Kaczynski's part—his conviction that his parents had abused him and made him a "social cripple"—Park saw rather as Kaczynski's opinion. There were no evident hallucinations in his history, and Park and Phil did not consider his obsessive anger at his parents to be delusions because they could not be proven to be objectively unreal. Dr. Johnson had also found that Kaczynski's extreme and consistent obsession with the damage technology was doing to human culture was delusional. If that were true, Phil and Park argued, millions of people with similar opinions through the centuries—many of whom wrote extensively about them—would appear to also have this specific delusion.

Sally Johnson herself was not present to discuss her findings, so I have no further information on the details of how and why she reached her diagnosis. It is true that delusions are part of what are called "positive" indications in a diagnosis of schizophrenia. Suffice to it say, there was and continues to be lively debate on the issue of whether or not Theodore Kaczynski suffered from paranoid schizophrenia.

I was frequently called upon as part of the panel to talk about the long law enforcement history of the UNABOM case, or to clarify things for the audience about some aspect of the investigation. Several questions from the audience came in the form of harsh criticism for the position that the government took in recommending publication of the UNABOM Manifesto in 1995. This question came to Bob but also to me, since I'd participated in the decision.

I reiterated the struggle we'd had over whether our conceding to a terrorist demand had set a dangerous precedent that would encourage the same kind of blackmail from other extremists—Lone Wolves or not—in the future. In the end, I said, the hunt for the Unabomber relied on using his own words against him once they were in print. The issue is still debated, and I still hear from participants in forums on terrorism that our decision was the wrong one. Over a decade later, I wonder what the consequences would have been and whether we would still be hunting the Unabomber. If the care Theodore Kaczynski took to cover every other bit of evidence he left had applied to this one lapse, we most likely would be. In the end, I believe it was his Lone Wolf's need to matter in a larger, social sense that led to his capture.

Workbench in Kaczynski's cabin.

The wood stove that heated Kaczyn-ski's cabin. Bomb components and writings were fund on the shelves in the background.

Selected Statements of Defendant

"A few days ago I finished making a twenty two caliber pistol. This took me a long time, for a year and a half, thereby preventing me from working on some other projects I would have liked to carry out. Gun works well and I get as much accuracy out of it as I'd expect for an inexperienced pistol shot like me. It is equipped with improvised silencer which does not work as well as I hoped. At a guess it cuts noise down to maybe one third. It is said that it is easy for machinist to make a gun, but of course I did not have machine tools, but only a few files, hacksaw blades, small vice, a rickety hand drill, etc. I took the barrel from an old pneumatic pistol. I made the other parts out of several metal pieces. Most of them come from the old abandoned cars near here. I needed to make the parts with enough precision but I made them well and I'm very satisfied. I want to use the gun as a homicide weapon."

GX 18-2046A, pgs. 43-45

Kaczynski's homemade pistol.

Detailed description of how Kaczynski built a pistol.

19

THE ARMY OF GOD

In January 1998, when Theodore Kaczynski abruptly pled guilty to all the UNABOM charges against him, Terry was already chasing the next Lone Wolf in the Nantahala Forest in North Carolina. In the fall of 1997, we'd moved the key components of the UTF to Sacramento to prepare for trial, and many of us had made a separate life there. Babies were born, engagements were announced, and since most of us were staying at the same Residence Inn, we were practically living together. It was a lot like being at college; although the pay was better, the work was harder.

Suddenly, it was over. Besides recording and maintaining the case file and the evidence, the UTF had no further mission.

Bob Cleary and the rest of the prosecution team breathed sighs of relief mingled with twinges of regret at not being able to fully present their case in court. A parade of evidence was ready to be demonstrated in compelling court exhibits that Maggie Stringer and the other analysts had produced, and a unique computerized presentation system was ready to be deployed for the jury. Now, we went from cruising at 100 miles an hour straight into a brick wall. The surviving victims and their families were disoriented by the plea agreement, wherein the government decided to waive the death penalty for Kaczynski in exchange for his plea. Many of them were with us on and off in Sacramento, and the family of the last UNABOM victim, California Forestry Association president Gilbert Murray, was in the courtroom every day. So were David Kaczynski and his mother, Wanda. Privately, I was glad that David and his family were spared the agony of being part of the federal case that would have led to his brother's execution.

We began preparations to return to normal life. It felt odd. For many of us, UNABOM had become our lives during the frustrating and fascinating years we'd worked it. I packed up and moved from the Residence Inn back to my Sausalito condominium with its view of the Bay and returned to counterintelligence work in the San Francisco Division of the FBI.

Coming back to the office was disappointing in a way. It became quite clear that many of our colleagues had gotten on very well without us, thank you very much, and their resentment against the UTF itself gained full expression as we all moved back into our offices. If you don't know what someone has been doing, you might assume they haven't been doing much of anything. The story now was that we'd wasted four years, a huge amount of money, and precious San Francisco resources until ·the Unabomber's brother came along to hand him over to us. We had laughed when one of the front office brass angrily accused a UTF agent of "stealing trash cans" when we made the move to Sacramento. Now our chickens came home to roost, and we came back to a decidedly chilly reception in good old San Francisco.

I worked back into life as I'd known it before UNABOM, luxuriating in long coffee hours at home on weekends and walks through Tennessee Valley out to Agate Beach. I spent time with people who hadn't lived and breathed UNABOM and discovered that life had gone on very well without us while we were gone. I began traveling again with the BAP Program to do behavioral work with my old pals from Washington, D.C., New York, Colorado, and Florida, and resumed working counterintelligence with a new team of agents young enough to be my kids. Happily, I was also working with Maggie Stringer again. Maggie noted ruefully that being on the UTF had been hard on her FBI analytical career, but I still felt the same way I had when I'd told Terry during the hunt for the Unabomber, "Whatever happens after this, it's worth it."

∞ ∞ ∞

It was déjà vu all over again when Terry called me from North Carolina.

"I need your help on this case, Kathy."

He'd had to leave Sacramento so quickly that he hadn't had time to say goodbye. The UTF got a letter of thanks from him and he was off to take over the hunt for the next Lone Wolf. Max spent a couple of weeks in North Carolina before Terry got there, and gave Inspector Turchie—Director Freeh promoted him before he left—detailed notes on the many obstacles presented by the complex structure of the Southeast Bomb Task Force and the separate fugitive hunt for Eric Rudolph. Terry faced many of the same politically delicate interagency issues he'd dealt with in UNABOM. He soon grabbed Joel away from San Francisco to come and help him, and they ended up spending a whole year directing the hunt for Rudolph in multiple states and even overseas.

Once again, Terry was frustrated with the profilers at Quantico. He had a distaste for the fiasco over Richard Jewell two years earlier, which in all fairness was largely media-driven from the start. Jewell later confirmed this by filing suit against the media, not the FBI.

But Terry was also irritated by the efforts of two Quantico profilers who'd suggested altering a witness composite of Rudolph—scruffed up to look like he hadn't shaved or cut his hair for a while—to make him look "less attractive" to the public.

Eric Robert Rudolph was young, fit, and handsome. And as a romantic outlaw figure, he appealed strongly to women as well as men. He still receives fan mail and marriage proposals at his permanent home in a cell on Bomber's Row at the Supermax in Colorado. Quantico was concerned that the composite emphasized his romantic outlaw image, and wanted to counter it in the public imagination by darkening and altering the image.

Although I understood their intent, I was incredulous when Terry called from North Carolina to tell me this.

"Didn't they see what happened to *Time* magazine when they did that to O. J.?" I asked.

Time's darkening of the image of accused murderer O. J. Simpson in an apparent attempt to make him appear more sinister had been the subject of wild and angry debate that featured accusations of racism for weeks on television and in the print media.

Terry sighed.

"That's just one thing. I want you to look at what we have. There are so many similarities to UNABOM in this—not the crimes, but in Rudolph himself, in his personality. He's not just a regular grudge bomber, like Moody in VANPAC. Some of this seems similar to UNABOM."

My ears perked up. I remained—and am still—fascinated by the mind of Theodore Kaczynski. If a young, former military, woodsman in North Carolina, who was placing bombs at abortion clinics and gay nightclubs, had anything in common with the genius mathematician from Chicago, who bombed strangers because he hated technology, I wanted to know what it was.

"I could probably come out for a couple of weeks and take a preliminary look at it," I said. We both knew the new SAC in the San Francisco Division of the FBI was already irritated that Terry had taken Joel—now supervising a White Collar Crime squad—away for months at a time. He was bound to say No to Terry's further diminishing of San Francisco's resources and manpower.

"Just come out here and do your thing," Terry said. "You get involved in this and there's no way the Southeast Bomb Task Force is going to let you go."

It turned out that Terry's faith in my abilities wasn't shared by Woody Enderson, the SAC running the Southeast Bomb Task Force that included all of the "Army of God" bombings in Georgia and Alabama over a two-year period. The fugitive hunt for Rudolph that Terry was now in charge of was only part of the total effort in the Atlanta and Birmingham offices of the FBI, who were often at odds about what should be done in the case. There were also dozens of other agencies involved, including the Georgia Bureau of Investigation, the Birmingham police department, and, of course, ATF.

Despite that, my two weeks in Atlanta, Georgia, and Andrews, North Carolina, were enough to convince me that Rudolph's personality did indeed have significant echoes of Kaczynski's, and in a very specific way.

Both of them were loners and relied exclusively on their own abilities, both intellectual and physical, to deal with the world. They were preoccupied by ideologies that transcended daily life, and were willing to go to extraordinary lengths to act on behalf of those ideologies at great expense of both time and money. Despite the fact that they acted alone, they presented themselves to the world as a group: Kaczynski as "FC," Rudolph as "The Army of God." Their primary aim appeared to be gaining the attention of the wider world to their ideology by stealthy acts of shocking, lethal violence.

I read what the task force in Atlanta had gathered of Rudolph's writings, which were found in his abandoned trailer in Andrews and in the "Army of God" letters themselves. They were few in number, and far less literate than Kaczynski's. Rudolph wasn't as verbose or eloquent, and he relied greatly on quotations from biblical scriptures as justification for his violence against "godless lackeys" of the federal government as well as abortion providers. But his ideology was just as fixed as Kaczynski's. At the same time, he was able to live for long periods of time without contact with anyone. Even his family— although unlike Kaczynski, he was close to them—often didn't know where he was. He didn't appear to feel it was necessary that they should know.

In her well-researched 2006 book *Lone Wolf*, journalist Maryanne Vollers probed extensively into the life of Eric Rudolph after he began corresponding with her from prison. She described his mind as "remarkable and frightening," and detailed his descriptions of how he survived completely alone in the Nantahala forest for five years. To me, the most striking image of his social isolation was in his relating to Vollers how he talked to himself and read newspapers aloud "to prevent his vocal cords from deteriorating during the years when he spoke to no one."

During the five years he was a fugitive, law enforcement as well as media representatives frequently announced that they thought Eric Rudolph was dead. Alternatively, they speculated, he might have escaped to Europe (he had traveled in the past to Amsterdam to buy high-quality marijuana seeds to grow and sell for income after he left the Army). It was incomprehensible to the public—and many "experts"—that he was still in the Natahala forest, alone, with no confederates and no one to talk to or spend time with. If he was still hidden somehow, he had to have help, they thought. Someone had to be sheltering or providing him cover in some way.

It's not surprising that most people had opinions like these. Human beings are social by nature, and for most people a place in society is part of survival itself. The fascination of stories like *Robinson Crusoe* is in the shivery thrill of thinking that one person could be alone so long without the understanding voices of his kind to sustain him. How amazing, then, to read in *Lone Wolf* Rudolph's matter-of-fact account of hearing only his own voice, and exercising it so it wouldn't become rusty from disuse. When many of us stand before a vast, echoing wilderness, what do we do? Call out and listen for an echo. Rudolph apparently did this for practical reasons only.

I did think Rudolph was more resilient emotionally than Kaczynski appeared to be. Rudolph gave no indication of the long torment Kaczynski felt from his failure to find a mate. I attributed this in my own mind to two major differences between them, neither of which had an impact on their determination to operate as Lone Wolves.

Kaczynski, bitterly estranged from his bewildered family for many years, agonized over his failure to successfully negotiate the social world. Rudolph, on the other hand, was secure in a large family that tolerated his solitary nature and was itself somewhat alienated from "normal" American family life. His mother searched for alternatives to suburbia and traditional religion, and her children were encouraged to think and live outside mainstream society.

Rudolph also never expressed any concern about finding a suitable mate. He was by all accounts successful with women sexually, but didn't seem to need them to complete his world. Where Kaczynski was puzzled by society, Rudolph was indifferent to it. There was none of the Asperger's Syndrome flavor in Rudolph's writings that suffused Kaczynski's.

What there was in both, however, was certainty. Neither Kaczynski nor Rudolph doubted the rightness of their ideology or their mission to further it. And both chose to capture the attention of society to their causes by using violence to do so.

The second week of my trip to Atlanta and North Carolina that year was dedicated to traveling with Park Dietz, once again the prosecution's choice for forensic psychiatric expertise in considering the mind of Eric Rudolph. He'd been a consultant during the investigation of the unsolved bombings and had linked the attacks as the work of one man. His profile of the offender had proven to be eerily on target for Rudolph.

Park and I drove out with the task force to the Andrews trailer Rudolph had left the morning he discovered he'd been identified in Birmingham by an alert citizen who'd seen him walk calmly away from the brutal bombing that killed Officer Sanderson and seriously maimed nurse Emily Lloyd at an abortion clinic.

We walked around the unremarkable interior, furnished much as Rudolph had left it. I noticed something by its absence, and confirmed that there had indeed been none found in the trailer: pornography of any sort. This was interesting to me, and Park and I discussed it. Kaczynski was in his early fifties when we captured him, and there was no indication that he'd had any such materials either. His inexperience with women hadn't meant that he was disinterested in sex; on the contrary, he'd expressed agonizing longings for sex with a woman over and over in his writings. But his cabin had been almost monastic in its contents, and Park and I remembered that he'd been scornful of *Penthouse* publisher Bob Guccione's offer to publish his manifesto, writing in a letter to *The New York Times* that people considered *Penthouse* "disreputable at best."

We learned that, in Rudolph's trailer, was a videotape of the movie *Conan the Barbarian*, and there was no literature or other media at a more prurient level than that in his belongings. Interesting, we thought, that Kaczynski and Rudolph appeared to share a certain imperviousness to what is often resorted to by red-blooded males of many nationalities in the absence of a social life of any kind. I make no judgment about this proclivity in any way, but it was surprising to me that it appeared to be absent in both these cases.

I believe that the absence of pornography in the homes of both these men was due largely to their single-minded devotion to, and their overwhelming preoccupation with, their occupations as Lone Wolves. They didn't need to be distracted, comforted, or stimulated. They experienced all of those in preparing for and accomplishing their missions.

One day during the week, Park and I went with a couple of others to view a very disturbing videotape that had been made by one of Rudolph's brothers, Daniel, at his home not far from Andrews, North Carolina. We stood in an evidence vault to watch it. Few had seen it, but it was important for Park to include it in his evaluation.

The tape depicted Daniel coming into a workroom, where he took off his suitcoat and placed it on the back of a chair. We learned later that this was a Sunday morning, and he'd just come from church. In the background, there was the low hum of a motor of some kind idling. Daniel sat down in front of the camera and said, slowly and distinctly, "This is for the FBI, and the media."

Without another word, he stood and began rolling up his shirtsleeves as he walked slowly around the room. He tied a tourniquet tightly around one arm—I don't remember now which one—and began breathing deeply and audibly. Suddenly, he walked quickly across the room and bent down just out of camera range. There was the sharp whine of a buzz saw, and then he lurched back into view, holding his arm up, covered by a towel. Shocked and horrified, we watched him walk around the room again, hearing him breathe in deep shudders. He'd cut off his hand. Park reeled a little in front of me, and I gave him a chair. He'd witnessed a lot of horror in his famous career, and we hadn't seen either the hand or any blood in the footage, but he told me later that it was one of the most chilling things he'd ever seen. I shivered next to him. I can still see the scene in my mind's eye, and it still makes me shiver.

We watched Daniel finally walk out of camera range and then heard the sound of a car engine start up. Incredibly, he drove himself to the hospital. Paramedics rushed to the scene and retrieved the hand, which was successfully re-attached in a delicate surgical procedure later that day.

The only explanation we ever had for Daniel's actions was that he'd felt guilty for betraying his brother by talking to the FBI and other law enforcement after Eric disappeared. Park and I discussed this at length. The religious and moral rigidity that had led Rudolph's brother to punish himself so ruthlessly might be an indication of the rigorous convictions of the family as a whole. Dedication to a cause seemed to be part of the ethos they lived by. We knew this had meaning for the dedication and defiance Rudolph was capable of.

Before we left, Park and I told Terry and the Assistant U.S. attorneys on the case that we were sure Eric Rudolph was alive and alone in the Nantahala Forest.

Mock-up of materials Eric Rudolph used in 1997 to construct a bomb.

Aerial view of the devastation of the Murrah Federal Building in Oklahoma City, April 1995.

Press photo of Timothy McVeigh being transported to his arraignment.

20

THE LONE TERRORIST

In 1999, the FBI under Director Freeh created a new investigative unit for the first time in many years: the Counterterrorism (CT) Division.

Terry had been back in San Francisco for less than a year, promoted to Associate SAC, when he got the call from Freeh in the summer of 2000 to come back to Washington, D.C. That fall, Terry called me about a specific project he had in mind.

"They're setting up new analytical units here, and there are a thousand things going on," he said, "but I want something definitive on the Lone Terrorist.

"I've talked to Dale Watson, CT Assistant Director, and he agrees that I can bring you back here for a few months," he continued. "The Director's already on board with it. What we need is a behavioral study on subjects like Kaczynski, Rudolph, and Timothy McVeigh—people who acted alone or nearly alone in significant acts of terrorism. We need to know more about them so we can develop a way to identify them before they kill dozens or even thousands of people."

"How much time would I have to complete the project?"

Terry hemmed and hawed a little. He was already late for another in the cycle of endless meetings at Headquarters, and I could hear papers rustling as he got ready to run out the door.

"If you can do it in a couple, say, three months, that'll be fine," he said. "Talk to you later."

I hung up the phone and stared out the window from my desk on the twelfth floor of the San Francisco Federal Building. In over 20 years with the FBI, I'd been part of a covert surveillance team;

been the "pigeon" (acted as the money carrier) in an extortion case and the girlfriend of an agent posing as an organized crime figure in another; searched the apartment of a KGB spy under his nose while I acted the role of a visiting friend to his neighbor; learned Russian; interviewed dozens of spies in prisons all over the United States, and worked dozens more challenging counterintelligence and espionage cases as a principal in the Behavioral Analysis Program (BAP).

It was in this last capacity that I found my real footing in combining the interview skills I'd developed with my hard-won psychological expertise. In the UNABOM case, I'd used every ability I had—and stretched past my training into the world of forensic psychology during preparation for the trial of Theodore Kaczynski. Completing and defending my doctoral dissertation was an advanced lesson in the art of social science research, and I'd made a number of good contacts with several prominent forensic psychiatrists and psychologists as a result.

Now I had an opportunity to use everything I'd learned to produce something that every future investigator confronted with the most elusive kind of terrorist could potentially use. It never even occurred to me to question whether it was a worthwhile project. For years, I'd wondered about the similarities between Theodore Kaczynski and Eric Rudolph, and I had an insatiable curiosity about what it was that made such different individuals tick in much the same way. I knew from experience that Terry would get me what I needed to get the job done.

I packed up a couple of heavy suitcases and shipped out at the end of February 2001. Washington was covered in thick snow within days of my arrival. It reminded me of the weekend we'd met David Kaczynski and his wife all those years before. I was given a desk in the Domestic Terrorism Section, next to an analyst and several desk supervisors who dealt with cases in the Field as well as national priority issues. It was a little cubicle in a warren of other little cubicles, towards the center of the floor and away from the windows. So this was the glamorous life at FBIHQ. I signed on to the computer system (because I had a project I didn't have to share a computer like most other agents on the floor), and called for files to review.

A big-wheeled cart appeared by my desk. Dozens of volumes were piled inside: case files, analyses, summary reports, and studies already completed on many known domestic terrorist groups. There was nothing on lone terrorists beyond the case files, and none of those had been looked at together.

I plunged in. For a couple of weeks I just read: files on the computer system, paper files that hadn't made it into the computer system, reports, analyses, and anything else I could find. Everything was about violent groups: left-wing, right-wing, racist, religious extremists, anarchists. They all cohered around a central theme or opponent: anti-government, anti-abortion, racist, white supremacist, radical religious. Every investigative file described the results of time-tested investigative techniques like informant development, undercover agents, physical and court-ordered electronic surveillance, all of which had proven time and again to be effective ways to penetrate and eventually neutralize dangerous terrorist groups.

Happily for me, I also had access to Federal Bureau of Prisons files on several inmates, graciously provided to me by Craig Trout, a detailee who'd been in the Domestic Counterterrorism Section at the FBI for over four years—an unheard of and very valuable tenure. These files included a limited amount of notes from prison psychologists that were like gold to me. I was also fortunate to have help from both ATF and the Secret Service, which led to a unique opportunity to review tapes of detailed Secret Service interviews of one of my subjects. There was a real advantage to being at the seat of power; everybody knew somebody from a dozen different agencies, and a lot of business was possible if you networked appropriately.

One day, I read a San Diego report about the "Lone Wolf Task Force" that detailed efforts by multiple law enforcement agencies— including the FBI—to investigate the rabble-rousing activities of a white supremacist named Alex Curtis. Curtis was using his Web Site to inspire his colleagues with a sure-fire method to evade law enforcement in striking out for the cause. One of his written diatribes, called "Advice for Lone Wolves," issued a call for a lone wolf who could strike under the radar and disappear into the woodwork, away from the group that was being observed and

penetrated by law enforcement. Curtis, who trembled uncontrolla-
bly when he was arrested in his parents' home, operated the Web
Site from his bedroom.

"Advice for Lone Wolves" was a stern directive from this desk-
bound terrorist ideologue that provided a checklist for avoiding
attention from law enforcement while performing stealthy acts of
lone terrorism for the cause (in this case, white supremacy). It was
grimly amusing to read. "Lone Wolves" were exhorted to live mod-
est lives, take menial and low-paying jobs, drive nondescript cars,
and avoid tattoos. They were instructed to avoid social gatherings
of the group at all costs, not to drink alcohol, or take drugs. Only by
this regimen, Curtis lectured, could they avoid surveillance, coverage by informants, or eventual arrest. Even so, they would eventually be caught or arrested. When that happened, they were to
accept their fates without complaint, never giving up the members
of the larger group, ending their lives in prison if it came to that,
without ever confessing to or cooperating with law enforcement.

"No tattoos?" I thought to myself. No drinking, no drugs, no
socializing? That didn't sound like the kind of scene most white
supremacists I knew of would be eager to follow. I wondered what
kind of human beings Curtis thought he was writing to, and
whether he realized the "Lone Wolves" he called for were creatures
of his own imagination rather than reality. Big parades, parties,
and bonfires were a big part of the social fabric that held his kind
of terrorist group together, and he was unlikely to have any real
takers for the strict discipline he recommended his Lone Wolves
exercise on behalf of the cause. I imagined readers of his Web Site
nodding their heads in approval of Curtis' admonitions while they
drank beer together at a barbeque or rally. They would certainly
respect such a selfless effort, but they were unlikely to take it on
themselves. Let someone else sacrifice enjoyment and a social life
for the cause; it was easier to shout epithets and wave flags to
show their support, and it certainly wasn't as risky. Freedom of
speech was still the law in America, after all.

After reading hundreds of pages about the "Lone Wolves" that
presented a secret menace to the public and a potential nightmare
for law enforcement, I came to the conclusion that, in reality, the
Lone Wolf was more fable than fact. To be a real Lone Wolf would

be a very difficult thing to accomplish, and it was certainly beyond the capacity of most human beings to stay away from the comforts and stimulation of society, sacrificing their own happiness in their selfless furtherance of an extreme ideology or belief.

If that was so, however, what about Theodore Kaczynski and Eric Rudolph? What about Timothy McVeigh? They'd all presented themselves as part of a group: Kaczynski was the anarchist (later terrorist) group "FC"; Rudolph was the "Army of God." There is now an "Army of God" Web Site that posts bulletins from Rudolph in his cell at the Supermax, but he was never part of it during his terrorist campaign. Timothy McVeigh had tried to recruit "soldiers" in his quest to spark a new American Revolution, but he'd ended up with a nervous and cuckolded misanthrope in Terry Nichols, who'd let him drive alone to Oklahoma City in a truck rigged to explode. None of them were members of an actual group.

What was it about these actual "Lone Wolves" that made them commit spectacular acts of terrible violence without being members of the terrorist groups whose ideology they appeared to share?

∞ ∞ ∞

After I'd plowed through dozens of files—including the Timothy McVeigh and Terry Nichols files under OKBOM as well as numerous files on violent anti-abortionists like Rudolph, who'd killed personnel at abortion clinics, and white supremacist spree killers, who'd shot numerous victims in Los Angeles and Indiana in the 1990s—I knew I'd have to clarify what I was doing before I got bogged down in case studies.

The most common law enforcement report is the case report, where thousands of tiny details illuminate the subject at hand but often don't extend the light past that individual case. Investigators think in terms of individual cases, the sort that form their entire experience. Although they may extract information that has a larger meaning from their experience—and may have a sophisticated understanding of a certain type of offense or offender—cases are King. When agents or cops get together and the "war stories" start, they always begin with something like, "I had this case . . . "

Psychological and other social science research is guided by a set of defined criteria, with meanings and definitions understood and agreed on before the work is done. I knew I had to clarify my study in my own mind before I could begin to lay it out for anyone else. I needed help in wading through this, and I knew just where to get it: Dr. Philip Erdberg, a world expert in complex methods of psychological assessment and a former consultant to the California Conditional Release Program for Mentally Disordered Offenders.

Phil was—and is now even more so—justly famous for the training he provides psychological professionals in the United States, Europe, and the rest of the world in the complex field of projective personality assessment. I'd taken a number of his classes, and I was particularly interested in his specialty: interpretation of the Rorschach technique.

Now, I called Phil in California to discuss the criteria for my study. Phil is a master at communicating complex ideas in plain language; and whenever I got befuddled by too much data or a foggy sense of direction, I could count on him to set me straight. He was fascinated by the idea of the study of lone terrorists. It fit in with his substantial interest in personality disorders. Phil's range of interests is broader than most, and he's very generous with his valuable time, always eager to discuss a new idea or project.

Phil spent hours with me on the phone over the next few months and made several critical contributions to my study. The first was in helping me set criteria to define precisely what characteristics generally apply to lone offenders, so I could isolate individuals from the case files. I also consulted Dr. Reid Meloy, a forensic psychologist in San Diego known for several published works on the psychopathology of violence. At the end of a week, we had established six criteria for selecting from the counterterrorism files the individual lone terrorists I'd be studying:

1. The terrorist act was conceived and executed by one or a few individuals not operating in the context of an organized group.
2. There was conscious acceptance of lethal violence as a means to achieving an ideological, political, or religious goal.
3. Although personal motivations for lethal violence might be present, accomplishing a larger ideological, political, or religious goal was always a primary objective.

4. There was conscious acceptance of the possibility of death or injury to third parties not associated with the primary target (what Timothy McVeigh called "collateral damage" when referring to the children who died at the Murrah Federal Building).
5. It did not appear that the perpetrator(s) intended suicide.
6. Homicide resulted from the act, or would have resulted had law enforcement or other circumstances not intervened.

The exclusion of suicide as part of the act subtracted from the "Lone Terrorist" definition what seemed at the time to be a significant number of "school shooters" at locations all over the country. The emphasis on ideological, political, or religious goals was a key selector in establishing my final study of ten subjects:

Joseph Paul Franklin
Buford O'Neal Furrow, Jr.
Michael Frederick Griffin
Paul Jennings Hill
Theodore John Kaczynski
Timothy James McVeigh
Terry Lynn Nichols
Eric Robert Rudolph
John C. Salvi, III
Benjamin Nathaniel Smith

It was clear at the outset that I would have to include subjects who'd killed staff at abortion clinics. Rudolph was the latest and most wide-ranging of these, but Griffin, Hill, and Salvi were also driven by an extreme form of anti-abortion religious ideology that was not generally classified as terrorism in the wider sense. The FBI had investigated their crimes under statutes governing hate crimes and civil rights violations. But they were terrorists under the criteria that defined my study, and they had acted alone. In addition, anti-government ideologues that included white supremacists and militia groups were making anti-abortion part of their cause, since in their view it resulted in diminishing their future numbers in the face of increased immigration and minority populations.

Ten subjects. In a way, it was encouraging; it was good to know that lone terrorists are relatively rare birds. But it was problematical from a research standpoint. I knew I'd have trouble making meaningful generalizations from such a small set of subjects. In the end, I was satisfied that, by holding to the criteria, I'd eliminated a large number of terrorist group members and "wannabes," who might otherwise have populated my sample and confused the results.

∞ ∞ ∞

Soon after I arrived in Washington, I had lunch with Dr. Steven Behnke, a Harvard Medical School psychologist who was then head of the Ethics Division of the American Psychological Association in D.C. Steve was one of several accomplished brothers that included John Behnke, who'd been Director Freeh's longtime agent assistant. As I described my reason for being in Washington, Steve listened intently, and then leaned forward and said in an earnest tone:

"You know that 90 days isn't anywhere near enough time to conduct this kind of study, right?"

I shrugged and smiled at him across the table.

"It's what I have, though. And the data I need isn't in the files. It's behavioral, personal stuff that no one's really looked at before."

I explained that I'd already taken a shot at getting in on an interview of Timothy McVeigh, who was scheduled to be executed that summer if he wasn't granted clemency and a full pardon for the Oklahoma City bombing. Longtime FBI profiler Al Brantley and Supervisor Mark White from the Dallas office were trying to arrange an interview as the clock ticked, and the politics of the situation were fierce. I'd stopped in Dallas on my way to Washington at the end of January and briefed SAC Danny Defenbaugh and White on my study and offered to assist in a behavioral interview. But I knew the ball was already rolling, and I would have had to get in the back of a very long line to get any kind of access to McVeigh.

"You know," said Steve, "I don't think you should even try to interview any of the subjects in the study directly. You don't have time." He looked thoughtfully at me. "What I'd suggest you do is consult instead with the forensic psychiatrists and psychologists who worked on the cases for court. It's the only way you're going to get a clear focus on the psychological angles, and they might share with you the specific behavioral information you're after."

I sat back in my chair. This was brilliant. It was also going to get me out of the Hoover building for a while, since I'd have to travel all over the country to consult and review data in the offices of psychiatric and psychological consultants for the court, the prosecution, and the defense.

"Reid Meloy is in San Diego," I said with a grin. Steve laughed.

"What an unlucky break," he said.

I bought Steve's lunch and headed back to the office, where I dove back into the files until most of the staff had gone home. It was about 7:00 p.m., and Domestic Terrorism Section Chief Jim Jarboe was packing up for the night. I walked in and told him I had good news and bad news.

"Terry really trained you well, didn't he?" he said sardonically.

I said the bad news was that the behavioral information I needed for the study wasn't in the counterterrorism files. He looked chagrined, until I said the good news was that I knew where to get it.

"We'll send you anywhere you need to go," he said. "Have you talked to Terry about it?"

I'd seen Terry only occasionally since I'd arrived. As Deputy Assistant Director for Counterterrorism, he spent most of his time with the Director and the Executive Staff. He was setting up a staff organization in the new Division that would streamline management and analysis. When I talked occasionally with some of the agents he had running special projects up and down the floors of the Hoover building, they always asked me the same thing.

"Does he always work this hard and fast?"

I told each one that it was a very different proposition, working for Terry. He moved things more quickly and wove teams together in a positive way that they'd appreciate even more in retrospect.

"Enjoy it while you can," I'd say. "There's nobody quite like him. Keeping up with him is a job, but you'll have fun. He makes things happen."

The fact that Director Freeh relied on Terry made it obvious that they'd pay attention to him in any case, but their appreciation of his abilities was good to see. He'd told me Headquarters was a rough place, and huge management and operational challenges presented themselves every day.

When I walked into his office one day he was on the phone; he waved me to a chair and said into the receiver:

"How many hostages are there?"

Hmmm, I thought. Maybe I'd better come back later for a chat. It turned out that several Americans were being held for ransom in South America, and my quirky observations on interesting items I'd found in archived files weren't any kind of competition for his attention right then. I knew he trusted me to do the right thing, so I wrote him a note: "Call me when you can; I have to go to Boston, San Diego, LA, and who knows where else." Then I left to plan my Lone Terrorist travelogue around the country.

21

THE ROADSHOW

By the end of February, I was ready for the road. I left the icy chill of Washington and landed in sunny San Diego, rented a car, and drove into town to meet with forensic psychologist and author Dr. Reid Meloy. His office was in an old California-style building that looked like a set from a 1950s film noir. The doors fronting on the long, wide halls were all wood with glass windows whose occupants' titles were painted in gold letters. I expected to see Sam Spade open Reid's office door, but, instead, a tall, tanned, and smiling Dr. Meloy welcomed me inside and introduced me to his office partner: a white Shepard dog who sniffed me carefully and decided I passed muster for the master.

He had the kind of office I'd always dreamed about: bookshelves and art lining the walls, windows open to the fresh, sunny air of southern California, and a dog on the carpet.

The Assistant U.S. Attorney on the McVeigh case, Sean Connelly, had given the okay to consult with Reid. In addition to his forensic work, Reid was an associate clinical professor of psychiatry at U.C. San Diego and an adjunct professor in the law school. We chatted about mutual friends—especially Phil Erdberg—and I was just about to begin my spiel about the study when Reid looked at his watch and announced it was time for lunch. We strolled down the street to a café that had outdoor seating and was dog-friendly. Having just spent a month in Washington, I was glad to soak up the California sun.

Reid was immediately interested in the project, and we discussed his consultation with the prosecution on the McVeigh and Nichols cases a few years earlier. When we got back to his office, he set me up in an adjacent conference room with a long table on which I laid out dozens of black binders filled with his notes and communications. He'd had access to information from prison psychologists, and some of the data included information I never would have been able to review if Reid hadn't provided it to me.

"Aren't they smart?" he said. He'd been impressed at the intellectual abilities of both defendants.

"They had a rough time in their personal lives, though." He pointed to several specific documents that depicted this, and then left me to surf through the binders alone in the quiet room.

A hard time in their personal lives, indeed. I knew that two reporters from upstate New York were writing a book about McVeigh. The scheduled publication was planned just prior to his scheduled execution for the Oklahoma City bombing that year. The Bureau was still trying to set up a last-minute interview with McVeigh that would have included Quantico Profiler Al Brantley's effort to gather at least some behavioral information from McVeigh himself. The SAC and supervisor in Dallas had told me that McVeigh was a "hardened warrior" who hated psychologists and "hates women." I knew that this latter point was intended to discourage me from seeking a role in the prospective interview, which I'd decided was a no-go in any case.

Reviewing Reid's files, however, which necessarily contained a lot of information and interviews from the investigation itself, didn't support the portrait of McVeigh as a hardened warrior. He'd been an apparently happy and social child, who became fearful of monsters in his closet after his parents divorced. At school, his response to a bullying incident from older and bigger kids made a huge impression on him. He later would characterize the U.S. government itself as a bully after the lethal standoff at Ruby Ridge and then Waco. He worked for money to buy land when he was still a teenager, and became interested in survivalism. His growing interest in weapons and the militia screed, *The Turner Diaries*, appeared to be less an expression of racism and more an assertion of the right to bear arms and to protect himself.

When he joined the U.S. Army, McVeigh took pride in being the "perfect soldier," staying in barracks and cleaning his rifle while his fellow recruits caroused in town. His "super soldier" reputation in the first Gulf War acquired more gloss after his marksmanship skills dispatched Iraqi soldiers at a distance. When he returned to the United States, he applied for Special Forces training. On the second day, after developing blisters on his feet, he dropped out—in much the same way a brief experiment with boxing in the eighth grade ended after his nose was bloodied.

I noted that, when he was arrested in 1995 as he fled the scene of the Oklahoma City bombing, there was no indication he'd intended suicide in committing the act. His careful concern for his own self-preservation appeared consistent.

McVeigh's relationships with women were striking in their courtly awkwardness. He was bitter about his mother and blamed her for his parents' divorce. But he expressed interest in girls, one in particular, who he seemed to put on a pedestal and toward whom he never really made any overt moves. His awkwardness appeared to me to indicate a reluctance to put himself on the line—to risk the possibility of failure or rejection—so, as he had in Special Forces training, he simply withdrew. His warrior pose allowed him to set himself honorably apart from the puzzling distractions of women and concentrate on bigger issues like the second American Revolution he wanted to spark.

I was fascinated. This was not the steely-eyed young man who looked out coldly at the world when, in a famous news photo, he was led in an orange prison jumpsuit to his arraignment. This was looking more and more like someone who needed to protect himself from harm, and who needed to believe that he mattered in the world despite his discomfort with a life inside it. His ideology seemed more romantic than malevolent. Above all, McVeigh seemed to be seeking recognition and accomplishment in the world.

I was particularly struck by accounts of the visit McVeigh and Terry Nichols made to the Michigan Militia a year or two before they assembled the bomb in the Ryder truck that McVeigh would drive to the Murrah Federal Building in April 1995. McVeigh exhorted the group to violence, saying the "massacres at Ruby Ridge and Waco" demanded payment in kind to the U.S. government. Michigan Militia leader Norman Olsen was quoted in a 1996 book called *All-American Monster: The Unauthorized Biog-*

raphy of Timothy McVeigh: "They were told to leave more than one meeting, because of that type of talk of destruction and harm and terrorism."

Later, McVeigh tried unsuccessfully to recruit members for his own "patriot group." In the final days before the bombing, he tried several times without success to call the National Alliance—a radical militia organization. He taped a note for attendees at a gun show that read "I'm looking for fighters" on a nearby transmission tower in the California desert. He remained alone. Even Terry Nichols didn't join him on his fateful drive to Oklahoma City.

Who'd have thought I'd find echoes of Theodore Kaczynski's personality in Timothy McVeigh? His awkwardness with women, his social isolation, and his total dedication to his ideology sounded ominously familiar. He didn't write down every thought he'd had like Kaczynski did, but there were persistent and compelling similarities in the way they saw themselves and their places in the world.

In the end, it would take two trips to San Diego to review all the material in Reid's office. I confess in retrospect that, if his office had been in Cleveland, like Phil Resnick's, I probably could have done it in one go, but I had other work to do in California, so I arranged to come back the following week.

That evening I had dinner with Reid and his wife and fellow researcher M. J. We were joined by a colleague of Reid's, who drove down from Los Angeles to see what I was up to. When Dr. Kris Mohandie, a Staff Psychologist for the LAPD, heard that my subject group included Joseph Paul Franklin, he said he'd videotaped an interview with him the previous year in Missouri, where Franklin was on death row. He offered to let me see it in full. After a short visit home to San Francisco, I arranged to meet him at his office in Los Angeles.

I checked in with Phil Erdberg when I got to Sausalito. We had lunch at a classic restaurant on Richardson Bay called "Horizons," which was famous as a hippie hangout in the 60s and 70s. He was interested and intrigued in the data from Reid's files.

I told him that, as well as the Franklin videotapes, the Secret Service had offered me a chance to review a long series of their videotaped interviews of Michael Griffin. In 1993, Griffin stalked and killed Dr. David Gunn at an abortion clinic in Florida. We were both elated at the possibilities. The Bureau had largely overlooked contributions from the Secret Service in the past, but I'd worked with them briefly in San Francisco on a threat case involving President Clinton, and I knew they had the best expertise when it came to looking at threats that came out of nowhere. They had a National Threat Assessment Center in Washington, and I was scheduled to meet with two of their psychologists when I got back to D.C.

Terry had made this happen in a characteristically diplomatic move. During a meeting with the Secret Service brass in January, he told them about my study. Afterward, I'd contacted Secret Service psychologists Drs. Marisa Reddy and Robert Fein, and drafted a letter for Terry to sign that was a formal request to review their data.

"This is shaping up in a very interesting way," said Phil. "Keep in touch and share with me what you can. I'll work with you on thinking through what all this means."

We said goodbye and he went back to his office; I went to my house to dust, throw away dead plants and things that had rotted in the refrigerator, do laundry, and my taxes. After a few days I was back on the road again, headed for LA.

∞ ∞ ∞

In the fall of 1999, Buford O'Neal Furrow, Jr., drove from Washington State to Los Angeles where he shot two adults and three children at a Jewish daycare center and then killed a "non-white" mail carrier before taking a cab to Las Vegas. After gambling and drinking "about ten" beers while he watched television news coverage of the shootings, he turned himself in to the FBI.

Furrow's attorneys had just reached a plea agreement with the government in January 2001. I'd already talked to the Assistant U.S. Attorney who'd handled the case for the government, Mike Gennaco, who agreed to my researching the case files as well as talking to Park Dietz & Associates, who'd done the forensic psych work. Mike noted that Furrow's plea agreement included an interview with Furrow himself, and he asked my advice about it. I told him I was sure Park would be interested in a subject interview, and that I would pass the word to his office.

When I arrived in Los Angeles, I got hold of case agent Steve Moore. He spread a cornucopia of information in front of me, including a detailed timeline he'd written about events in Furrow's life up to and including the offenses. Luckily for me, Steve was keenly interested in what made his subject tick, and consulting with him added a great deal to the project.

Furrow was an only child whose dad was an Air Force Chief Master Sergeant. When Furrow was 17, the family retired to Washington State. He did not belong to school clubs, did not play sports, and had no close friends. His father wanted him to join the Army after high school. Furrow did so, but was discharged due to an injury after 60 days in Basic Training. He eventually got an engineering degree and moved to California in the early 1990s, where he worked at Northrop Aviation.

In California, Furrow made his first serious attempt to join a group. He started to hang out with some men at work who rode motorcycles and camped in the desert. Conversation in the group increasingly centered around the sieges at Ruby Ridge and Waco, and its rhetoric emphasized anti-government posturing that, for most of the group, was purely recreational. Furrow, however, became fascinated with it. He began attending gun shows and reading literature that included racist as well as militia orientations. Dropping out of the group—they considered him too strange by this point—he bought a shortwave radio and began listening to KKK broadcasts at night. He heard about a Christian Identity group called the "Aryan Nations," and came to believe they were the group to join.

In mid 1994, he moved to Idaho to join up. Steve Moore told me: "He was so beyond any of the AN's mental capabilities that they initially thought he was an FBI informant. It was kind of like walking into a primitive culture and being named King."

Furrow became a figure of some note in the Aryan Nations. By 1995, he had married the widow of Robert Matthews, founder of the white supremacist/criminal group "The Order," who, in 1984, was killed in a shootout with the FBI on Whidbey Island, Washington. Furrow had practically no prior history of relationships with women; in one humiliating episode, a coworker at Northrop had told him she was a lesbian rather than go out with him. His marriage was effectively over within months, and his wife moved out. Furrow left the Aryan Nations the next year, saying they had become too permissive in terms of who could join the organization and hadn't done justice to the white nationalist cause. He returned to Washington State.

In late 1998, Furrow threatened staff at a psychiatric hospital and was arrested for assault. He signed a statement that he'd had "suicidal and homicidal thoughts for some time now," said he was a white separatist and that he'd thought of killing his ex-wife, who'd finally divorced him. In May 1999, after inpatient treatment, he was released on 12-months probation. He tried unsuccessfully to reconcile with his ex-wife. After a final argument with her, he decided to drive to Los Angeles and carry out his assault.

After his arrest, Furrow provided a statement that he'd wanted to "wake America up, to let them know the Jews have destroyed the country, and also how the non-whites are taking it over." He hoped that others would follow his example, and said that killing Jews was "a good thing for God." He added that he'd thought of shooting people at an abortion clinic, because abortion was "killing the white race."

Steve Moore told me that Furrow's prison time (he was sentenced to life) had been stormy, and although he'd tried to appear remorseful in FBI interviews since his plea agreement, he continued to threaten psychiatric staff and act aggressively toward others. Here was a lone offender whose mental difficulties were beyond dispute.

Later, I found that John Salvi—who killed two and wounded many others during a rampage within 48 hours at three different abortion clinics in Massachusetts and Virginia—was perhaps the most severely mentally ill of the ten individuals in my sample who met our criteria. I met with forensic psychiatrist Ron Schouten, M.D., and psychologist Robert Kinschereff, Ph.D., in Boston in March, both of whom agreed completely—despite the fact they worked on opposite sides in the court case—that Salvi had been severely mentally ill for a long time before his offense.

It was becoming apparent, however, that there was something shared by this group of ten lone terrorists that distinguished them from each other far more subtly than their socioeconomic differences. Salvi obviously had social difficulties related to his psychotic disorder (he was diagnosed as suffering from paranoid schizophrenia), but his diatribes at abortion clinics, and even during a service that a Catholic Church had not done enough to stop abortion, were similar to Furrow's accusation that the Aryan Nations weren't living up to their credo. All of these men were convinced that they had the direct line to the truest form of the ideology they espoused, whether it was anti-technology, anti-government, or anti-abortion. And none of them—whether they had been diagnosed with a mental illness or not—had successfully attached themselves to a group that shared that ideology.

∞ ∞ ∞

As socioeconomic groups go, the next subject of my study, Joseph Paul Franklin, was on a different planet from either Kaczynski, McVeigh, Furrow, or Salvi. But in my study, I came to consider him the occupant of one far end of the Lone Wolf curve.

In early March 2001, I met with Dr. Kris Mohandie at his office in LA. He was curious about how the study was shaking out. We had an interesting discussion over lunch about cases; "war stories" are always de rigueur in law enforcement.

When we got back to his office, he set me up in a conference room to watch the tapes he'd made of his own interviews with Franklin, as well as interviews done by a police agency and the media in Missouri in 1994 and 1999.

In the winter of 1975, Joseph Paul Franklin (born James Clayton Vaughn, Jr., he changed his name to honor Nazi Paul Joseph Goebbels and Benjamin Franklin) was kicked out of a rooming house in Maryland and decided to "do some killing . . . couldn't get a job . . . was going to pay some Jews back for it." He said he was influenced by Charles Manson in wanting to also "start a race war," but, instead of killing wealthy white people, would target interracial couples. He joined the KKK the next spring to learn how best to accomplish his mission. By the fall, he dropped out, after concluding that the Klan had abandoned its heritage and was now a joke.

Despite loss of vision in one eye due to an injury that had given him an excuse to drop of out of high school, he began acquiring weapons and taught himself to be a sniper.

In July 1977, Franklin began his mission in earnest when he bombed a synagogue in Tennessee. In August, he rammed the car of an interracial couple, shooting them at close range and killing them. During the three years that followed, he is believed to have murdered as many as 20 people, moving from state to state and changing his name, car, and hair color. In 1978, a round from his rifle paralyzed *Penthouse* publisher Larry Flynt, whom he'd targeted ever since seeing an interracial couple in the magazine. In 1980, he shot and wounded Urban League President Vernon Jordan.

He was finally caught (at a blood donor facility), convicted for several of these crimes, and incarcerated at the federal penitentiary in Marion, Illinois. When he felt he was in danger from other inmates, he started confessing to his crimes. He has enjoyed his notoriety ever since, while he awaits execution in Missouri. He avidly promotes his outlaw status, and has repeatedly bragged that he has "the same number of murders as Billy the Kid."

Franklin was the most cheerfully psychopathic member in my group, but I noted right away that he shared some interesting characteristics with the others.

His family was poor and his father an abusive alcoholic. He was quiet and withdrawn as a teenager when he became fascinated with religious extremism. While listening to the radio at night, he learned about and embraced a white supremacist ideology called British Israelism. In 1968, the same year he joined the National Socialist White People's Party (formerly the American Nazi Party), he married briefly, but his wife left after he began beating her. A brief second marriage led to the birth of a daughter, but he soon left them. He moved to Atlanta, where he listened to and admired the white power radio broadcasts of Dr. William Pierce, author of *The Turner Diaries*. It was there he joined the KKK for several months before leaving them in disappointment.

Again, the pattern is clear—repeated and unsuccessful attempts to join a radical group. Like Kaczynski, McVeigh, Rudolph, Furrow, and Salvi, this Lone Wolf saw himself as the best, truest believer in the ideology that had captivated him. Theodore Kaczynski had admired and quoted Eric Hoffer's *The True Believer* in both his journals and the UNABOM Manifesto, but he hadn't seemed to consider that its descriptions resonated in his own life and character. All of these men—despite wide variances in their backgrounds, education, and family origin—were beginning to look like they shared characteristics of thought and social development that appeared to predispose them to classic behavior as Lone Wolves.

∞ ∞ ∞

When I got back to Washington, I contacted Drs. Marisa Reddy and Robert Fine at the U.S. Secret Service to arrange a look at the data they had on two other lone terrorists who'd shot and killed personnel at abortion clinics: Michael Griffin and Paul Hill.

I met with Marisa and Bob and talked about what I'd found so far in the data. They were intrigued, and I was soon set up in a spacious conference room with dozens of videotaped interviews of Michael Griffin. It took me several days to go through the hours of tapes. I took detailed notes because Griffin's case was probably at the other end of the Lone Wolf spectrum from Franklin when it came to psychopathy.

In early 1993, Griffin and his wife became involved with John Burt, a lay preacher at their church. Burt, a former member of the KKK, had become the militant regional director of "Rescue America," a national anti-abortion organization. He also operated "Our Father's House," a home for troubled youth and unwed mothers in Pensacola, Florida. At his wife's suggestion, Griffin began doing odd jobs at Our Father's House, where he saw and was horrified by a video graphically depicting abortion.

Although others at the house later described him as a quiet loner who never showed strong emotions, Griffin said during the interviews I watched that the issue of abortion became increasingly intense for him over the next two months. He began to spend hours alone outside an abortion clinic targeted by Burt and his followers, on one occasion "for five hours in the rain with a gun in my pocket." He waylaid Dr. David Gunn on the highway one day and told him, "The Lord told me to tell you that you have one more chance." When he saw Gunn later at the clinic, he said Gunn was "sarcastic and adamant" when Griffin told him, "David Gunn, you're accused and convicted of murder, and your sentence is Genesis 9.6. (whoever sheds man's blood, by man his blood shall be shed)."

On the tenth of March, Griffin finished three long shifts at the Monsanto plant, went home to shower, changed into a coat and tie, and drove to the clinic where he shot and killed Dr. Gunn.

Michael Griffin first became affiliated with fundamentalist Christianity in his teens, to the distress of his father, a prominent dentist who was active in the Pensacola Presbyterian Church. He entered the Navy at 19 and was assigned to submarine duty, which he described as "prestigious." His final rank was petty officer. He had married his high school sweetheart right after joining the military. By the time he was discharged in 1988, they had two daughters.

Griffin said that by 1993 his wife was "acting strange, suicidal." She demanded that he leave her a gun when he went to work. He had discovered she was unfaithful to him two years earlier, after which he had filed for divorce and asked for custody of their two daughters. She had countersued, alleging that Griffin was a violent man who abused her, and she obtained a restraining order against him. After pastoral counseling at their church, both suits were dropped and the family reunited. But Griffin was bored and "uninspired" at work, which he described as "not prestigious." He began eating mounds of sugary junk food and gained 70 pounds. A pastor at one of the churches he'd attended told the press after the shooting that Griffin was "too radical . . . he'd have ideas and you couldn't reason with him."

By the time he was interviewed in 1997, Griffin appeared to be at a normal weight and was calm and soft-spoken. He expressed remorse for his crime, but was adamant that, if Dr. Gunn had only changed his ways, "I wouldn't have killed him." He was most sorrowful about his marriage breaking up. "I'd rather still have my marriage than not be in here," he said. He was given life imprisonment.

If Franklin was at the psychopathic extreme on the Lone Wolf continuum, Griffin was at the other extreme. I was reminded of the "twinkie defense" at the trial of Dan White, the former San Francisco City Supervisor who'd shot Mayor George Moscone and Supervisor Harvey Milk in 1978, my first year in the San Francisco Division. Griffin himself said his blood sugar was "really wild" at the time of the shooting.

Nevertheless, there was a stony aspect to Griffin's manner, an apparent conviction that his cause had been just and that he'd had no choice in pursuing his course of action alone, without counsel from anyone else. He'd described feeling like an outsider, and said he did work around John Burt's group in an effort to fit in, to be accepted by both the group and by his own wife. Despite his efforts, he said, he never felt that he was really a member of the group, or that his wife was happy with him.

∞ ∞ ∞

Back in my cubicle at the Hoover building, I turned my attention to the last of my Lone Wolves: Benjamin Nathaniel Smith.

There was no need to do a road trip to look at Smith. I'd already talked by phone with Bob Brown, the case agent in Peoria, Illinois, who said that everything they'd been able to surface about Smith was in the FBIHQ file, which was available to me on the computerized Automated Case System (ACS) in Washington. I called Terry and told him that I'd found a use for ACS, at last. He was unimpressed.

"How much more time do you think you'll need?" he said.

I thought about the conversations I'd had about the project with my psychologist and psychiatrist colleagues. When I was in Boston, I had dinner with Larry Strassberger, M.D., who'd just been elected President of the American Academy of Psychiatry and the Law. He was skeptical about my ability to get anything at all done in 90 days, and we discussed the methodological pitfalls that could bedevil such a hurried project. I knew that in the field of psychological research, what I'd done in the past two months would have constituted the beginnings of a research proposal for a study that would justifiably take years. I would only be able to stretch a few more months out of the Bureau.

"I think I'm going to need at least another month in D.C., I said. "Then I'll need more time in San Francisco to analyze it further and write a final report."

Terry was getting on a Bureau plane with the Director for a long trip abroad to discuss sharing information on terrorism with intelligence agencies in the Middle East and the former Soviet Union. I also knew by this time that he had decided to retire from the FBI. He'd been asked to run the Counterintelligence Program for Lawrence Livermore National Laboratory, and it was way past time for him to get back to his family. His new position would put him half an hour from home rather than 3,000 miles away.

"Okay, I'll get an extension," he said. "See you in a couple of weeks."

I went back to my files.

Case agent Bob Brown had told me that, as far as he knew, there had been no official "psychological autopsy" on Ben Smith. However, speculations about his psychology were all over the news at the time.

On July 2, 1999, Smith wrote World Church of the Creator (WCOTC) leader Matthew Hale a letter withdrawing from the church because he was "unable and unwilling to follow a legal Revolution of Values." Many thought later that Hale—sentenced in 2005 to 40 years for soliciting an FBI informant to kill a federal judge—had manipulated Smith into writing the letter to distance his actions from Hale and the Church. But Ben Smith didn't need to be manipulated into his reign of terror during the July Fourth holiday in 1999.

Smith drove his car to Chicago carrying two guns he'd bought illegally after failing a background check to purchase guns the previous month as well as a bulletproof vest, a military helmet, and a journal in which he referred to a "revolution on the Fourth of July." He shot six people at a Northside synagogue, then drove to Skokie where he killed a black man walking down the street with his children. He then shot at an Asian couple in a nearby suburb, and on July third shot two black men in two different towns. He shot and wounded an Asian man near a university campus, and then killed a Korean man near Bloomington, Indiana, on July Fourth. Running from the scene, he carjacked a minivan and crashed it during a police chase, which ended when he pulled to the side of the road and shot himself in the chest and chin. He died at the hospital later that day.

Benjamin Nathaniel Smith was the oldest of three sons born to a medical doctor and his real estate broker wife who also had a law degree. He grew up in an affluent Chicago suburb, where he had few friends as a child. He liked Dungeons and Dragons, and was often seen in the neighborhood carrying a crossbow and practicing with it in his back yard. He attended an elite public high school. Classmates described him as a quiet, intelligent student who "barely made an impression." By graduation, however, his year-book biography included the Lincoln assassin John Wilkes Booth's quote: "Sic Semper Tyrannis." (The South is avenged!)

Smith's "first racial awakening" was in the eithth grade, when he was "subjected to" mandatory study of the Holocaust. "There wasn't a single incident that traumatized me, he told a reporter in college, "it was just a love for my race." He read *The Turner Diaries* as well as *Mein Kampf,* but it wasn't until he read *Nature's Eternal Religion*—by the founder of the WCOTC—that he said he finally found what he'd been looking for.

Smith was attracted to WCOTC's opposition to Christianity as well as to Judaism, and its condemnation of all racial minorities and immigrants as lesser beings. When he was unsuccessful at starting a group of his own, "The White Nationalist Party," he turned fully to the WCOTC. He began distributing leaflets and wrote numerous letters to the campus newspaper, explaining that his goal was to "wake up my race and achieve a pure white America."

Faced with expulsion after beating up a girlfriend and using marijuana in a dorm room, Smith enrolled in the criminal justice program of another university and continued his letter writing and leafleting. WCOTC leader Hale named him "Creator of the Year" in 1998, and he did an on-camera interview with the media in 1999 near his childhood home. His only known employment, in May 1999, was a brief stint with a construction company in the Chicago area. His arrest records— for physical fights with a WCOTC woman who lived with him until he beat her once too often—reflect that antidepressant medication was found in his car. He became increasingly estranged from his parents. A witness later said that in the Fall of 1998 he heard Smith tell Matthew Hale that he wanted to "kill Jewish people," and that Hale told him that the WCOTC "did not condone violence." Another witness said that, after Hale was denied a legal license at the end of June 1999, Smith called Hale to reiterate his intention to kill Jews. Hale alleg-edly replied, "Make sure you get enough of them and then get out of there."

∞ ∞ ∞

It was after 10 p.m., and it was quiet in the office. My desk lamp was the only one still on, and the rest of the room, with its dozens of cubicles, was in shadow. Everyone else in the Section had gone home hours ago.

I thought about the howling loneliness that was the social world these Lone Wolves lived in. Each of them had tried numerous times to connect to other people, and despite their relatively high levels of intelligence, they repeatedly failed. I hadn't anticipated that I would feel any compassion for them, given the savagery of their crimes. Looking at the choirboy faces of Timothy McVeigh and Ben Smith, it was wrenching to think that they had grown from children into monsters by following their dark visions. I remembered the anguish in many of the thousands of pages Theodore Kaczynski had written, and the matter-of-fact descriptions from Joseph Paul Franklin of his own desolate life. I thought of Eric Rudolph listening to the sound of his solitary voice for five years in the Nantahala forest. There had been a stony, haunted look in the eyes of Michael Griffin as he described shooting Dr. David Gunn, and I winced when I thought about the desperate frenzy in the minds of John Salvi and Buford Furrow.

My task now was to figure out just what it was that they had in common, this handful of men from vastly different backgrounds, who were driven to commit societal-level acts of stunning violence alone.

I closed the file on Smith and stared at the charts I'd put up on the wall behind my desk. There were lists of files, names of contacts, and a calendar with days marked off in red. I'd taken to working nights to stay out of the normal business of the office, and to have the space that was crowded and busy during the day quiet and to myself so I could work. I had a growing awareness that this was a little Lone Wolfish of me, but I told myself I'd become a social being again after this was over. The hallways of the Hoover building were mostly quiet at night, although there were always others around doing some sort of work. Lots of people burned the midnight oil at the Bureau.

My days in the FBI were now numbered. Terry had called me while he was on a trip home to California and offered me a job at the SAFE Program at Lawrence Livermore Lab. I'd chuckled initially, sure he was kidding. I lived 60 miles from Livermore, and I'd escaped having a long commute to the office for 23 years.

"You can't be an FBI agent forever, Kathy," he said.

I turned out the light and headed home for the night.

John C. Salvi, III   Joseph Paul Franklin   Paul Jennings Hill

Benjamin Nathaniel Smith   Timothy McVeigh as a teenager

22

THE LONE TERRORIST UNMASKED

Although I began my analysis of the data I'd gathered while I was still in Washington, I finished in San Francisco. Burning the midnight oil at the Hoover Building had only gotten me so far. While on the phone one day with Phil Erdberg, I said nervously that I was running out of time, and worried that I wouldn't make my report deadline at the end of April.

"Kathy," Phil said softly, "What is the reason for the April deadline? Is there any real reason you have to have it done by then?"

I thought a second.

"No," I said. "You're right. I need more time."

I called Terry, who was packing up his office, and asked him to intercede on my behalf with the brass in San Francisco, since I was likely to have a full caseload land on me the minute I got back. He called, and the SAC back home agreed that I could have the summer to finish the study. I felt a huge weight adjust on my shoulders. It wasn't gone, but it shifted so I could deal with it. I was already interviewing for the job at Livermore Lab, and I knew now that I could give the study my all as my swansong project in the FBI rather than doing a rushed and slapdash job.

I was on the phone with Phil regularly now, discussing details of the lives of the Lone Wolves I'd researched, their crimes, their statements, and their histories. It was critical for me to use him as a sounding board to check my thinking. His ability to digest the meaning of what I was looking at in psychological terms would be the key to the findings in my final report. Busy as he was—and I knew he was still mentoring graduate students, consulting for numerous agencies, as well as conducting training seminars in the United States and abroad—he was as generous to me with his time as if he was on a long cruise somewhere with nothing more urgent than relaxation on his mind.

I couldn't discuss with Phil all the information I had. Some of it was proprietary to the FBI, or part of a case file and not for public release. At the time, for example, Eric Rudolph was still at large, and some of the information I referenced from the case file led to my study being initially classified by the Bureau as "Law Enforcement Sensitive" after I'd finished it.

What Phil and I worked through together was understanding and demonstrating the psychological dynamics behind the lethal actions of these Lone Wolves.

All ten subjects acted alone, or with a few confederates, to commit acts of terrorism outside the structure and direction of an organized group.

Throughout history, thousands—if not millions—of violent criminals have placed or sent bombs, shot, or otherwise killed their victims. Many committed their crimes alone. But there were two things right off the bat that differentiated the Lone Wolves in my study from other solitary offenders.

First, their crimes were big: violence at a societal level, with a capital V. Kaczynski had tried at least once to blow up a plane in mid-flight. Rudolph planted a bomb in the middle of an Olympics venue. McVeigh's truck bomb destroyed an entire federal building and killed many of its occupants, 19 of them children. Franklin, Furrow, Salvi, and Smith went on rampages that took them through streets of multiple neighborhoods and even multiple cities and states. The shot Griffin fired was the first by a religious zealot that killed an abortion provider. Paul Hill was inspired by his act, and landed an appearance on the Phil Donahue show to applaud it for being "as good as [Nazi] Doctor Mengele being killed. A year later, Hill shot two more at another Florida clinic.

Second, they were shaped and motivated by ideology. They didn't know their victims, and they weren't out for money or any personal gain outside the notoriety of their acts. Whether or not the Lone Wolf attacks of Ben Smith or Eric Rudolph would have been applauded by someone like Alex Curtis, who openly sought such services for his own cause, would have been completely irrelevant to either Smith or Rudolph. They weren't in the game to gratify anyone else but themselves.

Why was it that ideology framed the actions of these real Lone Wolves and set them apart from other offenders who commit acts of criminal violence? What was it about ideology that gave them what they needed to act alone?

∞ ∞ ∞

Jerrold Post, M.D., directs the Political Psychology Program at George Washington University in Washington, D.C. His many publications on the psychology of terrorism emphasize a key point: "The Cause is Not the Cause":

Individuals are drawn to the path of terrorism *in order to commit acts of violence* [emphasis mine], and their special psycho-logic, which is grounded in their psychology and reflected in their rhetoric, becomes the justification for their violent acts. (From *Origins of Terrorism*, Cambridge University Press, 1996)

If altruism and dedication to a cause were enough, there would be no end to the supply of selfless and dedicated terrorists who were ready to surrender their lives and even die for their ideological causes. But I believe that such individuals are actually rare. I would submit that even the international terrorists who preoccupy us most—like the hijackers on 9/11—are distinguished by their own needs, and their actions are unlikely to be selfless.

The throngs of suicide bombers who were supposedly poised to enter the United States to conduct waves of terrorist attacks against soft civilian targets after thousands died at the World Trade Center, the Pentagon, and in a field in Pennsylvania have not—nearly six years later—unleashed those individual attacks. At the same time, suicide bombings in the wartorn Middle East continue, and videotapes record their martyrdom for their families and friends, their dedication and sacrifice for the group. They achieve something they would not if, instead, they made a secret and solitary voyage to a distant land to die unrecognized and without the status accorded a martyr by family, friends, and the larger social group in their own culture.

It became more and more clear to me, as I looked at the life stories of the lone wolves in my study, that each had primarily served his own needs in inflicting deadly violence. Their ideology, which was a banner they flew to elevate their own status above that of ordinary men, served their need to *matter* both to themselves and in a social context. Why? Because they'd been *unable to matter socially* all their lives.

∞ ∞ ∞

The subjects in my study ranged in age from 21 (Smith) to 40 (Hill and Nichols) at the time of their first (or only) offenses. Two (McVeigh and Nichols) had parents who divorced during their childhoods. Franklin had an abusive and alcoholic father, and Smith's parents were said to be distant and reclusive. McVeigh considered his mother to have abandoned him; Kaczynski was convinced (against all evidence) that his parents had mistreated him emotionally. But Rudolph was extremely close to his mother and adopted many of her religious beliefs. Franklin was the only high school dropout; all the rest had some college. All of them were described as having at least average intelligence, and most had above-average intelligence. Kaczynski, whose IQ was in the genius range, earned a Ph.D. in mathematics.

They were so different on the surface. Their ages, birth order, family histories, socioeconomic backgrounds, and educational levels were generally dissimilar. Despite this, they committed crimes of striking similarity according to the criteria we'd drawn for the study, and they represented three primary ideological themes: anti-government, white supremacist, and anti-abortion.

Why did they seem so different on the surface when their crimes were so similar? Did they have anything at all in common in their backgrounds?

The developmental similarity that first struck us was that all of them were described as having few friends and being quiet and withdrawn as children. I thought at first that McVeigh and Hill were exceptions to this, but then found that, as he grew past boyhood, McVeigh was increasingly described as a loner. As an adult,

Hill began spending most of his time "alone in the attic writing sermons and speeches."

In all the subjects except Hill, their social isolation was linked to and compounded by a lack of satisfactory relationships with women. Kaczynski and, apparently, McVeigh had no physical relationships with women at all. This wasn't accompanied by indifference; all of them self-identified as heterosexual and were interested in women. Hill's marriage was successful largely because his wife shared his extreme ideology, although the family was forced to move from town to town when Hill's extreme orthodoxy alienated his parishioners (he was an ordained minister who was eventually excommunicated for his extreme fundamentalist views).

All ten subjects were assessed as somewhat to highly intelligent. Phil pointed out to me one day that, as intelligence goes up, the likelihood increases that the "locus of control" (Terry would call this psychobabble, but bear with me) is internal rather than external.

This means that the more intelligent a person is, the more he is able to look to his own ideas as authority for his actions, rather than to the direction of others (such as a government or an extremist group). Although these subjects had trouble affiliating with other people, they weren't directionless as a result. They were able to form their own ideological variants of the agendas of an extremist group and interpret and adapt them to their own uses.

All ten subjects used this intellectual ability to compensate for being unsuccessful in their social lives. They needed to *matter* in the world, and if they couldn't do it socially, they needed to make their mark in another way, a way that would be noticed. A big way.

I was continually struck by the fact that even though none of these ten were successful in affiliating with a group, they never stopped trying.

Franklin tried the Nazi Party and the KKK, and communed with the author of *The Turner Diaries* himself before he struck out on his own campaign of gruesome violence. Furrow spent several rocky years jockeying for a position of authority and status within the Aryan Nations before declaring they were too permissive and drifting back to the Northwest, from where he launched his solitary assault.

McVeigh and Nichols both tried unsuccessfully to fit into the Michigan Militia, and McVeigh tried repeatedly—and fruitlessly—right up until the Oklahoma City bombing to connect with others in the militia movement. Both McVeigh and Rudolph craved the status of being in the Special Forces in the Army, but for different reasons: McVeigh for self-protection and Rudolph apparently out of sheer orneriness. Neither could adjust to it.

According to people who knew him as he grew up, Rudolph was always looking for the perfect church. Park Dietz told me that although Rudolph couldn't join groups—and relationships were threatening to him—his image of himself as a guerrilla soldier in the Army of God let him avoid having to deal with an actual group.

Smith tried and failed to start his own white supremacist group and turned to the World Church of the Creator after reading a book by its founder. He was named a model "Creator" by the WCOTC before he resigned and left it to begin his deadly rampage. Neither Griffin nor Hill ever achieved the status and recognition they craved; Griffin had a low-status job and troubled marriage, and Hill's path to glory in the antiabortion movement was assured only when he followed Griffin by doubling the body count at another Florida abortion clinic.

Even Kaczynski wrote in his journals that he wanted to start an anti-technological organization, adding that, if it weren't for his social disability, he probably would have.

∞ ∞ ∞

Time out, I thought. I had to step back and take a look through a different lens. All ten of my subjects had wanted—and save for Kaczynski had repeatedly tried—to affiliate with extremist groups. Despite repeated failures, they continued to try.

I thought of the motley crew that makes up the crowd at rallies of extremist groups: the "skinheads," the Aryan Nations, wannabe Rambos in the militias, and the KKK in their robes and hoods. How hard could it be to join these guys? And if you were more intelligent than most, like the men in my study, why would you want to?

I pulled out the materials I'd gathered from my talks with the Secret Service. In 1999, Drs. Marisa Reddy and Randy Borum published an article in the journal *Behavioral Sciences and the Law* that provided a succinct and well-worded answer:

> Why is it that individuals join groups—extremist or otherwise—in the first place? [They] gain some reward for doing so. Groups generally provide social acceptance to individual members . . . the identity of 'group member' can be used to augment or substitute for an individual's personal identity, a benefit that may be particularly appealing for those who's own identities have not been socially successful in the past . . . An individual who joins a group can take pride in the group's achievements, find meaning in the group's mission, and derive self esteem from their affiliation with the group and its identity. (From "Assessing Threats of Targeted Group Violence: Contributions from Social Psychology.)

This made very good sense to me. I hadn't studied much social psychology, but anyone who's lived in any society has a pretty good layman's sense of how individuals operate in society simply by being one of them.

It's important to remember that extremist groups are also social groups, which are important to their members for purely social reasons. However strongly they may believe in the ideology that provides the group's ostensible reason for being, the main reason people attend rallies, wear uniforms and insignia, perform ceremonies in honor of tradition, and the rest of what groups do is largely because they like doing it. Their social needs are met, and they feel they have a place in the world that defines them as part of something important, something that *matters*. For most of them, just being part of the group is enough. Although they may posture and spout extremist rhetoric, and they may cheer loudly when others commit violent acts in service of the cause, most are happy to let someone else do the dangerous and bloody work of terrorism.

I called Phil.

"Are you packing up?" he asked.

I looked at the boxes around my desk.

"I guess you could say that," I said. "Listen, Phil, I want to read you something."

I read aloud to him the paragraph I've quoted above from the Secret Service work on group affiliation. As always, he gave me his complete attention. Notably agile of mind, he started processing it for me as soon as I got it out.

"That's interesting, Kathy," he said. In my mind's eye, I saw him sitting back in his chair to consider this. "In the context of your study, there are some even more intriguing aspects to that."

I started scrawling notes on paper as he talked; I always had a few pages of notes after talking to Phil about almost anything.

"You know, the thing that intrigues me here is that one of the things that is shared by the members of an extremist group is a strong, shared paranoid stance. There's a lot of suspicion and distrust—and hatred of those who are different from them."

"That's certainly what holds the group together," I remarked. "These guys are focused on 'the other'—the ones different from them— as evil and dangerous to them."

"Precisely," said Phil. "This article talks about the sense of belonging, of the social connection to the group as a powerful motivator for people who are attracted to join it. It's interesting to note that the search for connection—connections, really—is a hallmark characteristic of the paranoid personality."

"Like my guys," I said. "They're paranoid all on their own."

I thought about the hundreds of people I'd talked to over the years while on complaint duty in the FBI. As a public service agency, the Bureau is open to the public during business hours, and every agent is "on complaints" from time to time, spending time in sterile little offices near the reception room with local denizens who make the rounds of federal agencies with one complaint or another. Many of them are homeless, and many are also mentally ill. I was impressed many times at the overwhelming waves of fear and desperation from these people as they sat across from me in the office that they must have considered as representing both menace and solace to them. They feared the FBI, but they were far more fearful of whatever they came in to report.

Paranoid personalities are characterized by enduring patterns of distrust and suspicion in their thoughts and behavior. This leads them to believe things are connected, but in a dangerous and malevolent way. The human mind is built to make meaningful connections between things, but paranoid personalities go far beyond observable reality in connecting the dots. Conspiracy theorists of all stripes are like this. I know from experience that, however hard you try, it's impossible to dissuade someone sitting across from you, rigid with fear and the complete conviction that he is at the center—or has put the critical pieces together—of some huge conspiracy that has preoccupied his every waking moment for years, that he's wrong.

Since I was always interested in psychology, I usually spent more time with "walk-ins" in those tiny interview rooms than most agents on complaint duty. Now that I'm retired, I can confess that sometimes there was a little voice in my own head that whispered, "What if it's true?" The eyes of the person across from me held such conviction— and terror. They usually talked as fast as they could, because they were used to getting thrown out of government offices. I used to see a flicker of relief in their eyes when I let them talk. Maybe this time they'd convince someone. Maybe this time the alien invasion—or the evil that was stalking them on the street—would be stopped.

Phil brought me back to the moment.

"These groups are all distinguished by a certain ideological framework, aren't they?"

"Right," I said. "They all have a central ideology that drives their rhetoric. They share it; it's part of the social cement that holds them together."

"And the ideologies are generally paranoid in nature, aren't they?" Phil continued. "They're characterized by 'us versus them,' by distrust and suspicion of people who are different from them."

I nodded as I listened, then added, "They all have their special hatreds. They enjoy gathering and having hate fests together."

I thought of the white power rallies, where racist slogans were as much a part of the atmosphere as tattoos and mayhem.

Something started to take shape in my mind. Phil was now prodding me to make a connection of my own. "Connections," I thought. I had an image of a public television program from years ago, where the British science writer James Burke took audiences through historical events that were connected to each other in unlikely and fascinating ways. I seemed to remember one show that began with London's Big Ben and ended with the development of the atomic bomb. The show was called "Connections," and I used to watch it with my family at home.

"Phil," I said thoughtfully. "What happens if you make the internal paranoid connections—in your own thoughts—but you can't connect to the group that shares them?"

"That's right!" he exclaimed. "You can't complete the social connection part of the equation."

It clicked. We both saw it. Phil took it further.

"You're still paranoid," he said, "You still need to make those connections. What is there left to connect to?"

"Ideology," we said together.

Excitedly, we processed the concept further.

Consider an essentially paranoid personality who can't successfully affiliate—for reasons having to do with his own psychological makeup and social difficulties—with the group whose ideology he shares. Just because he fails in joining the group doesn't end his desire—his need—to do so.

Being part of a group, besides making him feel good, would give him power and importance outside of himself. He could claim the stature of the group, and he would *matter*.

But his characteristic problems with social relationships keep him alone. Isolation is threatening to most human beings, whose vulnerabilities are increased when they're alone. The drive for connection is strong; and after multiple failures to achieve social connection and acceptance in a group, there's one aspect of the group that is still available to the Lone Wolf: its ideology.

As noted earlier, the more intelligent someone is, the more able and inclined he is to adapt ideology to his own uses. He becomes an army of one, or a few—but not because he follows the exhortations of people like Alex Curtis to become a Lone Wolf. His motivation is personal and very persistent over time. He makes the attachment he craves not to a group, but to the ideology itself.

The attachment is intense. Since ideology won't reject him—as people in a group might—he is able to fully give himself up to it. He becomes the "true believer" of the ideology. His dedication to it is undiluted by debates, dissension, and distractions that are part of the social culture of any group of human beings. The isolation he has felt all his life is replaced by a sense of strong belonging to the cause, the ideology itself, and he can focus all his energy and attention on action in its service.

I felt a rush of blood to my head as we processed this. It felt like my brain was clicking on all cylinders.

"This is amazing," I said. Phil and I began to discuss the subjects in the study, one by one:

Joseph Paul Franklin: Disappointed by "the joke" he thought the KKK and the American Nazi Party had become, he began his own campaign to "start a race war" that would purify the country.

Buford Furrow: Initially captivated by the Aryan Nations and for a time one of its luminaries who also married the widow of a patron saint of the movement, he became disillusioned by the group and his marriage failed. He decided to "wake America up" on his own.

Michael Griffin: Stuck in a "low prestige" job with no likely advancement and betrayed by his wife, he became so obsessed by the antiabortion cause that he committed murder in its name.

Paul Hill: Chafing at his excommunication from the established church that had ordained him, he seized Griffin's example as a beacon and demonstrated his unique dedication by saying, "The Lord has done great things through me," after he shot three people at another Pensacola clinic.

Theodore Kaczynski: Tortured by being "a social cripple," he blamed his family and spent nearly 20 years getting revenge on "the technological society" he couldn't live in by sending increasingly sophisticated bombs to total strangers he'd read about in newspapers or looked up in *Who's Who* that seemed to be connected to the things he hated in society.

Timothy McVeigh: Self-protective and wary, he came to consider the U.S. government itself a bully and the enemy of freedom after he was unsuccessful at becoming an elite warrior in its military service. Instead, he took up the militia cause after the siege at Waco.

Terry Nichols: A fellow soldier of McVeigh's, the older Nichols came from an area that was a hotbed for militia distrust of the government. He failed to establish himself financially and was cuck-olded by his wife; his growing anger at the government served as a scapegoat for his lack of social and financial success. Although he helped McVeigh assemble the truck bomb, he declined to help deliver it and turned himself in to police to avoid an arrest by the FBI.

Eric Rudolph: Another who failed his bid to join the Army Spe-cial Forces, he was so comfortable in his social isolation that he spent five years in the woods without speaking to another human being before he was finally arrested for his terror campaign against abortion and the "ungodly" U.S. government as the "Army of God."

John Salvi: His severe and undiagnosed paranoid schizophre-nia drove him to become the self-described avenger for the Catholic Church despite what he saw as its insufficient and weak opposition to abortion.

Ben Smith: Convinced that his mission was "to wake up my race and achieve a pure white America," his inner turmoil caused him to abandon leafleting for the World Church of the Creator in favor of killing "Jews and non-whites" during a savage rampage that ended with his own suicide to avoid being captured by police.

Phil and I sat in momentary silence as we finished our review. Static hissed faintly over the phone line from Washington to Cali-fornia. Within an hour, we'd processed what we suspected was the essential finding of my study.

"Wow," I said, not very eloquently.

"Yes, indeed," said Phil. He rang off, finally admitting that I'd kept him from attending to his own business for an awfully long time. I sat back in my chair and closed my eyes briefly. The weather in Washington was balmy now, and I left for a last walk down Pennsylvania Avenue to a nearby park where I'd often taken my lunch and watched the tourists mingle with the local business-men, bureaucrats, and politicians.

This was the last time I would spend any protracted time in Washington, D.C. In the mid-1980s, I'd gone to Russian language school here and had several temporary assignments here, but within days I was heading back to the West Coast for good. I looked around at the bustling crowds on the sidewalk. In the minds of many of them, this was the center of the world. I remembered with amusement the shock Terry described on the face of the editor from *The Washington Post* when he heard how few newsstands in the West carried his paper on a daily basis. Hundreds of people in the FBI spent their whole careers within 50 miles of this place. I'd never tired of exploring the nearby countryside, visiting inns and civil war battlegrounds with my friends as I tried in vain to enjoy Virginia wine and extract the meat after clobbering little soft-shell crabs with a wooden mallet. Now I missed the fresh taste of California Chardonnay and Dungeness crab with crusty sourdough bread by the windswept bay in San Francisco. It was time to go home.

∞ ∞ ∞

When I got back to San Francisco, I began writing. I kept in touch with Phil and rechecked information I'd gotten from the case agents, attorneys, and forensic psychiatrists and psychologists I'd consulted for the past few months. Terry was already taking the reins of the counterintelligence program at Lawrence Livermore; and because of his background, he was equally as involved in counterterrorism issues there. My application was in the works, and I was adjusting in stages to the idea that I would soon surrender my FBI credentials to Headquarters so they could return them to me in a frame with the word "Retired" stamped on them. I'd carried them for 23 years, and the picture they bore was still the same: a 27-year-old California blonde with an inappropriately wide grin. I'd been embarrassed over the years to read people their rights after an arrest or prior to an interview after flashing that picture; everyone else's credential picture was more appropriately serious and agent-like. Now I would turn in my Bureau-issued weapon and other gear and become a civilian again. For five more years I'd work counterintelligence and counterterrorism, holding higher-level security clearances with the Department of Energy than I'd ever had in the FBI. But the end of my FBI career was just months away, and it was the end of a momentous era in my life.

I finished writing the study in July and gave it the ponderous title "THE LONE TERRORIST: The Search for Connection and its

Relationship to Societal-Level Violence." My old colleague, analyst Maggie Stringer, helped me print out and bind a number of copies.

I decided to use all of my accumulated annual leave and spend the whole month of August in Hawaii. I rented a house on the North Shore of Oahu and hosted family and friends there; by the time I left I almost felt like a local. I got back to the office at the beginning of September, 2001. My last day in the FBI was September 30th.

On the 11th of September, I immediately thought I'd postpone my retirement. I called Terry at Livermore, and we had a long discussion about the events of that terrible day. I put off making any changes until later, and it was probably a good thing that I did. San Francisco was well away from the heat and movement in the investigation of the terrorist attacks, and I was assigned initially to an interview team that was headed by one of the young agents who'd worked with us on UNABOM years earlier. He called me at home to rally the troops, and I pointed out gently that if he called everybody in to stand by in the office immediately, he'd have no reserves for a second or even third shift. I went into the office that night. Joel had changed my assignment and arranged for me to join the team in the Emergency Operations Center that was coordinating all 9/11-related investigation in our area.

Within a week, I realized I wasn't critically needed. At least, the San Francisco Division didn't appear to view me as such. I called Terry and confirmed that I'd be processing out and would begin work at the Lab in Livermore in the middle of October. Terry said I'd be busy there; there was heavy concern about the vulnerability to terrorist attack of nuclear weapons facilities, and Livermore was among those at the top of that list.

I hand carried a copy of my study to the Associate SAC, who smiled as he took it and put it on his bookshelf. There was no time for him to read it then, and the attention of the FBI—as well as the attention of the entire U.S. government and the American people—had shifted dramatically away from the threat posed by domestic terrorist lone wolves.

TRACKING THE FUTURE

Tracking down a Lone Wolf requires significant and dedicated psychological and behavioral support, combined with an innovative and often nontraditional management approach that is unusual in law enforcement.

We discovered in the hunts for the Unabomber and Eric Rudolph that a multidisciplinary approach—used by a unified task force that brings multiple agencies together in nonbureaucratic ways—is by far the most effective technique. Kathy's event-related behavioral assistance in UNABOM, and later in North Carolina, validated the operational plan Terry and Don Bell devised. As a result, we believed—in spite of strong opposition to the contrary from other law enforcement entities and elements in the FBI itself—that Rudolph would hide out alone for as long as he had to in the dense Nantahala Forest that was so familiar and comfortable to him.

In preparing her study on "The Lone Terrorist," Kathy forged relationships with highly respected and well-known forensic psychologists and psychiatrists, as well as representatives from the Bureau of Prisons, the U.S. Secret Service, and the ATF. The multidisciplinary and multiagency approach that had served us well in both UNABOM and the Rudolph cases proved again to be the most effective and efficient way to delve deeply into and illuminate what appear to be hallmark characteristics of Lone Wolves.

The Lone Wolf operates outside the observable structure of a group, not because he wants to but because his peculiar psychology makes it impossible for him to fit in anywhere. He adopts a hate-filled ideology as a life companion instead of other people, and he becomes its deadly advocate.

Although he has no connection to his victims—has never even met them—he sees them as representing a threat to him and his ideology. His dedication to his cause is pure; he's smart and he's careful. He protects himself from discovery as well as from physical danger.

He's outside society, but his need to matter in the world is strong. He sets himself on a higher plane than the groups who share his ideological beliefs. If he can't get a sense of belonging from others, he inspires their dread. His mission is fueled by the need to prove his own, deadly importance to himself and to society as a whole.

How many Lone Wolves are out there?

Once again, in an attempt to answer the question, we can usually rely on an overwhelmingly powerful countervailing force: human nature.

The vast majority of people who hold extremist views—and may display them on the Internet, at rallies, and everywhere else—will never commit a terrorist act because of their ideology. Most human beings are preoccupied with living their lives among other human beings, and mere preference for a solitary life is not at all related to committing violence.

Extremist groups spouting radical ideologies are everywhere, but they're visible, and being in a group makes them susceptible to vigilant law enforcement in jurisdictions all over the United States.

Because of this, radical groups have long dreamed of stealthy lone wolves doing their bidding without implicating the group. Luckily, their ideal remains for the most part a fantasy.

Why?

Because being a Lone Wolf terrorist is such a difficult thing to be that only someone who had no choice would be capable of doing it.

Living alone for most of 25 years in the Montana wilderness was what Theodore Kaczynski did, but he did it because it was the only thing he thought he could do. He made numerous attempts over the years to re-enter society, and wrote endlessly about how unhappy he was to be a "social cripple." His longing for a woman to share his life filled hundreds of pages of his journals. His failure to belong fed his anger at the world, and he was determined to get his revenge for the unhappiness he felt as a result. Whether or not he suffered from mental illness, he was uniquely capable of careful planning and execution in a series of bombing attacks lasting nearly two decades.

Why did he resort to terrorism? He laid it out in one of his letters to *The New York Times:*

> To make an impression on society with words is almost impossible for most individuals and small groups. Take us (FC) for example. If we had never done anything violent and had submitted the present writings to a publisher, they probably would not have been accepted. If they had been accepted and published, they probably would not have attracted many readers . . . in order to get our message before the public with some chance of making a lasting impression, we've had to kill people.

Eric Rudolph had dreams of being an Army Ranger, but he couldn't conform to Army life. His relationships with women were superficial, and he had been stewing for a long time about abortion, homosexuality, and the government handling of these matters:

> For many years I thought long and hard on these issues and then in 1996 I decided to act. In the summer of 1996, the world converged upon Atlanta for the Olympic Games. Under the protection and auspices of the regime in Washington, millions of people came to celebrate the ideals of global socialism. . . the purpose of the attack was to confound, anger, and embarrass the Washington government in the eyes of the world . . .

Rudolph didn't join one of the thousands of antigovernment or antiabortion groups; he wasn't cut out for a group. He soldiered on alone, and staged his deadly attacks as the "Army of God."

Both Kaczynski and Rudolph operated under group identities: the "terrorist group FC" and the "Army of God." Timothy McVeigh yearned to be part of a special group, as well. His bombing of the

Oklahoma Federal Building was intended as the spark for a "new American Revolution," and he saw himself as the instigator.

In claiming responsibility for their acts of Lone Wolf violence, all three gave themselves the group identities they longed for but could never achieve in their actual lives.

∞ ∞ ∞

We have a tendency to regard the idealized image of rugged individualism as peculiarly American. We look at older and more communal cultures around the world and assume that Lone Wolves would be unlikely to independently evolve outside Western culture.

But there is no geographical barrier to the development of a Lone Wolf terrorist. Ideologies cross cultural barriers, and so does every element of human psychology.

We can't afford to make the mistake of thinking that the interpersonal difficulties that characterize the social development of Lone Wolves in America aren't present outside the United States.

In fact, a "social cripple"—as Kaczynski described himself—in a culture that values the group over the individual to a greater degree than in America would be under even greater interpersonal stress. In many other cultures, to live outside the group is literally a matter of life and death psychologically as well as physically.

In the same way that these American Lone Wolves were compelled to take up their solitary campaigns, it's logical to assume that extremist ideologies from abroad will be adopted by one or more new Lone Wolves who decide to commit acts of societal-level violence as a result. They may be homegrown or they may be immigrants, but they will be every bit as motivated to strike out alone for their cause as Kaczynski, Rudolph, and McVeigh were.

As the world becomes more connected and the technology of violence continues to evolve deadlier and more compact instruments, Lone Wolves will be increasingly able to cause grave destruction all over the world. Because of this, it will be increasingly difficult to differentiate the acts of homegrown domestic Lone Wolves from those of international Lone Wolf terrorists.

A world where domestic and international terrorism collide will be an increasingly dangerous one. Since 9/11, the primary U.S. response to attacks from international terrorists has been from the military. Civilian law enforcement has been overwhelmed by the challenge of preventing terrorist acts on American soil, and extraordinary techniques have combined under the hastily passed Patriot Act and executive orders from the White House in an attempt to monitor the vast number of potential terrorist targets in the country.

The collision of international with domestic terrorism has already had serious consequences for the delicate balance between security and freedom in the United States. In early 2006, FBI officials told *The New York Times* they were overwhelmed with leads generated from NSA eavesdropping, most of which led to innocent citizens or dead ends.

We learned in working the most difficult homegrown terrorism cases of the last two decades that we can free our citizens from the threat of terrorism without depriving them of their own freedoms.

If we continue to retract the liberties that have made this country strong for over two hundred years because of our fear of terrorists, then we will be the ultimate losers in the war on terror.

We should never lose sight of the irony that Theodore Kaczynski and Eric Rudolph now sit in isolation at the Supermax in Florence, Colorado.

They were always isolated in a psychological sense. But their physical isolation, now and for the rest of their lives, is a result of independent American law enforcement strengthened by an independent and aware public.

And that is the successful combination that will protect U.S. citizens while preserving their civil liberties into the new millennium.

Moving Kaczynski's cabin to safe ground, 1996.

INDEX